P9-CDD-913

88 Mistakes Interviewers Make . . .

88 MISTAKES INTERVIEWERS MAKE . . .

. . . And How to Avoid Them

Auren Uris

A James Peter Book
James Peter Associates, Inc.

amacom
American Management Association

This book is available at a special
discount when ordered in bulk quantities.
For information, contact Special Sales Department,
AMACOM, a division of American Management Association,
135 West 50th Street, New York, NY 10020.

Library of Congress Cataloging-in-Publication Data

Uris, Auren.
    88 mistakes interviewers make—and how to avoid them.

    Includes index.
    1. Employment interviewing. 2. Interviewing.
I. Title. II. Title: Eighty-eight mistakes interviewers
make—and how to avoid them.
HF5549.5.I6U73   1988   658.3'1124   88-47702
ISBN 0-8144-5906-4

A James Peter Book
James Peter Associates, Inc.

Printing number

10 9 8 7 6 5

CONTENTS

114062

Foundation Factors

Hiring

Terminations

ACKNOWLEDGMENTS

This book addresses a complex subject crucial to all organizations, from the small enterprises to industrial giants. For this reason it cannot spring from the knowledge and experience of one person. My sources include authorities I know only by name in print, professional colleagues both of long acquaintance and those newly met in first-time interviews, and friends and family members with business experience. Most of these collaborators are mentioned in connection with their contributions. To some I owe a special indebtedness for personal and material assistance with this work.

Doris Reichbart Uris has extensive experience interviewing and auditioning people in the film and television industries. She added firsthand knowledge along with a wifely interest in advancing the project.

Margaret Arthur is a good friend who supplied numerous anecdotes drawn from her intimate knowledge of the work scene. Her professional experience also helped in the physical preparation of the manuscript.

Evelyn Mertens, Mildred Sherwood, and Betty Russo provided a range of secretarial services at various stages of the book's development.

Print research benefited from the vast resources of the New York Public Library, the capable staff of the American Management Association library, and the Mercantile Library in midtown Manhattan.

Special thanks go to Nancy Brandwein of AMACOM, whose masterful editing made a significant contribution to the clarity and coherence of the manuscript.

And finally, I am grateful for the contribution of a group of executives and authorities steeped in the daily practices of one-on-one business communication, especially George Black. As executive vice president of Poppe Tyson—an advertising and public relations company of Morris Plains, New Jersey—he enlisted and coordinated the efforts of many of the contributors. All the following people answered questionnaires designed to elicit their experience and opinions on the present and future practice of interviewing in all its diversity. They also participated in follow-up contacts by phone and in writing:

Philip Agisim, advertising and marketing consultant, New York City; Lester M. Bornstein, president, Newark Beth Israel Medical Center, Newark, New Jersey; Joanne Conforti, director, Corporate Human Resources, Bozell, Jacobs, Kenyon & Eckhardt, New York City; Martin E. Daniels, president, Bozell, Jacobs, Kenyon & Eckhardt, Yellow Pages, New York City; Michael D. Drexler, executive vice president, Bozell, Jacobs, Kenyon & Eckhardt, New York City; Jack Faber, consultant, Briarcliff Manor, New York; Valerie Friedman, director of marketing, Nabisco Brands, Parsippany, New Jersey; Terry M. Gruggen, senior vice president, Bozell, Jacobs, Kenyon & Eckhardt, Minneapolis, Minnesota; Gerald Lewis, president, Vanton Pump & Equipment Company, Hillside, New Jersey; John McCooe, president, McCooe & Associates, an executive search firm of Ridgewood, New Jersey; Barbara Pittfield, styling consultant, Red Hook, New York; Richard H. Schreiber, district sales manager, National Institute of Business Management, New York City; Michael Silverstein, senior vice president, Marketing, Bozell, Jacobs, Kenyon & Eckhardt, New York City; Robert M. Sok, Skinner Engine Company, Erie, Pennsylvania; Bettina Uris, president, Enterprise Realty, Honolulu, Hawaii; Edward A. Wiler, vice president, Marketing, Rowe International, Whippany, New Jersey.

Every one of these people made a significant contribution to this book, and I would like to thank them all.

INTRODUCTION

Interviewing isn't just talk. If that were all it would be an aimless art. The quality that distinguishes the interview from ordinary conversation is structure. The former has a beginning, a middle, and an end, and at the manager's command are a wide range of techniques to guide and control the proceedings.

In theory the course of an interview is clear and results are easily attained. But too often, obstacles cross up the interviewer, and frustration and a poor payoff are the return for effort expended.

The Interview Concept

Interviewing can be a most human and unusual experience. It can put you in closer touch with another person and establish greater rapport than in many more permanent relationships. In the course of a good interview you have the opportunity to communicate with trust and empathy at a level at which ideas, information, and insights come readily, sometimes with the impact of revelation.

A perfect interview is a beautiful thing, but unfortunately is rare.

Too often interviews are haunted by errors, misjudgments, oversights, in short, damaging mistakes. These may occur at any stage, may stop an interview cold, or may cause difficulties so subtle as to be identified only by the poor results. The pages ahead present eighty-eight faults, selected on the basis of their frequency and importance. Identifying them and learning how they can be avoided guarantees a better interview and gets managers, for whom interviewing is a major operational tool, closer to perfection, and certainly to greater effectiveness.

Each unit is introduced by a Mistake. The device is used for two reasons:

1. It broadens your understanding of the subject. You become aware of the dark as well as the bright side and so see the hazards and limitations as well as the "right way."
2. By avoiding the mistakes others have made, you can skirt areas that afflict an interviewer with that embarrassing ailment that has been called, so colorfully, foot-in-mouth disease.

Broadening Your View

This book focuses on the four most-used reasons for an interview: hiring, termination, performance, and problem solving. However, other types of one-on-one meetings can benefit from being considered as interviews. The advantage is that once you adopt the broader view, your one-on-ones become susceptible to all the techniques of the form, from that of control by the manager to developing an agenda and an outline for covering crucial elements. Some examples include:

- *Fact finding.* The CEO of a large organization queries each member of his staff to learn what lies behind a surge of employee grievances.
- *Raise request.* This can be a crucial event in the relationship not only between manager and subordinate but also between the subordinate and the organization.
- *Negotiation.* Many situations may require a give-and-take between interviewer and interviewee.

To repeat, considering these face-to-face situations as interviews makes them susceptible to control by established methods.

A Panel of Experts

The experience and wisdom of a group of highly qualified executives are represented broadly in this book. Members filled out questionnaires and participated in subsequent interviews that, it is hoped, give to its pages an invaluable true-to-life impact. Their contributions have been noted in the text as well as in the Acknowledgments.

The guidance for fine-tuning your skills has been further enriched by the know-how of experts in the art/science of interviewing—personnel executives and outstanding managers at all echelons. They have been tapped by questionnaires and in-depth conversations to sharpen the recommendations offered in the pages ahead. Their contributions have been confirmed in the text.

It should also be pointed out that the Cases in Point in almost all instances use fictitious names because the sources usually requested anonymity, for the understandable reason that the examples illustrate mistaken procedures, the ingloriousness for which few wanted the credit.

Format

Finally, a word about the structure of the presentation exemplified by the four headings, *Mistake #, Case in Point, Analysis,* and *Effective Action.* The format was devised to simplify and streamline content, to afford condensed information in a context that ensured coherence and logical sequence and made them readily understandable to the time-pressured reader.

PART I

Forward to Basics

We learn in strange and complex ways. Consider some basics in interviewing, such as preparation, objectives, time pressure, and closing. Managers who interview (which is about 99.9 percent) have learned these both as concepts and procedures. And by practice they have imprinted their knowledge kinesthetically on their muscle and nerve patterns.

Practice Makes Perfect?

And yet practice, which supposedly makes perfect, also can make imperfect. We get bored with the craft and stop doing what we know is the thing to do. Further, we forget the rationale of old procedures: "Been doing it for years, but I seem to have forgotten why." Lost our way, is the old phrase. And we blunder into the errors of our rookie days.

We become lax about goals: "I must be slipping," an executive tells himself, coming out of a hiring interview. "I didn't really get that candidate in my sights. I felt she had good possibilities, but. . . ."

Veteran managers may suddenly find they make a botch of a termination interview, or a performance review, or the dozen one-to-one sessions that are not called interviews (such as encouraging a subordinate or discussing suggestions) but are.

The edge is lost, and what managers have learned well and applied skillfully becomes a routine performed in mediocre fashion. Fortunately, the deterioration is not irreversible. The youthful verve and excitement of being tuned to the same wavelength as another person—of living briefly in a microcosm with the other, trading information, perceptions, and insights in the meaningful context of the world of work—may be retrieved. None of us can be made younger. All of us can renew the freshness of experience. We do it not by going through the old motions but by putting a new edge on old skills and perceptions.

Welcome, Newcomers!

Part I is designed to revitalize interest and fine-tune the basic techniques of experienced managers in that exciting confrontation known as interviewing. But younger managers and those who aspire to the profession need not become restive. The same wisdom and savvy calculated to renew the zeal of the seasoned practitioner offers newcomers learning of value—the distilled know-how of experts in practical form.

"You will put beginners on a par with ten-year veterans in short order," said an admirer of this book in its manuscript form. Undoubtedly an exaggeration, but the point is noteworthy: Material relevant for past masters holds for the novice not only knowledge of concepts and procedures but equally important, standards of performance and judgment at a professional level.

REVVING UP

MISTAKE 1: LETTING TIME PRESSURE RUIN YOU

In the opinion of Philip Agisim, a management consultant who hires for his client companies, pressure-free time is essential for interviewing success. How to create a depressurized climate for your meetings? The benefit lies in identifying the causes of the pressure and minimizing them. But some executives fumble in deciding on the way to go.

Case in Point

Adele Ritter prides herself on her briskness, sees it as a professional virtue. However, she understands that interviewees must not feel rushed. She tells a colleague, "I try to insulate the interviewee from pressure, but I do use subliminal cues to keep things moving. For example, I have a large clock on the wall. [Some managers are less restrained. They ostentatiously place their wristwatches on the desk.] Then, no armchairs. I want the other person to feel alert, not comfortable. And I keep the conversation friendly but businesslike."

Ritter surely misreads the effect on her interviewees. The cues may be subliminal, but the message isn't. "Let's get it over with fast," is what they hear. The only thing that builds is tension.

Analysis

Seasoned managers are sometimes good actors. They may feel rushed, but disguise it successfully. However, feelings of pressure are not easy to hide. When the interviewee's own sense of tension is added to by the interviewer's,

- Rapport suffers and it becomes difficult to foster the exchanges that take place at a deeper and more meaningful level.
- Many interviewees react by mentally pulling out and the conversation becomes superficial because, feeling that the interviewer doesn't have the time to be receptive, they are less able to express their ideas.

Effective Action

The following guidelines can help create a more relaxed atmosphere.

1. *Accept the rule of communicability of tension.* If you feel uptight, the other person will be affected. This means you must be pressure free. Try to avoid interviews when you are rushed or otherwise under strain.

2. *Schedule in an adequate time slot.* "Providing enough time for a meeting," says Philip Agisim, "is essential. Avoid tight fits, putting an interview between two pieces of business that are likely to put the squeeze on the meeting."

3. *Keep in mind the interviewee's sensitivity.* If you seem to be rushing to get on to your next task, the other

- Assumes the interview isn't high on your priority list.
- Feels he or she doesn't rate the courtesy of your attention.
- Believes the subject, whether it's to discuss a new assignment, a departmental situation, or whatever, is unimportant to the interviewer.

4. *Be prepared for additional time needs.* If a meeting goes past its intended limit, consider whether to push other matters aside and continue, or to have a second get-together. If the latter, it should be reasonably soon, otherwise the lag may undercut what has already been accomplished.

MISTAKE 2: FORGETTING THAT THE INTERVIEWEE AFFECTS THE INTERVIEW

Mike Slosberg, nationally known executive in the field of direct marketing advertising says, "In a strange way the quality of the interviewee has a great deal to do with the quality of the interview."

It's unavoidable. It may even be desirable. Yet it's too often neglected by interviewers. "It" is the fact that the behavior or the personality of the other person tends to influence the tone and direction of your talk. You should be prepared to take advantage of this phenomenon.

Case in Point

VP Ted Sullivan, a strong-willed manager, likes to interview because he enjoys the feeling that he is in complete charge. As a result, he is unaware of how much the interviewee influences what he says and does. Two examples:

• In discussing an idea brought to him by one of his staff, he steamrollers the assistant, making abrupt and arbitrary comments that throttle rather than encourage the other's thinking.

• In a career-development session with Tim, a subordinate for whom he has high hopes, he allows his subordinate to take control. Tim has been taking courses in management information systems and reports progress. "Next semester I'd like to study wood sculpture," Tim says, and counters Sullivan's obvious surprise by asserting that it would help his creativity. Such whimsical ideas may or may not be practical.

Creativity is a "go" word for Sullivan, and he tries to get the company to pay for the sculpture course as it does for the MIS study. But when he makes the request, his boss just laughs. "If we paid for that, we'd have to mortgage the building to underwrite courses in mudpie making and everything else."

Pondering the situation, Sullivan agrees that Tim has been playing him for a patsy. "How did I get into this?" he wonders.

Analysis

Two important observations can be made about the interviewee's influence. One is that managers who believe they have total control of the interview are probably mistaken. Even if subtly, the other person modifies what and how things are said. The other is that if the manager does have full control of the session, it's likely that it soon deteriorates into a Q-and-A meeting. While many facts may emerge, the psychic interaction that is a crucial factor in rapport will be missing.

Mike Slosberg says, "If you can get positive about the other person, you tend to get deeper into the nuances of thought and feeling and certainly can learn more about the him or her." "Getting positive" usually means making mutual contact at a below-surface level.

Effective Action

You can do a number of things to turn the influence the interviewee exerts into a favorable factor.

1. *Expect and welcome it.* Don't regard it as an interference, a usurpation of your authority or role.

2. *Stimulate it.* In some cases, where the other is shy, or hesitant, you may have to encourage him or her to participate more actively in the session. You do this by:

- Asking questions that require substantive answers: "You say you enjoy challenge. Please give me one or two examples of assignments in your previous job that illustrate that."
- Asking questions that reveal attitudes and values: "How would you handle recalcitrance or overargumentativeness by a subordinate?"
- Praising openness: "I appreciate your telling me about the disagreement you had with your boss. In this company we don't think bosses always have the right answers, and subordinates who avoid rubber stamping are especially valued."

3. *Decide on how much participation you want*—that is, the degree to which the other person affects the movement and quality of the conversation.

The limits of participation—from the upper one, where you hand over the reins, to the lower, where the individual is completely passive—offer a broad middle range. In a brief, sharply focused fact-finding session you might encourage minimum participation from the other. In a selection interview, where assessment of the other person is the goal, the more the other enters into the conversation, the more revealing and useful his or her efforts may become.

4. *Hand over the reins, temporarily.* One way to maximize the other's role is recommended by one executive: "In some instances, I say, 'You probably have questions you want answered about the job, the company, and so on. Why don't you get them off your chest now?' "

Of course, the conversation that touches on what the other's influence is to be can, in itself, help in your assessment of his or her cooperativeness, initiative, and ability to communicate. A person who hesitates to share the substance and direction of input shows lack of assertiveness and possibly a tendency to be intimidated by authority. The one who jumps right in and shares the development of the conversation suggests greater emotional maturity and a potential for leadership.

MISTAKE 3: MAKING SNAP JUDGMENTS ABOUT PEOPLE

Judging people is one of the more crucial skills of the executive repertory. Most of your interviews require that you appraise people, as in a selection interview, for example. But even with those you know, as in a performance review, you must evaluate: Is the other capable of leveling with you? Is he or she making a promise that will be kept?

A hasty judgment may be less accurate than one given time to cook. And the situation itself provides a context that may influence the interviewee's behavior and your perceptions.

Case in Point

Lita Green tells a colleague, "I just interviewed Al Stoner, and I could tell he was right for the job. Pete agreed to let him transfer. With his experience, Stoner should be able to clear up my record-keeping mess in no time."

"His boss must have sold you a bill of goods."

"You're kidding."

"Weren't you told that Stoner has a lousy attendance record and that he's always messing up?"

"I had him sized up as a straight arrow."

"If Stoner was OK you wouldn't get him. I guess Pete was glad to get rid of a problem employee."

Analysis

Lita Green bought too soon. Quick judgments can be like judging a cake by the cherry on top. You need a bigger sample for a sound opinion.

There are several reasons, usually needless, for managers to rush to judgment:

- All managers feel they are good at evaluating people. Most are, but that still leaves some who aren't.
- It is easy to be impressed by surface appearances, which feeds directly into the urge to save time.
- Managers feel quick assessment makes them look good, gives them an aura of being sharp at their job. If two managers are equal except that one visibly has faster reflexes, the speed merchant generally gets the higher rating.

However, don't rule out the snap judgment per se. When haste precludes more effective procedures, your methods may be improvable.

Effective Action

What you do depends on how much of a problem snap judgments are for you. Take the time to review how relevant this mistake is in your case. If you discover that you are less than perfect, consider these guidelines:

1. *Fight the "snap".* Mike Slosberg, president of direct media, of Bozell, Jacobs, Kenyon & Eckhardt of New York City, stresses the dangers of overly quick decisions about people. He says, "If the person being interviewed is smart and articulate, it tends to 'inspire' me," by which he means that he tends to shortcut on appraisal time. He offers these ways of fighting the impulse:

- Remember the results of past judgments. If hasty has been wrong, modify your decision making.
- Search out the negatives. Fortunately or otherwise, a fast "no" usually gets you into less trouble than a quick "yes."
- Set yourself a time limit, such as, "I shall firm up no hiring decisions until one day after the interview."

2. *Check your motivation.* Review the reasons given to justify impulsive judgments:

- *Saving time.* What's the rush? If time is really a factor—you are under pressure to conclude your interview to get on to other matters, for example—OK. But to speed up a decision to save a few minutes or hours, when the alternative is to be stuck with long-lasting hurtful consequences, is clearly undesirable.

- *Playing hunches.* If you are an intuitive person and experience shows that your spontaneous judgments of people tend to be accurate and useful, keep going. Like love at first sight, snap judgments save time. But review the last several intuitive decisions you've made. What's your score? If you are batting high, stick with what you've got. Otherwise, take your time, use cognitive thought as a check on your intuitive approach.
- *Preserving your image.* Your ability to judge people quickly may be a plus in your professional dealings. If you're doing all right, no reason to change. But if a review suggests that you are being hampered by your people judgments, start considering how you can turn over a new leaf. You could take up a mini research effort. Consult sources to stimulate your perceptions and understanding of people. (I recommend *Behavior Management** by Lawrence M. Miller or *Executive*† by Harry Levinson. Your librarian may be able to make other suggestions.)

3. *Be aware of various elements of people-judging.* Two that are particularly relevant in the interview situation:

- *Evaluating physical characteristics.* You can judge by a variety of sensory cues—appearance, manner, speech, grooming—how well or badly a person matches up to the standards in your part of the world. If you're on the West Coast, individualized attire, use of first name, and a relaxed manner are the norm. Your opposite number on the East Coast is more formal. You then translate your observations in terms of the practicalities required.
- *Estimating potential.* In some cases your judgment of people is based not on the past or present but on the future. How will Joe B., with whom you are conducting a disciplinary interview, behave in the days ahead if you let him off with a warning? Can you depend on the promise of your "enemy," the manager of the department next door, to keep her word to share the secretarial pool and copying facilities?

In *The Executive Interview,* Balinsky and Burger‡ point out the kinds of projections made in hiring:

* Lawrence M. Miller, *Behavior Management* (New York: Wiley, 1978).
† Harry Levinson, *Executive* (Cambridge, Mass.: Harvard University Press, 1981).
‡ Benjamin Balinsky and Ruth Burger, *The Executive Interview* (New York: Harper & Brothers, 1959).

The best interviewers are able to estimate potential for learning and continued self-development. It is not often that you will be selecting among people who are clearly tops in every respect. Nor is the reverse true, fortunately. The middle grounds take the most territory. It is in these borderline cases that you will want to estimate how much people can develop and the conditions needed for their development.

Judgments about how people will perform in the future require more imagination than those based on direct observation for immediate needs, but both may benefit from intuitive perceptions, and both may be improved by rechecking by considered review and cognitive thought.

4. *Avoid the unconscious-bias factor.* An overly quick conclusion may come from bias, either positive or negative. For example:

You dislike slow-talking people and equate their speech pace with slow thought processes and difficulty in putting thoughts into action. You may unjustly, and at a cost, act on this bias, and fail to hire the one genius you will ever meet.

You like people who are witty and spice their conversation with clever remarks or colorful language. You hire an assistant with whom you have established an immediate rapport, but in a few weeks you feel you've made the worst possible choice. She is bright, very social, and decides she hates the work and quits.

You may decide that the slow talker won't do for an assignment as liaison with another department, or that the witty person is just right to give a speech at a seminar you have to bow out of at the last minute. Both judgments may be right on the money. However, if you are objective and you relate their qualities and abilities to needs and give yourself time to consider, the odds favoring success become better.

MISTAKE 4: BEING AFRAID TO PROBE

Edward A. Wiler, vice president, Sales of Rowe International of Whippany, New Jersey, nominates ineffective probing as the most persistent problem in interviewing. Certainly for some managers it's a fault that limits results. Getting below the surface is essential where the interviewee plays up appearances and attempts to cover up facts, faults, and failures. The manager who cannot probe deeply enough may never get more than half the story.

Case in Point

Sid Tryon is very impressed by a candidate for a field selling job. The man has a good appearance, is well spoken and intelligent, and his references and résumé paint a favorable picture. However, after a long interview, Tryon still feels he hasn't gotten a clear picture. He decides to check with the candidate's previous boss.

The other is friendly and speaks well of the applicant. "He's very well liked, got along fine with his regular customers."

Sid Tryon continues the conversation—actually a fact-finding interview conducted over the phone. The longer they talk, the more loquacious the sales manager becomes. Finally Tryon asks, "Would you hire him again if you could? He said he left for personal reasons."

Pause at the other end, "Actually, we're cutting back on staff," is the answer. "Well, I'll level. He's a nice enough guy, but as far as selling, he's a poor closer. I often had to go along to finalize the deal."

A salesman who has trouble closing is like a fish who can't swim; anyone who knows selling will tell you that.

Sid Tryon's problem in interviewing is not too different from the candidate's. They both have trouble getting to the nitty-gritty. Tryon did not discover the man's weak point on his own. The interviewer had let a favorable impression stand in the way of incisive probing.

Analysis

Interviewers may be held back by a variety of deterrents. In Sid Tryon's case, he hesitated to spoil a favorable assessment. Perhaps he was tired of seeing prospects, and chances seemed good that he had found the person he wanted.

Another executive might say, "I don't want to invade another person's privacy," a seemingly commendable but obstructive feeling. Or, in a perverse way, some managers identify with the other person so that if he or she has something to hide, they feel uneasy about uncovering it. Or, if probing might cause pain, the oversensitive manager doesn't want to inflict it.

Another barrier: Some managers cling to a self-image that sees them as liked and admired. They hesitate to do anything (such as being tough in an interview) that seems harsh and unfeeling. But where there is a vital and relevant fact to be uncovered, probing is the way to get to it.

Effective Action

Those for whom seeking below the surface is not easy may take liberating action on two fronts:

1. *Mental adjustment.* People can't change basic attitudes easily, but habits that interfere with the attainment of desired goals may be modified by rethinking. For example:

- Be aware of the handicap. Look back at past interviews you have conducted. Do you recall any hesitation to pose an incisive question that came to mind but remained unasked for fear that it might hurt the other person or shake up your relationship? Or, after an interview, have facts emerged that might have materially affected the outcome? If your self-assessment suggests less than a desired level of probing skill,
- Figure out exactly what the bind is. The Analysis suggests some of the possible reasons for a hesitation to probe. Do any of those apply? A possibility not mentioned, that may sound plausible to some, far-fetched to others: "I try to keep emotions out of the workplace," asserts one manager, who applies the principle to probing in interviews of various kinds. Is this view yours to any extent?

2. *Procedural adjustment.* Developing a procedure that imposes a desired behavior is a common method of self-discipline. In the context of overcoming probing hesitations:

- Select probing targets for a given interview. In a hiring session, for example, you have two sources:
  — A résumé or other documentation about the job applicant.
  — Statements or responses made in the interview that you find suspect.
  An illogicality or contradiction may not be damaging in itself, but may call for a clarification that extends your knowledge of the other person.
- Devise a "probing checklist." This is an idea Edward A. Wiler of Rowe International uses in his interviewing. First, he makes a distinction between a closed probe, which are questions that may be answered by yes or no, and an open probe, which starts with words like how, why, what.

Here are the kinds of questions one executive suggests for an open-probe list for a performance review situation:

- How do you plan your work?
- Do you feel you work better with a team or by yourself? (Whichever the answer, he adds Why?)

- What did you like most about the assignment you just finished? Least?

Few people you interview expect a syrupy session. They don't expect to be beat upon, either. But it's perfectly practical to probe effectively between these extremes.

MISTAKE 5: UNDERESTIMATING THE INROADS OF SHAKY CONCENTRATION

We all have limited attention spans and other impediments to total concentration. Losing the conversational thread, going off into mental byways, gums up the works. If necessary, special efforts must be made to keep your mind on track.

Case in Point

Jerry Cohen has just come back from the hospital where he has seen his radiant wife and their newborn infant. "Jerry," his secretary tells him, "you have an appointment with Pete Ward to discuss his ideas for a new storage system."

Ward comes in and Cohen apologizes for being late and asks about the storage idea. Ward goes into a detailed description. When he stops, the manager realizes he hasn't heard a word. His head is where his heart is, back in maternity. He does the wise thing. He explains why he's out of it, and reschedules the meeting.

Analysis

Few people would fault Jerry Cohen for his mental state. But whether distracted for good reasons or bad, the interview demands concentration. "But what can I do?" asks one manager. "My attention span is shorter than average. My mind wanders in long interviews." Fortunately, concentration can be controlled.

Effective Action

Here are a few remedies for some concentration destroyers:

1. *Decide whether poor concentration is your problem.* Ability to

concentrate, like many personal qualities, tends to be unevenly distributed. Some people have good powers, others range from poor to extraordinary. For managers whose focus tends to blur, the following recommendations can be especially worthwhile.

2. *Take care of the controllable factors.* For example, observe these concentration protectors:

- Don't go into an interview dog-tired.
- Don't prolong a meeting past the fatigue point.
- Don't interview if, as in Jerry Cohen's case, you're so preoccupied, you're out of touch with the here and now.
- Watch out for serial sessions. "Some people can't stay interested after several consecutive interviews," says Tracey Etelson, CEO of Special Service Freight Company, of Bridgewater, New Jersey. She suggests spacing the meetings or having another executive help in preliminary screening.
- Bar distractions. Saying "Hold all calls" can help you retain mental balance. Tell others, including your boss, "I'll be interviewing between two and three o'clock. Unless it's urgent, contact me after that time." Intrusions are not always caused by people. For example:
  —Noises from adjoining offices. If you can't quiet them, consider moving your meeting site.
  —Street noises, traffic, jackhammers getting at pipes below the road surface. If they get to you, find a quieter site.

3. *Try not to be distracted by the other person's behavior.* Toe-tapping, frequent trips to the water bottle, a cold that requires constant nose blowing, even the signs that the other person's attention is wandering, can wreck your train of thought. The best remedy is to raise the conversation to a higher level of intensity. For example you say, "Would you mind sketching that floor layout on the easel chart?" Changing the position of your seating, changing the light, or opening a window, can improve matters.

4. *Know your own attention span.* If it is indeed limited, divide a long meeting into two or more parts, with a ten-minute rest between. Even if you ordinarily can stick with long sessions, excessive temperature, poor air circulation, routine and even boring conversation may make it difficult to keep your mind focused. Anything you can do to break the pattern will dissipate the murk that weakens your sharpness.

5. *Watch for the signs.* Like the fog, inattention may come on little cats' feet. If progress seems unnaturally slow, if you don't feel sharp,

ask yourself whether woolgathering is taking its toll. If so, can you screw your mind to matters at hand? Most people can bear down, exert effort that increases concentration, at least for a while, which may be all the time you need.

6. *Be aware of the other person's attention.* The other's woolgathering can affect you and the conversation. If the other's inattention is temporary or if the cause is simple (he or she hasn't had enough sleep the night before, physical fatigue), try livening your conversation, making a challenging statement. But if these don't work, scheduling another meeting may be your best bet.

MISTAKE 6: MAKING FALSE ASSUMPTIONS

We often mess up our thinking by mistakenly accepting an idea as a hard fact. "Of course the earth is flat," said an ancient ancestor. "If it weren't, things would fall off of it." False beliefs can become mental land mines. In interviewing, they can cause major misunderstandings and turn conversations to cross purposes.

Case in Point

Executive Maria Rodriguez sets up a meeting to talk to Hal Riley, whose performance has been sagging. She knows Hal well, and believes she has diagnosed his problem. She gets right down to brass tacks: "Hal, I can understand that you're upset because Carla got the job you wanted. Now your work has begun to suffer. . . ."

"Hold on," Hal says. "I know I've been doing a lousy job the last few weeks but I couldn't care less about the promotion. I've got the shakes because my kid brother lost his job and he and his family are staying with us. Do you know what it means to be awakened by crying kids after your own have become teenagers?"

Rodriguez, embarrassed, tries to pick up the pieces.

Analysis

Incorrect assumptions may be formed before, during, and after your interview. And when they are used as a basis for asking a question, you may find yourself out of the ballpark. For example:

Ed Salter is closeted with an employee who has come to him with a complaint about the poor ventilation at his workplace. After he's listened to the details—no window close by, fumes from the cafeteria below making his office smell like a hamburger joint—Ed assumes the other wants some kind of air exchange equipment to improve the situation. He suggests having engineering look into it, but the employee says, "I don't mind the food odors. It's the two people down the hall who are heavy smokers I want you to do something about."

It's impossible to live day to day without making some assumptions: If the report calls for fair weather, we leave for work without an umbrella. If a job candidate makes an appointment for the maintenance mechanic's job, you assume the caller has some qualifications. Both assumptions may be wrong.

We are usually tricked into our off-base assumptions. The misleading factor may be the interviewee's attire or some other detail. A confession of a young personnel assistant is revealing:

"I assumed he wasn't a college graduate because the spelling on his résumé was awful. Later I learned he graduated during an era when spelling was downgraded and some collegians turned in term papers on sophisticated subjects with spelling at a high school level. He turned out to be one of our brightest copywriters."

Effective Action

A false assumption gets in your way at any interview stage. Watch out for them both before and during:

1. *Don't take things for granted.* Often we fill in gaps in our knowledge by filling in from related matters. "He talked a good game," a manager tells his boss to explain the failure of a newly hired supervisor. "He looked honest," a manager asserts, following the theft of her handbag by an office temporary.

2. *Conduct a false-assumptions hunt.* Seek out and eradicate mistaken ideas in advance of a meeting by moves like these:

- Don't assume that an applicant who has most of the essentials has them all. Verify. Before setting up a hiring session, pin down for yourself the education, training, and experience you seek and examine the résumés or query callers as to their qualifications. Major discrepancies suggest no meeting.
- If there are any stresspoints to the job—hours, location, overtime requirements—don't assume these will be acceptable to inter-

viewees. Use them, not too late in the conversation, to see if they are knockout factors from the other's point of view.

- In a problem-solving interview (you want to get to the bottom of an unsatisfactory work situation) hold back on premature conclusions as to what you think is wrong. Better to leave the range of possibilities wide open and test them one by one.

3. *Check your own understanding during the conversation.* If you have lost the thread, don't assume it's your fault. It may be the speaker's. Here's what to do about it:

- Ask for clarification of statements you don't understand. You are not the only person who can get mistaken ideas. Particularly in complex or abstract matters, check the other person for understanding. If you are not satisfied that he or she is on the right track, ask for an example, a diagram, or an explanation of what's involved.
- Double-check replies or statements that don't make sense. "You say you were in your last job for five years. But that means you must have started there at the same time you say you were in the army."
- If you start getting replies that don't seem to mesh with previous statements, go back to the point where the confusion started and recheck your understanding of what was said.

4. *Check "evidence."* You can assume most people are honest most of the time. But in critical matters it becomes especially important to examine assumptions, both your own and others'. Of major relevance in this connection: a well-meaning subordinate may substantiate an assumption by "evidence." For example: You are conducting a fact-finding investigation following a theft. "Sure I know it was Tom. I saw him go in and out of the supply room where the theft took place."

It's possible you've just heard one of the common logical fallacies, known to the ancient Romans as, *Post hoc, ergo propter hoc,* which roughly translated means, "After something, therefore caused by that thing." You would check more thoroughly before accepting the assumption that Tom is guilty of anything. Some questions to try to answer: When did Tom go in? Why? Was anyone else seen entering the room? If what was stolen was of any substantial size, how could he have hidden it?

It's impossible to get through the day without making assumptions. If you ring the bell, the elevator will eventually come; if you advertise for help wanted, you expect applicants. The mistake to avoid is making assumptions unnecessarily and acting on them in important matters.

MISTAKE 7: BEING UNAWARE OF THE BENEFITS
OF CONFRONTATION

Most interviews proceed in harmony between the executive and the other person. The usual mood is one of businesslike directness and a mutual desire to achieve the goals of the meeting. But occasionally, emotions boil over, and decorum is ruptured.

Some interviews—termination, for example, or dealing with an irate complainant—bear the seeds of trouble. Disagreement over an issue may cause a crisis. And in all interviews, the arousal of negative emotions may put managers at loggerheads with the other person. In some quarters confrontation is a dirty word. Yet it can have positive value, and ability to deal with it is an essential interviewing skill.

Case in Point

This case is told from the interviewee's viewpoint, the better to illustrate the causes and effects of confrontation.

Roger Ellison applies for a job as assistant purchasing agent with an electronic-parts supplier. His qualifications and experience are right on target, but his record is not without its flaws. He does reasonably well in his first interview. He is pleased when the session concludes with the staff member saying, "I'd like you to get together with the head of the department."

The meeting is set up, and Ellison is uneasy. Not a word has been said about his problem. Maybe they hadn't checked his references after all.

"Well," he tells himself, "do or die."

The head of purchasing greets him courteously, but Ellison shortly realizes that he is a tough probing interviewer. Then comes the blow: "Your credentials are impressive," the other says, "although our requirements are quite stringent. Now, to the personal area. I understand you have a drinking problem."

This man doesn't pull his punches. "I had a drinking problem," he says. "I was in treatment, and haven't touched a drop in three years. Check with my previous employer on that point and on my performance. And since you've been so direct, let me say that I like what I see, and I could do a great job for you."

Roger Ellison was hired. He tells his wife. "When it comes to interviews, give them to me straight and tough. If my new boss hadn't confronted me with my drinking past and cleared that up, I never would have been hired."

(The executive who starred in the case above had been with the firm for twelve years and was chief purchasing agent when he talked about it. The name, of course, is fictitious.)

Analysis

Confrontation, both unplanned and as a considered tactic, can be useful or disruptive. In cases like that of Roger Ellison, it can break through obstacles that block interview progress. It may emanate from the interviewee as well as the interviewer. To deal with it requires an understanding of what it represents both as an interaction between you and the other person and as a part of the interview process.

Effective Action

Consider the following guidelines as an assist to gaining the benefits and avoiding the undesirable consequences of confrontation:

1. *Know the several uses of confrontation.* Confrontation may originate with either of the two parties. You should be prepared to take the initiative or to respond to it.

- To accuse. "I believe what you did was irresponsible . . ." Regardless of the previous conversation, the interviewer's statement now lays it on the line.
- To defend. "Are you implying that I am telling a lie?" demands an interviewee. The manager who has been asked the question must decide between two possible courses: (1) to back off, and disclaim the intention; or (2) to intensify the crisis by a statement such as, "Call it whatever you like, but what you are saying is completely implausible." It's still the other's move. What happens next depends on which of the two is willing to moderate his or her stand. The interviewee may reword the statement to make it more acceptable. The manager may shrug and say, "Let's get on with it." But if the confrontation isn't ended, the session may end, or the person in authority may make a definitive move: "We won't continue unless you . . ." and he or she states the condition.
- To correct. "What you just said contradicts your earlier statement." Is the interviewee lying, or has a mistake been made? Your assertion makes it possible to set matters straight.

- To shake loose an important fact. "We can't proceed until you tell me exactly what happened." The importance of a key piece of information can be emphasized.
- To assist in self-examination. In a counseling interview, for example, the manager may point out, "You've been saying that you like your job, yet you want to get into some other line of work. Which is it?"
- To end an emotional crisis. A subordinate tells her boss in a performance review, "I've been at loose ends. Will you tell me now where I stand in my future here?" It's up to the manager to respond, by giving an direct answer, explaining why one can't be given, or by naming a date or period of time in which an answer will be forthcoming.
- To reveal feelings. "I'm extremely angry," a manager tells an assistant, "at the way you treated that temporary. Such insensitivity is inexcusable." The battle is joined. What happens next depends on just how far the manager wants to go.

2. *Develop a personal policy on confrontation.* It may seem like a formalistic approach to a matter-of-fact situation. But if you don't think through your ideas about confrontation, you may be unprepared to handle it when it comes.

"I'll just do what comes naturally," one manager says. But that may be exactly the wrong thing to do. In clarifying your ideas about confrontation in interviews, you can tell yourself when and to what degree to use them and just how strong you want to make your responses to the other's confrontational tactics.

3. *Decide on the situations in which you don't want to be confrontational.* These will vary from manager to manager. In making such a decision, take into account the degree of comfort or discomfort you feel. In their book, *Professional Interviewing,* Downs, Smeyak, and Martin write, "Many interviewers shy away from confrontation, but this desire to avoid an unpleasant situation creates a bias in the interview."* By bias the authors mean an unbalance because of an absence of one of the basic building blocks of communication.

Choose from among the items on the list below—to which you can add, to suit your own values—the instances in which you would not want to confront an interviewee.

- Punishment. The manager lets the other have it right between the eyes. "That was a stupid thing to do" doesn't leave much latitude for response.

* Cal W. Downs, G. Paul Smeyak, and Ernest Martin, *Professional Interviewing* (New York: Harper & Row, 1980).

- Weakness. When the other might not be up to weathering the stress of the confrontation.
- Purposelessness. If the manager has no specific intention in mind, confrontation for its own sake is undesirable.

Finally, consider your ideas about confrontational tactics by your interviewee. That fountainhead of human-relations wisdom, the Bible, counsels that "a soft answer turneth away wrath." The soft answer may indeed be mollifying, and secondarily, gives you a chance to decide on your next step.

MISTAKE 8: FAILING TO LISTEN TO YOURSELF

Interviewees' self-projection is frequently discussed in the literature. Everything from their comfort to suggestions on loosening their inhibitions and getting them to speak up are covered. But what about interviewers? Somehow, it is assumed that they as a class are close to perfection, faultless in speech and language. The publisher's and author's interest in offering this book suggests the contrary.

Case in Point

Says an executive,

> I tape-recorded the first draft of a talk to be given at a meeting of the board of directors. Later I played it back and was astonished. I heard myself clearing my throat frequently, sounding like an angry frog. That unpleasant voice on the tape paused, stopped, went back and repeated himself, mumbled and stammered. I thought, "Good grief, if that's what people hear when I'm interviewing, I've got a serious communications problem."

Analysis

Some things we say and how we say them may become obstacles to interview progress. None of us can be completely sure of our faultlessness unless, as in the case of the executive above, we listen to ourselves speak.

Many people fail to realize that they sabotage their interviews by speech or behavior. The basic types of distortions are:

- Auditory habits—throat clearing, sighing, and so on.
- Obstructive speech patterns, such as over-long sentences, or incoherent word sequences that fog up the sense of what is intended.
- Nonsense phrases. "You know," a speaker says repeatedly, and you don't know. Actually, it may be a filler to give the other time to think, to grope his or her way through the complications of putting thoughts to words, or is intended to be ingratiating.

Walter Menninger, in a syndicated column,* wrote, " 'You know' is more refined than 'uhhh.' The phrase may also be used to provide a bridge between the speaker and the listener."

More likely such interjections put people off. Add to the list such gratuitous usage as, "In other words," "The thing of it is," and the "Wows" that may pepper the speech of younger humans.

Listening to one's own speech need not be narcissistic, but remedial. We think we know how we sound and don't. Listen to the exclamations of people who hear a recording of their own words. "Is that me?" is the most common reaction. And it is often followed by specific discoveries: "I never realized my delivery was so bad. I sound so stilted!" or speak too rapidly, or too slowly, or don't pronounce words clearly.

In all cases the consequences are the same. The speaker doesn't come across as well as he or she might, the sense of the interview is muddied, and results are minimized.

Effective Action

The good thing about this hazard is that detection is three quarters of the remedy. Here are some things you can do:

1. *Hear what you say and how you say it.* The simplest and best way is to follow the example of the executive who tape recorded his planned speech. Another recourse: Have your spouse or a colleague critique a verbal presentation. Ask for specific comments.

- Don't read from printed material. First of all, this does not parallel the interview situation. In addition, such vocalizing tends to be studied and stilted, and doesn't represent your ordinary speaking voice.
- If you can record an interview, with the other person's permission,

---

* Walter Menninger, "Do You Actually Realize What You're Saying?" (Overland Park, Kans.: Universal Press Syndicate, 1976).

go ahead. Most people soon get used to the presence of the equipment, and what you hear on the playback will be an accurate measure of your normal speech.

Another way to get a line on your speaking is to get it from friends and colleagues. Their opinions are likely to be subjective, and lend themselves to inaccuracies, but every once in a while you can pick up a tip. Just be wary. The comments you get may be overly favorable, and you may not be given the full picture.

2. *Eliminate the eliminatable.* Some habits can be restrained or minimized, once you spot them. For example, once the "You know" plague, or other undesirable habit, has been identified, the average person can screen it from his or her speech.

3. *Minimize to the irreducible core.* If you tend to be a frequent throat clearer, you may not be able to stop altogether. In some instances the habit is the result of a physical condition, such as a postnasal drip. One sufferer clears his throat before starting a session, which gives him about twenty minutes of hawk-free time. He breaks briefly for another throat clearing, and that's pretty nearly the limit of an average interview.

4. *Reinforce clarity and meaning.* Keep in mind that the damage by poor speech and delivery is done to clarity and therefore to the meaning of what you say. In the course of the self-assessment suggested in the recommended procedure, look for opportunities to further improve the clarity of your verbal communication. Your self-review by tape recorder can start a more general speaking improvement that goes beyond your one-on-one schedules.

MISTAKE 9: NEEDLESSLY LIMITING YOUR VIEW OF THE INTERVIEW

The dictionary defines "interview" as "a formal consultation usually to evaluate the aptitude, training, or progress of a student or prospective employee." Since that definition was devised, additional applications have grown to include performance reviews, the firing and exit interviews, and one of the more controversial forms called management counseling.

Hiring, terminations, and performance reviews get major attention in this work by examples, extended discussions, and so on. However, there is an advantage in broadening your concepts and thinking about other possible areas of application.

Case in Point

Executive David Chen comes in Monday morning, remembering that it's first day on the job for Sid Grant, a new manager for the department next door. Almost unconsciously he finds himself jotting down a few questions he would like to ask his new neighbor. For example, the department Grant will run has an unusual mixture of computers and production equipment. What kind of education, training, and experience has he had to qualify for the job?

It goes well, with David Chen convinced that he and Sid will be good friends. As he leaves, he realizes with surprise that their conversation, which he thought of as a get-acquainted chat, has paralleled a hiring interview.

At first he's chagrined. Is he misapplying a professional technique to a social situation? Then he decides, "Why not? My thinking of it as a 'get-acquainted interview' helped the conversation flow and we got to know each other better not only because I got to ask some of the same questions I ask in hiring but because I used some rapport-building techniques. What's bad about that?"

"Nothing," he concluded.

Analysis

For two strangers to meet in order to get to know each other, a relaxed exchange is required. And for David Chen and Sid Grant it was, despite Chen's use of professional techniques.

"David Chen must be insecure to make up an agenda for a friendly chat," some might say. But Chen shows no sign of self-doubt or awkwardness, and what he did worked. The case suggests that other one-on-one meetings can benefit from wider application of the business-interview approach.

Effective Action

A broader use of interview procedure requires changing your perception of one-on-one meetings. The following guidelines can help:

1. *Be aware of interviewing potency.* Remind yourself of the benefits of the standard procedures. Ask yourself, "What does any interview—hiring or otherwise—gain from structuring?" Answer: "Not a straitjacket that limits conversation, but a logical track along which the talk flows toward desired goals."

2. *Look for broader application.* A meeting ordinarily not thought of as an interview may benefit from interviewing techniques if it has two characteristics: (1) It's about something, it has a subject, and (2)

it has goals, e.g., facts to gather, problems to solve, and decisions to make.

3. *Know the range of possibilities.* Some meetings not generally accepted as being "interviews" that lend themselves to the standard procedures include:

- Meeting to get acquainted (like the Chen-Grant contact)
- Praising a subordinate
- Encouraging someone whose spirits flag because of failure
- Motivating
- Negotiating (a raise, for example)
- Developing ideas jointly with a colleague
- Critiquing a project by a subordinate

- Add your own: _____

4. *Focus on technique.* Be clear on the specifics of converting meetings to the interview mode.

- Preparation. You needn't walk into an encouragement interview empty handed if records or other data strengthen your case.
- Goals. Tell the other your idea of why you are meeting: "It's about time we got together to coordinate the security procedures between our two departments."
- Leadership. Use interview control methods to steer the conversation and to turn it over to the other when that would be helpful.
- Pace. Don't let the conversation be too discursive or too hurried. Either means loss of meaningful content.
- Tracking. Is the conversation headed toward productive goals? In a general way, at any rate, you want to stick to business.
- Closing. Conclude at an appropriate time and in an appropriate manner.
- Follow-up. Tie up loose ends.

With this heightened awareness of broader applications, you can undertake one-on-one contacts with more specific ideas of where you want the conversation to go and how to get there. Also, by broadening your applications, your handling of all interviews becomes both sharper and more flexible because of more practice and better perspective.

FOUNDATION FACTORS

MISTAKE 10: PREPARING INADEQUATELY

For some interviews, all you need is a quiet corner. Others require research, updated information, a written agenda. The circumstances suggest what is needed, but whatever the requirements, failure to plan threatens results.

Case in Point

Jim Stevens, manager of manufacturing for a midwestern firm, tells of interviewing for a production engineer.

> We were getting out a huge order, and I didn't have time to prepare. However, the candidate was impressive and I decided to hire him. When I told personnel the salary I had committed us to, I found I had promised considerably more than was intended. In our second interview I explained the error—which he wasn't too happy about. He began asking for specific information, everything from health benefits to our policy on continuing education for professionals. I wasn't up on our benefits program, and I could see that my "Don't knows" were souring him. I got angry at him and myself, and the conversation went badly. The deal fell through. He was a good man. It was a definite loss.

Analysis

Preparation is critical for the smooth progress of every interview. Some require more preparation than others, depending on the type of interview, the situations involved, and their complexity. Personnel specialists suggest that a meeting be postponed if you are not set for it.

Effective Action

The preinterview checklist below, developed by Mary Marlin, head of the internal communications department of a major insurance company, will help you plan for just about every interview.

1. ☐ Do you know as much about the interviewee as is necessary?

   Name and title_____

   Nature of responsibility or function_____

   Name of company and what it does_____

   _____

   Work experience, accomplishments_____

   _____

   Special interests, objectives_____

2. ☐ Have you arranged a suitable time and place?
3. ☐ Have you informed others who should be aware of the meeting?
4. ☐ Have you invited others who should be present during the interview?
5. ☐ Do you have all the information and data you might need at hand?
6. ☐ Have you taken steps to minimize interruptions?
7. ☐ Do you have a list, mental or written, of points to cover?
8. ☐ Are you clear on the objectives you want to achieve?
9. ☐ Do you know the objectives of the interviewee—what he or she hopes to gain from the interview?

10. ☐ Have you decided to what extent you want to help satisfy the interviewee's objectives?
11. ☐ Are there others who should be informed of the outcome of the interview?
12. ☐ What follow-up steps should be taken? Memos sent? Ideas pursued? Actions taken?

_____

_____

13. ☐ Should a record of the interview be made?
14. ☐ If the interview is one of a series, should you note the ideas gained that can be used in subsequent interviews?

MISTAKE 11: FAILING TO SPECIFY GOALS

The personnel head of a large airline says, "Recently a manager terminated an employee and was halfway through before he explained the reason for the session. Also, he failed to give reasons for the firing. Not surprisingly, the man stormed into my office claiming discrimination."

Some people are able to freewheel and meet all their objectives, others muddle along. "Not having interviews goal-oriented," says the personnel executive, "is like taking a plane up without knowing where you're going to land."

Case in Point

Executive Stan Lubinski phones assistant Lily Damon. "Lily, got something I'd like to discuss. Can you come in now?"

On her way down the corridor, Damon thinks, "The boss sure is steamed. I wonder what's up?"

Coleman doesn't hide his excitement. "I passed by that small storage room near the elevators this morning," he says, "and I realized it's a key spot. You know about our copying bottleneck. That room would be great for a second copier . . ."

Damon interrupts, "It certainly would cut down on waiting time. Would you like me to do a little feasibility study?"

"Well, no. That's not necessary."

"Shall I check purchasing to see what type of copier—"

"I've already done that."

"Then what?"

"Would you please see where we could put the materials that are now stored in the room?"

"Sure," Lily says, and nodding, walks out talking to herself.

Analysis

Being clear on objectives and points for the agenda to reach them is obviously a prerequisite for streamlining your sessions. In a problem-solving interview, a small number of points may get you to your target. Information-gathering may require only a few points, hiring may require dozens. Asking yourself, "What do I want to cover?" can keep you on a fast track.

Effective Action

To minimize the murky-objective difficulty:

1. *Don't be satisfied with a "pretty good idea" of what you want to accomplish.* "In general, I know what I'm after," a young manager tells himself, but his sessions meander. Clear and comprehensive goals insure more efficient interviews.

The Lubinski-Damon case shows that it may be just as time-wasting to oversupply background details as to offer too little. Also, Damon's confusion suggests that it may be wise to start with a one-sentence statement of purpose to provide focus for the information that follows: "Lily," Lubinski could have started, "I'd like you to find a location for the supplies now in the storeroom near the elevators. Here's the background. . . ."

2. *Write down points to cover.* If you have difficulty in putting your targets into words, they probably require further consideration. In some cases this may mean discussion with your boss or other colleagues. Also, you often can preplan agenda items that might not occur to you during the interview.

One manager's agenda for an interview to patch up misunderstandings with another manager looks like this:

Agenda for a Peace Interview

- Don't stir up old embers. (Emphasize the positive.)
- Don't place blame. Dishonors are usually equal.
- Express regrets for things I did wrong, for example, my memo to Mr. G. accusing Bill of lying about the shipping foul-up.
- Explore areas in which we can join forces.
- Discuss what to do in case of future difficulties.
- Discuss how to cool off our staffs, get them into the peace process. (Note: Get Bill Smith's ideas on this.)
- Suggest regular sessions (monthly?) to discuss common problems and opportunities.

Imagine holding an interview on a subject with as many facets as the above, and you can understand the value of written goals. In delicate matters such as termination interviews, it might be wise for the manager also to write out the wording of what he or she will say. These days you must operate with one eye on the antidiscrimination laws. To be avoided are statements such as this one, which got one manager into hot water: "You've gotten too old for the job."

3. *Don't oversimplify.* Simplification is often desirable because it tends to eliminate unimportant details. But in some interviews it is exactly those details that must be considered. Failing to bear down on the specifics, sometimes even to the point of boredom, may mean slurring over crucial matters.

4. *Be aware of the multigoal possibility.* An interview may have two or more aims. For example, in conducting an exit interview, manager Jim Slade knows he faces an embittered, upset employee. He correctly anticipates that he will have to give the other a chance to voice complaints, and claim unfairness. Slade keeps this part of the exchange brief and goes on to the next phase, which is to provide help in finding new employment.

5. *Remember that goals may change.* In a succession of interviews for the same purpose, objectives may vary. For example, your objective may broaden or narrow as a result of the people you are evaluating. Mary Rooney, head of a word processing department, is meeting with job candidates. The last prospect is extremely well qualified and has had some management experience as a group leader. She decides to hire her with the expectation that in a few months she may promote her to assistant, and reshuffle the assignments of some of the others on her staff.

Point 5 emphasizes the desirability of staying flexible and modifying your interview objectives if unexpected blockage or opportunities present themselves.

MISTAKE 12: MAKING DESTRUCTIVE SEATING ARRANGEMENTS

Just as the want of a nail may lose a war, the seating arrangement, supposedly a minor factor, can nevertheless spoil an interview. Where the other person sits in relation to you, along with other seating considerations, should be as carefully planned as any other key factor in your meeting. Seating can be a hidden handicap, undercutting effectiveness of your interview before you start and continuing right on to the end.

Case in Point

Manager Mae Hollis thought her meeting with the new assistant purchasing agent to review purchasing procedures had gone fairly well, despite some unaccountable hesitations. The man seemed to have some difficulty with his neck. But as she descends in a crowded elevator on her way to lunch, the assistant and a colleague enter. The former is complaining, "She had me stuffed into a corner, and I had to keep looking around the clothes rack to see her. I could hardly wait to get out of there." Hollis, hidden behind separating bodies, is pretty sure that she is the "she" referred to.

Analysis

Most managers instinctively know the basics of good seating for their interviews, but the refinements sometimes escape them. For one thing, offices may be small, and don't offer much latitude in arrangement. But a review of some principles of effective seating can further improve the degree to which you can remove obstacles to communication.

Effective Action

Let's get the basics out of the way, and go on from there.

   1. Comfortable chairs. Chairs should be comfortable enough to

permit an hour-long meeting without the squirms and shifts the body undertakes instinctively to eliminate possible aches and pains. An armchair is usually better than an armless one.

2. Supporting furniture. If your interview requires the other to refer to written materials, small models, or even to run a portable computer, a side table will increase convenience.

3. Clear sightlines. Your position and the other's should not be visually blocked (as by a clothing rack in the Hollis case or objects on your desk across which you are both sitting).

4. Interviewer position. Should you be sitting at your desk? Executives who have "conversation pits," a couch and armchair around a coffee table, for example, usually conduct their interviews away from their desk to achieve a feeling of informality, as well as more comfortable seating.

5. Position relationship. There are various possible ways to align two chairs.

- Face to face. This arrangement is possible at a desk or away from it, in a conversation area or other open space into which two chairs can fit. Usually it's simplest and best. You can make direct eye contact, and body language can flow freely between you.
- Alongside. Interviewer and interviewee may sit side by side, facing in the same direction. Conversation is possible by each turning to the other. It's not a recommended position. Not only is the neck craning uncomfortable, and continued for any length of time, painful, but it lacks both the eye contact possibility of face-to-face and blocks body language.
- Two on a couch. When you occupy one end of a couch, with your interviewee at the other, the resulting informality somewhat offsets the awkwardness of the body-twisting required to get you face to face.

6. Who's higher? Another practice to avoid: chairs of uneven heights. It's a problem either way. If you sit in the higher of the two, you gain the psychological advantage of dominance. But this very result can make the other uncomfortable.

Reversal can be just as bad or even worse. For the interviewee to look down at you suggests his or her control of the situation, at the very least, a puzzling contradiction of actuality. Both chairs at the same level is best to neutralize the psychological complications that may otherwise result.

See Mistake 42, on the stress interview, to see how improper seating has been used as a stress device by some possibly unwise interviewers.

MISTAKE 13: MISUSING THE FIRST PRECIOUS MINUTES

The first minutes of your interview can be critical to the success of the meeting. They can be used to start building rapport, to point the conversation in optimum directions, and so on. This doesn't mean that a lot of disparate actions must be crammed into the first 300 seconds. You may even want to spend the time simply putting the other person at ease and building and fostering friendliness.

Case in Point

Executive Ethel Wayne is confronted by department head Hank Cramer, who resents her recent promotion to a job he coveted. Despite his negative feelings, Wayne has suggested a joint planning session to eliminate bottlenecks caused by unclear responsibility for overlapping areas. She senses his hostility and decides on immediate efforts to avoid a get-nowhere session. She must act quickly before matters get out of hand.

"Hank," she says, "this is the first time we are working together. I'd like T.R. (the big boss) to see how well we perform as a team. It could do both of us a lot of good. Since you have had more experience in this area, why don't we agree that although it's a joint project, you will call the signals. . . ."

Analysis

The very start of your session is the time to build the platform on which your conversation will prosper. In the Wayne–Cramer case, Wayne rightly decided that overcoming Hank's hostility was an essential first move.

The nature of the interview tells you what your opening keynote should be. In a hiring situation, a friendly start to make the other comfortable is generally best. In a morale-building session, where the other is likely to be suspicious, one executive got right to the heart of the matter:

"Joan, I'm sure you know the whole department is upset by the layoffs in the last few weeks. We're hoping that's behind us. We want to get back to normal, and the better our performance as a team, the brighter our future can be. Now, in your case . . . ," and the executive proceeds to point out the encouraging factors for Joan and the department.

Below is a list of starting items that you can arrange, in your mind or on paper, into the sequence and time allotments appropriate for a given interview.

Effective Action

Here are a few major points to cover. You can number the boxes according to the priority you wish to give each; or cross an item out if it doesn't apply to the case at hand:

☐ *Hidden reefs.* Previous events may threaten prospects for a constructive session. In a performance review, a subordinate's festering resentment of injustice, real or imagined, can stop a session cold. Failure to face up to this situation at the outset may result in superficialities that get nowhere. Confronting it can assure an outcome satisfying to both parties.

☐ *Greeting.* Formal or relaxed, crisp or easygoing.

☐ *Name.* How you address a person is an instant clue to your attitude. A first name suggests informality, using last names shows respect, and so on.

☐ *Attitude.* Getting a fix on the other's mood can be of considerable help. An enthusiastic person can make a discussion of ideas take off quickly. A person whose manner is best described as "bearing a grudge" needs some leavening before you can expect much teamwork.

☐ *Opening keynote.* "It's about time we got together to settle this minor tangle. . . ." You've stated the purpose of the get-together and described the goal in a constructive way.

☐ *Outlining.* In a planning session, a few minutes devoted to discussing the importance of the session; past experience in the subject; and short-range and long-range goals can clear the way for a running start. Anticipate sore spots: "Let's take the time to settle the question of who will take responsibility for the production of the report, once we have a draft."

☐ *Expectation disclosure.* What you and the other persons hope to accomplish are best voiced early to prevent disappointment and misunderstanding: "I'm hoping that one thing to come out of this meeting is better communications between our two departments." And go about eliciting the other's ideas in this regard.

☐ *Self-revelation.* If you and the other person are strangers, as might be the case in a job interview or in a meeting between supplier and customer, provide some relevant facts about yourself to help get acquainted: "I've been with this company for over ten years. I started in sales and switched to service years ago. In my opinion, how you treat a customer after you've sold him is the key to a good relationship. . . ." The fewer the mysteries about yourself and the other person, the better you will get along.

MISTAKE 14: FAILING TO RECOGNIZE THE HIDDEN AGENDA

Most managers are familiar with the hidden agenda phenomenon, now standard in management training programs, under the headings of both interviews and group meetings. Even managers who have missed out on the advantages of formal study are no longer puzzled by a colleague interjecting an unexpected, even irrelevant subject into a conversation. Less well known: how to deal with it.

Case in Point

Manager Susan Lane is conducting a performance review with Al Gerald. The conversation is going along smoothly. They are discussing goals for the next quarter when Lane is startled by a tirade from Al Gerald:

"If you want me to be more productive, I'll tell you what to do. Renovate my office. It needs painting, better lighting, and ventilation. And a new desk and chair would help. I go home every night with an aching back."

Susan Lane is startled by the outburst. Why is the statement so abrupt and belated? If Al had a back condition aggravated by an unsuitable chair, why hadn't he mentioned it earlier? Were the communications between them so poor? And finally, she is bothered by his vehemence. The repressed rage scares her.

Analysis

Hidden agendas appear in one-on-one interviews, and in small and large group meetings. They consist of an idea, request, complaint, demand, or accusation catapulted into the conversation. Usually the speaker has been repressing it for some time. But it is not always offered in anger. In some instances the subject is introduced calculatingly, with a shrewd sense of timing, when the agendaist feels it will get optimum attention.

Some agendas are helpful, others are irritating or destructive. The manager who knows how to deal with them in whatever their guise has an opportunity to show his or her managerial capability to good advantage.

Effective Action

Three steps can lead to a successful counteraction: recognize, analyze, utilize.

1. *Recognize.* Not every digression is an instance of a hidden agenda item. In some cases the other person may say, "I've just had an interesting idea. It's not directly related to what we've been discussing, but. . . ."

Unlike a hidden agenda item, this kind of deviation is spontaneous, and the speaker is likely to be as surprised by it as you are. Enthusiasm, the excitement of a discovery, often accompanies the idea. On the other hand, the hidden item typically has been on the person's mind for some time, and its tone reflects the feeling he or she has about it; resentment, anger, hostility. If it is a ploy to embarrass you, it may have a sly quality.

2. *Analyze.* You have to make a judgment before you can proceed. Key questions put you back on track:

- Exactly what has been said? In the situation faced by Susan Lane, she must figure out the substance of Al Gerald's statement. On its face it is a request for renovation of his office, and that seems quite clear. But . . .
- Why is it being said? Here the trail is obscure. Lane's guess is that it reflects a dissatisfaction with the way the review has been going. Al Gerald has performed poorly for reasons that seem to reflect lack of motivation.

  In your own situations, use what you know about the individual to decide his or her mood. Is it constructive, or is it hostile? Or, does it reflect outside tensions—such as those at home—for which you are a convenient sounding board? If the reason for the digression remains unclear, consider a direct approach: "Why are you bringing up that subject?" It may be a good question to raise in any event.

- Why now? The timing of the statement may reveal something about the speaker's feelings and intentions. Lane believes Gerald suffers from both failure and guilt, and the complaint is intended to explain and excuse his poor showing. If this is true, then she sees she has to work more closely with Al so that she can supply both support and stronger direction. And she intends also to look into another key question:
- Is the statement justified? Hidden agendas may appear unbidden and even out of line. But you must make an immediate decision according to three possibilities:
  - —The subject is off base. For example, a subordinate, in the course of a performance review, tells her boss, "I think the company should include a course on chart and graph making in its supervisory training program." The manager may say, "That's out of my hands," or say, "Why don't you send a suggestion to the training department?" Or, "If you like, I'll mention it to the head of training next time I see him."
  - —The subject is relevant. If the subject is pertinent, or would add a constructive note, discuss it then and there as a regular agenda item.
  - —The subject may be worth exploring. If so, set a later specific time and place. If others are involved—another manager or staff member—tell your interviewee your suggestion for a meeting with these people.

3. *Utilize.* A hidden agenda subject may mean opportunity. You can learn of a colleague's repressed resentment, a secret aspiration, a cherished idea breaking through the veneer of everyday communication. You get a new understanding of the person. And the statement itself may lead to a productive follow-up.

What has been revealed? Usually something of special importance to the speaker. Then ask these key questions:

- Real, imaginary, or a bit of both? In the Lane-Gerald case, checking may show a certain amount of fact in the complaint and some fantasy. Does it suggest follow-up?
- How can the revelation be put to use? For example, Susan Lane arranged to meet with Al Gerald to discuss his suggestion. She made no attempt to find fault with the request or even separate the logical from the illogical aspects of the complaint. She began a fact-finding interview, addressing the problems that she decided

needed attention and could be resolved. In the end, Al got a new chair, desk, and better lighting. His performance improved sharply. Lane attributes that to his more suitable working situation and the feeling that he was getting personal recognition from his boss, which heightened his self-esteem.

MISTAKE 15: NEGLECTING THE BENEFITS OF AUDITIONING

It's a traditional method of hiring in the theatre. A director wants to know how well an actor or actress can do a part. He or she is given a script and the time to study it. Then comes the performance. Now the director needn't be concerned with background, training, experience, or other indirect factors. The judgment is based on what is seen and heard on the spot.

Not every job lends itself to the auditioning test. However, many do, and if not in their entirety then in crucial aspects. Even executive job applicants can prove themselves by the way key elements of a job are handled in an interview demonstration. For example, a candidate for an overseas position uses Japanese, Spanish, and Italian to show language capability. A candidate for a management job with a freight forwarder is given some typical shipments specifying materials, weights, points of origin, and destination. He rattles off the transportation he would use, and estimates the cost and time for delivery.

Cases in Point

1. Architect Calvin Berg is hiring a junior member for his staff. When applicant Elaine Gardner comes in for an interview he hands her a folio of photographs of the company's most recent structures and asks what she thinks of them. She praises admirable features and points out aspects with which she finds fault. Berg not only is impressed by her critique but also admires her tact in using mild terms to express unfavorable reactions. Her incisive and sophisticated judgment wins her the job.

2. Failure to give a hands-on test to some job applicants can get you into trouble. Helga Flint, a director of television commercials, recalls an early error in hiring:

> I was doing a job that needed six women to perform a simple water ballet in a pool. I picked them from a large group, using size

and shape as my criteria. "Can you swim?" I asked each finalist. All assured me they could. In the first take in the water, two had to be fished out to keep them from drowning.

Analysis

A performance test in hiring has obvious value. The two examples above show, in positive and negative ways, how the procedure may be used. Your ingenuity in reviewing the job and determining which elements may be tested broaden possible applications.

Another aspect of "reality testing" should be considered. Not only job procedures but such elements as the office or workstation, co-workers, and physical matters such as closeness of washrooms and eating facilities may be important judgment factors both from the employer's and employee's standpoints. For example:

An executive, after considerable interviewing, felt she had finally found the perfect assistant. As an afterthought, and to clinch the deal, she took the assistant to the office that would be hers.

"We just had the place repainted and refurnished. You could help choose the pictures."

The other shook her head sadly. "I'm awfully sorry but I couldn't work here. The office is too small and there's no window. I suffer badly from claustrophobia."

Effective Action

The theory of performance testing is simple. The applications will depend on the nature of the job and the imagination of the manager in extracting from the job appropriate elements. Steps like these, some derived from examples above, can pave the way:

1. *Be aware of the pros and cons of reality testing.* In the TV director's casting, ability to swim was essential. She hadn't expected that applicants would fudge on such an essential requirement. The idea was, get the job, worry about doing it later. There is an old saying in the job-hunting tradition: "A new employee can do a job as well as his or her friends can help to do it." The nonswimming extras couldn't benefit in this case. In most cases, however, auditioning provides the employer with evidence of degree of capability.

But take into account the possibility of nervousness or other interference. For example, a manager was looking for a technical clerk with experience in using spreadsheet computer programs. A candidate assured him that he was knowledgeable but botched a test. "Give me a few pointers on this equipment and let me try again," the candidate asked. The manager agreed, and the other gave a convincing demonstration.

2. *Understand that exposing applicants to the realities of the job gives them a chance to assess the setup.* By making it possible for a candidate to discover a job element that is a knockout factor for them, like the claustrophobic applicant mentioned earlier, they can save themselves and you wasted time and effort.

3. *Make the test fair.* Fairness, in this instance, consists of two factors:

- Don't just go through the motions. "Do you think you can do that?" asks a factory supervisor of a young woman applying for a job running a kickpress (a punchpress operated by a foot lever). She watches others operating and says yes. A week after starting she quits. "It's too hard for me. My legs are too short."
- Keep in mind the difference between a test performance and ability to do the job. For most people the audition brings out true ability; a few tense up in the audition spotlight. Managers may recognize this fact and have a candidate back for a second appraisal if they suspect "test tension" has spoiled the showing of an otherwise desirable prospect.

MISTAKE 16: FAILING TO SEEK LEVELING

When an interviewee says, "I'll level with you," the interviewer is likely to get all the information and insights required to explain an otherwise puzzling situation.

Leveling signifies the removal of a major obstacle in communication. The term is different from honesty and rapport. It suggests openness plus specificity. A person who levels with you is going to deliver a revelation that unlocks a mystery.

Case in Point

Executive Jane Ward is in a fact-finding session with Len Carver. "I still don't understand," Ward says, "why you didn't tell me about your trouble with Personnel."

Carver shrugs. Ward persists. "Come on, Len. You can trust me."

"I'll level with you," responds Carver. "People who pick fights with that crowd usually get it in the neck. Look what happened to Roy. He had that big disagreement with Smith, and a month later he was out on the street."

Carver's leveling meant a confession that helped explain otherwise murky behavior. It is now up to Jane Ward to ameliorate the situation to which Len Carver has referred.

Analysis

Leveling means a number of things. These phrases are synonyms:

"to play it straight . . ."
"to deal frankly and openly . . ."
"to come clean . . ."
"to tell it like it is . . ."

The vital element in leveling is that the other becomes willing to speak up despite a previous hesitation. Persuading a person to level may be the only way to break through a barrier of secrecy or coverup. It may hold the key to the success of the interview.

Effective Action

There are three ways to get the leveling response when the other is giving you a hard time:

1. *Make an emotional appeal.* "In all the years we've known each other," a manager says, "I've never betrayed a confidence or let you down . . ." Striking a chord of reassurance, perhaps of confidentiality, may loosen the barrier.

2. *Underline the benefits.* "If you level with me," says the interviewer, "you will be helping every person in this department. And we may be able to end this backbiting that has been so damaging to morale . . ." However, it is important to stress the advantages of leveling in terms that will be meaningful to the other. Peace and harmony in the department may mean little to one employee—for whom improved chances for advancement would be persuasive.

3. *Ask.* Interestingly enough, of the three approaches, the direct

request is often the one that works best. You look the other in the eye and say firmly, "This is important, I want you to level with me." Somehow, it's a request difficult to refuse.

MISTAKE 17: DISCOUNTING COURTESY

You don't have to shake your fist in the face of an interviewee to seem threatening. Failure to be pleasant can have the same effect. Courtesy is more than a hollow gesture in the interview situation. The manner and procedures that represent courtesy in action lay the groundwork for a good relationship. A smile and a handshake are just the beginning.

Case in Point

Consider manager Ralph Griff as seen by his latest victim, Lisa Corey, a candidate for a job opening available to transferees from other departments.

As Lisa knocks at Griff's door his neighbor from across the hall calls, "He said he'd be back late from lunch. Wait in the reception room."

Eventually Lisa spots Griff coming off the elevator and she follows him to his office. She is invited in, but seeing no place to sit—the two available chairs are taken up by books and files—she remains standing.

He removes just enough of the impedimenta so that she can sit on the edge of the seat. "Kind of busy," he says, and sorts through a pile of papers for her application. After skimming it he says, "Looks good. When can you start?"

"I'd like to know a bit more about the job."

"Oh, so you're the suspicious type," he says, but she doesn't appreciate the humor.

After a brief description of the duties he says, "That's it. Yes or no?"

"I wouldn't be at my best in the kind of work you described," she says, "but thanks for considering me." Later she tells a colleague, "I'd no more work for that boor than I would eat fish eyes."

Analysis

Courtesy for courtesy's sake is not at issue. Courtesy for the sake of a productive climate is. A hospitable manner is important not only to put the other person at ease, but it also shows that the executive cares. Below the surface, in hiring and exit interviews, for example, are vital concerns. The interviewee's job future, possibly his or her career, is at stake. A show of caring suggests the other's interests are respected. A friendly manner creates a harmonious tone that builds good communication.

Effective Action

Some of the old formal courtesies are obsolete. However, hat-tipping and opening doors for women are not the question. Contemporary good manners require relaxed and open friendliness. A sense of equality between members of the same or opposite sex is the key.

One executive, whose rapid progress is credited largely to her skills with people, suggests these observances:

1. *Physical amenities.* Prepare for the other's comfort, not only a place to sit, but one where the light is good, the sight lines from interviewer to interviewee clear. For example, a desk lamp that shines in the other's eyes and is on a line between executive and visitor is thoughtlessness that interposes an obstacle to a satisfactory outcome.

Other signs of consideration:

- Refreshment. Especially if the other has traveled a distance refreshments are a kind gesture. Fruit juice or soda, while not the most elegant of drinks, will be welcome on a hot day. Coffee or tea go in all weathers. Stay away from alcohol for the practical reason that even a slight high might interfere with normal conversation.
- Note pad and pen.
- Materials that bear on the visit. For example, in a retirement discussion, brochures on health, finances, and so on, at the very least show your willingness to be helpful. Or, for a job candidate, printed matter about the company and its products or services makes the same point.

- Add your own: _____

2. *Psychological factors.* Everything you do that suggests that the visitor is expected, and that you are prepared for the occasion is a desirable ego stroke. For example:

- Be on time for the meeting. If you are delayed, let the person know how long the wait will be.
- Have on hand résumés, correspondence previously exchanged, reference material likely to be required. This makes last-minute searches or interruptions to your conversation unnecessary.
- Open the meeting in a friendly manner. A pleasant greeting—even if the get-together is based on controversy, as for hearing a complaint—can minimize the tension. And if appropriate, a brief aside also can improve matters, anything from weather talk to "I understand you just got back from vacation," or, "I see from your résumé that you graduated from Annapolis. I tried for an appointment, but wasn't as lucky as you were." Personal comments are fine as long as they are innocuous.

"Be pleasant" is a somewhat ambiguous, certainly a general directive. Your judgment of the situation and the other person helps you supply the how and how much.

MISTAKE 18: BECOMING A VICTIM OF THE BROKEN-RECORD SYNDROME

Managers who interview with any degree of frequency may find they repeat themselves. For example, a string of hiring interviews may tend to become uniform and monotonous. One undesirable result: the interviewer gets stale, and what is said and questions asked become unstimulating. The interviewees are treated in the same way, overlooking the very differences that eventually help select the best candidate.

Even if interviews are not frequent (as when a manager calls in a subordinate to praise him or her for outstanding work), the sessions fall into a routine, and the manager may slur over the uniqueness of each subordinate's effort and accomplishment, which is the essence of recognition.

Case in Point

"The only thing Nick Costa lacks in his one-on-ones," the executive's subordinates agree, "is a teleprompter." They chafe at the assembly-line repetitiveness of the sessions. They compare notes and find that falling asleep in Costa's interviews is a real threat. Whether it is an idea-developing session or project planning, for Costa, it is only the occasional initiative of some interviewees that adds spark to meetings. He doesn't realize that the automatic repetition that makes things easy for him bores his group to death.

Analysis

Nick Costa doesn't vary his methods for two reasons: (1) He doesn't realize that what he thinks of as "keeping on track" actually is staying in a rut, and (2) in his desire to touch all bases, he uses the same list of points and covers them in a routine manner. As a result, he minimizes natural turns of conversation and the written agendas straitjacket the sessions.

Since rigidity gets in the way of communication, Costa's methods badly need an overhaul, not unusual for executives with a heavy interviewing load.

Effective Action

Don't guess about the vitality of your interviewing technique. The self-rating quiz below can provide a rough but useful measure of this important quality.

YOUR FLUIDITY INDEX

		True	*False*
1.	I don't like my interviews to run too long, so I always keep a tight rein on the conversation.	☐	☐
2.	I tend to keep the interviewee on the straight and narrow and discourage digressions.	☐	☐
3.	I permit no interruptions when I speak.	☐	☐
4.	I prefer interviewees who are businesslike and brief.	☐	☐
5.	I feel uncomfortable at minor revelations from an interviewee, about personal or family matters, for example.	☐	☐
6.	I encourage small talk about the weather, and so forth.	☐	☐

7. I don't hesitate to strike off in an unexpected
conversational direction, even though
   (a) it may waste time   ☐   ☐
   (b) it may not lead to any useful information.   ☐   ☐

[*Scoring directions: All "right" answers are False, except for numbers
6, 7a, and 7b. Give yourself 10 points for each correct answer, 0 for
"wrong" ones. If your score is below 50, consider adopting some of the
suggestions below.*]

Each of the suggestions below can help make your sessions more
stimulating, productive, and pleasurable.

1. If you use outlines for extensive and repeated interviews, consider
updating them from time to time. Or, for a change, might it be desirable
to hold a performance review in your subordinate's office, where he or
she can show-and-tell in describing projects? Be imaginative, even
daring. Your new ideas may flop, but also may invigorate you and your
interviewee.

2. During the session, take a quick reading of the liveliness or
interest factor. If you perceive drag in the conversation, take a break
and use it to add a new element to your agenda; introduce a new line
of questioning; or ask an unexpected question: "What would you do
about that if you were in my position?"

3. Give the other person more latitude, get below the surface of
bland answers: "You say you are satisfied with the progress of your
new project. Are you being too easily pleased?"

4. Use a simple but neglected measure of the success of an interview:
"How strong was my own interest?"

MISTAKE 19: FEARING THE INTERVIEWEE'S SILENCE

*Gerald Lewis, president of Vanton Pump & Equipment Corporation
of Hillside, New Jersey, says that while a halt in the conversation
may create a feeling of strain, an interviewee's silence may bring
unexpected benefits. It can mean resistance to the discussion or
presage introduction of a new element. Being aware of the other's
silence—and learning what it means—can get to the heart of an
important matter otherwise hidden.*

Case in Point

Frank Delaney, a young manager eager to shine in the executive fir-
mament, is pleased with his interviewing skill. His satisfaction is based

not so much on results, which he finds only vaguely measurable, but on the ease with which he elicits responses from interviewees. But he hits a stone wall in a performance review with assistant Emma Miele. After some one-word answers, the interview stops dead. Delaney hastily tries to rekindle the conversation. More silence that Miele abruptly breaks: "I think the new supervisor you appointed is ruining the department." The outburst reveals what is really on the assistant's mind and starts a new line of productive talk.

Analysis

Silence is often seen as uncooperativeness, even hostility on the part of the other person. But:

- It may suggest boredom or disinterest.
- The interviewee may be gathering thoughts or marshalling memory.
- A question you ask puzzles the other, and he or she hesitates to confess that it is not understood.

The typical interview develops with a natural continuity. If the interviewee does freeze up, there may be a misunderstanding or an obstacle that you must uncover before progress can continue.

Effective Action

In dealing with disconcerting breaks in the interviewee's flow of talk,

1. *Ask yourself, "Can I reap a benefit?"* Whatever the cause, consider the other's silence as an opportunity rather than a threat. There may be something to be learned, some useful action to be taken. For example, the other person may be preoccupied with matters that make the interview seem unimportant. When you get the other to explain, your next best move may be to switch subjects.

2. *Don't act prematurely.* One or two minor hesitations may mean nothing. But if long halts persist, stop pursuing your agenda and deal with the blockage.

3. *Seek the cause.* Check these possibilities:

- Faulty communication. Listen to one sales manager:

I asked Tom to come in to discuss an error he made in taking a customer's order. After get-nowhere talk with him staring at the wall, he abruptly said he resented me second-guessing him. He had done what he thought was right at the time. I said I wasn't there to find fault, but to learn what had actually happened. With that point made, we were able to agree on how to handle that sales situation next time.

(Note how the interview focus switched from fault-finding to problem identification.)

- Loss of interest. A job candidate loses interest in the job being discussed and stops participating.
- Resentment. An employee in an exit interview deeply resents the separation, or a subordinate feels that an information-gathering talk is an invasion of privacy.
- Doubt about objectives. Rather than blunder and grope toward uncertain goals, the subordinate stops talking. This is easy to handle: clarify the purpose and you're on the way.

You may not have to probe or guess at the reasons for the silence. A simple query gets to the heart of the matter: "You don't seem comfortable with our conversation. Can you tell me why?" If you get the answer, you may bridge into a high-payoff subject area.

4. *Decide whether you should be the one to break the silence.* Valerie Friedman, director of marketing for Nabisco Brands of Parsippany, New Jersey, suggests, "Force yourself not to fill in the conversation gaps." If the halt is overly long, she may toss the ball to the other person: "Is there anything you'd like to say at this point?"

5. *Question your technique.* Inexperienced managers may lack the skill to keep a conversation moving. If this is the reason for silence, some form of training is called for. At a minimum, drill in the particular kinds of interviews he or she conducts will help.

Even a seasoned interviewer may be fazed by a continuing silence. If this happens and you can't figure out why, or, you know the difficulty but can't offset it, try another line of discussion or reschedule the meeting.

MISTAKE 20: UNDERESTIMATING YOUR OWN SILENCE AS AN INTERVIEWING TOOL

Bartlett's Familiar Quotations *lists over 150 references to silence, suggesting that poets and interviewers have a mutual interest. Your silence can be a most effective interviewing tool. However, it is a slippery one, and getting a handle on it may not come easily. This unit can help reinforce your understanding and feel for it.*

Case in Point

Alex Bryson tries to put some life into a review of Bill Heinz's performance, but it just limps along. Heinz seemed glad to have the meeting, but once in Bryson's office, he talks and talks but says little. Bryson asks, "Have your feelings about your work changed any?"

"I'm not sure," responds the other and stops, watching Bryson expectantly. The manager says nothing. Heinz twists uncomfortably in his chair, looking hopefully at his boss. Bryson remains silent.

Suddenly Bill Heinz blurts out, "It's not my work," he says. "I like my job."

"Glad to hear that," Bryson responds, and again is silent.

"It's home," says the subordinate. "Our teenager is down with some disease the doctors can't diagnose. And we're running out of money. . . ." Tears roll down his cheek, and the manager doesn't interfere. Finally the subordinate says, "I feel better getting that off my chest."

"Let's table the meeting for now," Bryson says. "Let me know how things are going and whether I can help in some way."

Analysis

The Bryson–Heinz case shows how silence can jar information loose. Heinz had talked aimlessly in his reluctance to voice what was really on his mind. The questions being asked were too removed from where his heart and mind were. Silence created the opportunity to talk.

"Well-timed silence is more eloquent than speech," said a nineteenth-century essayist. It is incorrect to think of silence as a mere vacuum. It can be threatening, healing, provocative, or an invitation to speak from the heart.

Effective Action

In thinking about your use of silence as an interviewing tool, consider these guidelines:

1. *See silence as an eliciting tool.* It tends to bring out responses that may be difficult to get by questions.

2. *Understand that the interviewee's response to silence has two phases.*

- Discomfort. There is a feeling that he or she is on the spot, is expected to say or do something that is not specified.
- Reaction. What the other says to fill the conversation gap is usually an idea or feeling that represents something of importance to the person, therefore of interest to the interviewer.

3. *Know the points in an interview at which silence can be constructive.*

- When the other stops talking and waits for you to take over. Instead, you extend the silence, and it's up to the other.
- To let a statement or line of reasoning sink in. If you continue talking, it may lessen the weight of what you've just said.
- To give you time to think over the import of something the other has said, or vice versa.
- To assess what has been achieved at a particular point in the discussion, particularly if you are dissatisfied with progress. By tossing the ball to the other, you get feedback that explains where the session is at.
- When you need a bridge into another subject or area of interest.

If efforts to elicit conversation are unsuccessful, you may want to state the obvious, that if the other is unwilling to contribute, the interview must end. If the other has a hidden agenda or repressed feelings, or a subject on his or her mind, he or she may then speak up.

MISTAKE 21: ASKING STALE QUESTIONS

Terry M. Gruggen, senior vice president of the Minneapolis branch of Bozell, Jacobs, Kenyon & Eckhardt, asserts that "asking questions that every interviewer asks" is a turnoff. Cliché questions are an invitation to boredom and lackluster responses.

Of course, one manager's cliché may seem incisive and useful to another. You have to know the clichés to avoid them. The example below illustrates one of the worst, with more to follow subsequently.

Case in Point

Says a recent job hunter,

I needed a job, but when a young manager, thinking to be professional, started off with, "Instead of my asking a lot of questions, just tell me all about yourself," I decided who needs this man as a boss and said, "Fine, you tell me all about yourself first." Needless to say, I left shortly thereafter.

The reaction shows the damage that can lie in old phrases that are not only turnoffs but putoffs as well.

Analysis

Clichés and tired phrasing make poor conversation. Successful interviewers are those whose language reflects the interview's basic strength, that it is a get-together of two human beings to communicate thoughts and feelings on a subject of mutual interest. This goal is reached most readily when the conversation is responsive and both parties can speak openly in a freewheeling exchange. It's as simple as this: tired language dulls a conversation; freshness brightens and sharpens it.

Effective Action

Every interview can be made spontaneous and attention-holding. It is easy to slip into ruts worn smooth by habitual use. But observe the theater, where the same words and actions must be repeated at every performance. Do the members of the audience, even the actors themselves, die of ennui? No, the actor's skill has been described by Sir Laurence Olivier as making each performance seem the very first one.

To give your interviews an internal vitality:

1. *Use fresh language.* Remember the old roller towel? It had to be pulled down to a clean area. Make the effort to avoid "used" vocabularies.

- Try to get the other to avoid bad habits you eschew. For example, don't let him or her slip into superficial or vague answers. "Interesting," as a response to, "How did you like your last job?" can be decidedly ambiguous. "Nice," can be a no-answer answer, as in, "I had a nice boss."
- Be aware of your tone of voice. The greatest bore in the world is the speaker bored with his or her own subject. If you talk in a friendly, encouraging, possibly enthusiastic way, your conversation will become a lively exchange.

- "Personalize" your speech. Use the other's name, say "As you just said," for a tight continuity. Put yourself into the conversation occasionally: "I share your feelings about that . . ."

2. *Keep the interview simple, sincere, free of tired old gambits.* Instead of, "Tell me about yourself," a roundhouse shot that suggests you're after an autobiography instead of information, narrow the focus. Broach general subjects as openers, to provide a framework. Instead of "Tell me about your work experience," then silent waiting, try, "Now about your work experience. Where and when did you first get into sales promotion?"

Additional verbal abysses include:

- "What are your weaknesses?" Likely response: "My main weakness is that I'm so enthusiastic about my work that I don't have time for my personal life."
- "What are your strengths?" It's no coincidence that if you let it be known you're after a go-getter, the other is almost sure to be "strongly result-oriented."
- "Where do you see yourself in five years?" Don't be surprised if you hear, "Sitting in your chair," or some such drivel.

Of course, the main thing wrong with stale questions is that they get stale answers.

MISTAKE 22: GETTING CAUGHT FLAT-FOOTED BY THE OTHER'S MOOD

It doesn't happen often, but when it does it requires action: The interviewee comes into your office in a mood unsuited to the occasion. He or she may be angry, frustrated, depressed. Whatever is wrong, you must deal with it, but how? The one thing you're sure of is that the interview is threatened.

Case in Point

Executive Quint Martin awaits Art Hale, a design engineer with whom he wants to discuss his idea for a new welding jig. He and Hale have met at various company functions, and Martin knows the other well enough to see that as he comes in, he's seething. The executive hesitates.

Should he query the engineer about his upset? Instead, thinking to lighten the atmosphere he utters a pleasantry about the weather.

"Let's get on with it," Hale snaps. "What's the big brainstorm?"

Taken aback, Martin hesitates, then hoping that ignoring Hale's manner may make it go away, he says, "You know that welding operation is a bottleneck. If we put our two heads together, we might be able to develop this idea of mine."

Hale's laugh is more like a snarl. "You executive types. Haven't you anything better to do than sit around thinking up dumb ideas?"

Martin is startled by the other's attack. He says lamely, "I thought we might have a productive discussion. . . ."

"Glad you put it in the past tense," the engineer says. "When you straighten out your thinking, call me," and stalks out.

Quint Martin stews over the incident. Finally he calls Art Hale's boss. "Stan, this is Quint Martin . . ."

The voice at the other end interrupts: "I know, you were supposed to have a meeting with Art Hale. Well, he had a quarrel with his wife, and I guess things fell apart for him."

Martin feels sorry for Hale but is irritated by his inability to deal with the encounter. What might he have done differently?

Analysis

Newly-generated anger or frustration isn't always as obvious as Art Hale's. Martin noticed the symptoms on sight, but in some cases, behavior is faked and emotions suppressed. Symptoms may appear as sarcasm, argumentativeness, or illogical reasoning and incoherent speech. If the interfering mood is depression or anxiety, the interviewee may attempt to shrug it off, but usually fails.

If the mood is rage, the interview situation, with its privacy and a captive audience of one provides a convenient setting for venting destructive feelings, as in Art Hale's case. The attempt to continue despite the interviewee's emotionality seldom produces a successful meeting. Regardless of the exact nature of the upset, if it persists the manager must make immediate decisions.

Effective Action

You have three courses open to you when confronted by an interviewee victimized by his or her mood:

1. *Take direct action.* Forget the interview you had planned. Make a tentative statement that shows your awareness that something is wrong: "You seem upset. Can I help?"

In some cases you can wean the other out of his or her black mood. But when the emotion is deep and bitter, it may be impossible to dislodge. If your move doesn't work, and the other responds either by denial or by a hostile reaction, move on to the next option.

2. *Test for intensity.* How strong are the emotions? An executive who wants to learn just how far out of it a subordinate is, asks, "Would it be better to postpone our talk?" Any response other than yes can lead to an airing of feelings and agreement on the next step, whatever it might be.

3. *Cancel the interview.* Don't put the onus on the other person. Whatever the specifics are, ease the other off the hook. One executive relates, "I was about to start a performance review, but it was clear that my subordinate was in bad spirits. I told her, "Mary, I feel the vibes are wrong for a good meeting. Let's make an appointment for tomorrow."

Postponing the interview is a good move and may even be initiated by the other person. For example, a job candidate is justified in asking for a raincheck: "I'm eager to have this meeting," is the opening, followed by, "because I think we both have a lot to gain from it," then suggesting another appointment. For what reason? Most are perfectly acceptable: a temporary malaise, serious family problems, a bad hassle because of traffic. Even a poor reason is acceptable for a wise move.

MISTAKE 23: NEGLECTING THE AWAY-FROM-THE-OFFICE INTERVIEW SITE

You probably do your interviewing in your office. Most executives do. You may even have several arrangements to provide seating flexibility: a chair directly across the desk for formal matters; the same chair moved to the side so you can swing around for greater informality. Larger quarters may provide couch, coffee table, and armchair that form a conversation pit in still further contrast with the standard across-the-desk axis.

But for some interviews, the office, no matter how well equipped, may not be suitable. Fashion consultant Barbara Pittfield, with experience in hiring for a range of industry needs, says, "For some jobs, only meetings away from the office suggest serious intent."

Cases in Point

These cases are distinguished by locale:

• *Restaurants.* Executive Adele Morgan is looking for a person to bring into her publishing company at the top. She wants to sound out Hank Yale, VP of a competitive firm, who has the marketing experience she is after. An invitation to lunch is accepted. Morgan has been subtle about it, and Yale understands it isn't a social matter.

They meet at a quiet dining place known for its excellent cuisine and well-spaced tables. This last means, to Morgan and her guest, an absence of loud restaurant chatter and the chance to talk freely. Occasionally, important deals have been shattered by a casual eavesdropper who overheard a conversation and passed it along to unfriendly parties.

• *Airports and railroad stations.* For some one-on-one meetings transportation terminals have a particular virtue. They are convenient if either party is from out of town. Also, meeting in such crowded places paradoxically offers anonymity.

• *Hotels.* But not if interviewer and interviewee are of the opposite sex. Even the most broadminded principals would hesitate at the questionable appearance of such a meeting. However, if a third party is present, as in a group interview, a hotel room offers privacy, comfortable surroundings, and room service.

Analysis

Off-premises interviews are not uncommon for higher-echelon hiring particularly when the exchange is meant to be secret or confidential. Or, the interviewer wants to signal the importance of the meeting.

Two additional benefits may be gained from a restaurant setting:

1. *An opportunity to impress a job candidate favorably.* A company anxious to gain the services of a individual may count on outstanding food and posh surroundings to polish the company image and suggest its affluence, a favorable quality in an employer. You might not think that an expensive lunch would make much of an impression on a prospect who is out for a salary of $50,000 a year or more. It often does.

2. *The opportunity for the hiring executive to size up a candidate's social behavior.* What? Judge a job candidate by his or her table manners? Absolutely. It happens every workday of the week. And for certain jobs,

in which the incumbent will be calling on customers or making key contacts, which often means dining out, the company's image and reputation may stand or fall on the way the representative addresses the waiter, what dishes he or she orders, and what and how much is drunk.

For meetings other than for hiring, some managers say the removed site can work wonders.

• *Patching up a misunderstanding.* When colleagues have had a falling out, one may take the initiative and suggest a meeting at a local dining place. The physical distance from the office, the change of atmosphere, the ritual of eating together, relaxes tension and supplies a therapeutic perspective.

• *Disagreement about performance.* The subordinate maintains that all is well, the boss insists he or she should do better. Attempts to resolve the differences in the office have failed. Either may initiate an off-site meeting, both may benefit. The subordinate's contentions and the manager's differing opinions seem less in conflict as food and the atmosphere affect body chemistry, making the individuals more susceptible to compromise.

The potency of a changed locale is explained by two sets of factors:

1. *Pair dynamics* (see Mistake 79). Interactions between the two are obviously affected by the new and neutral surroundings. More relaxed attitudes and better perspective tend to develop.

2. *The physical fact of privacy.* The latitude to talk without interruption or being seen or overheard by third parties, is another benefit.

Effective Action

The cases and analysis above suggest the rationale, applications, and benefits of off-site interviewing. The guides for this arrangement are summarized in key points, some of them already made.

1. *Consider the away-from-the-office meeting place* for interviews that may not have worked out in the office or might benefit from a nonbusiness setting.

2. *Be aware of the benefits: privacy, informality, lack of business interruptions, less tension.* One factor not mentioned earlier: you and the interviewee are doing the equivalent of "camping out," creating a

kind of camaraderie and rapport that can be of special help in forging a meeting of the minds.

3. *Remember to bring along all relevant documents and materials.* If you are hiring, you don't want to find yourself five miles away from the desk drawer that holds the other's résumé, work history, and newspaper clippings that celebrate his or her proof of public recognition.

4. *Be prepared to assume all the duties of host, including picking up the tab.*

MISTAKE 24: BEING UNCERTAIN ABOUT CLOSING

Every element in the interview is important; the closing phase is crucial. Usually the wrapup is the element on which the outcome of the entire exchange may hinge. Three major mistakes may mar an otherwise successful session:

1. Premature closing
2. Belated closing
3. Failure to tie up loose ends

Cases in Point

Three vignettes dramatize the pitfalls:

1. *Premature closing.* Executive Alf Moore starts a problem-solving interview with section leader Ann Mara, who has been having difficulties with a new assignment. He hopes to keep the meeting short but a half hour passes with no end in sight. Mara is about to begin another phase of her problem when Moore interrupts:

"Ann, we've covered the major hitches. Don't you think you can take care of the rest of it yourself?" He stands up. "Let me know if you need any further help."

Ann Mara leaves, frustrated. "Need any further help! That's a laugh." She feels she's been brushed off. Perhaps it's her own fault. A prepared list of questions might have speeded things up. She hates to do it, but will probably have to ask her boss for another meeting.

2. *Belated closing.* The new employee is having an orientation session. The first fifteen minutes are fine, the next fifteen drag, and after that it's just plain boredom. "I hope," the subordinate thinks, "this isn't typical of company procedures." Lacking in the interview

was any effort to condense the information, and put into writing factual material in the form of a small handbook.

3. *Failure to tie up loose ends.* Cal Newton says to Ted Reedy, "Guess we've taken care of everything. Good meeting, right?"

But outside the door, Reedy stops dead. There are a dozen decisions left hanging. Back in his office he starts making a list:

- Who is going to get an OK from Mr. Rackley on the new report format?
- The revisions of the report require retyping. Will Newton authorize that, or have his secretary do it?
- Who is going to tell Helen Breen she is no longer needed on the task force? And who is going to deal with the disappointment he knows she will feel?
- Why hadn't he, Ted Reedy, insisted that they settle the question of whether or not to bring someone from Personnel into the task force full time? The pickup consulting had wasted a lot of time.

Ted Reedy has rediscovered an old truth: Loose ends that show up after an interview session for planning, problem solving, and so on, seriously handicap an ongoing project.

Analysis

The closing minutes of an interview pose a special challenge. You must assess the conclusion as carefully as a master chef watches a soufflé. Failure to terminate at the right time, and in the right way—because of prematurity, letting the interview drag on, or leaving loose ends— can mean failure. The errors may result from inexperience, poor interviewing technique, or forgetting. For many executives, touching all bases is a habit. But even the most experienced interviewer, under pressure, or diverted by other matters, may suffer lapses. The points made below can remind you of the essentials of successful closing.

Effective Action

Each of the failures requires its own specific remedies:

1. *Avoiding prematurity.* Concluding an interview before all its purposes have been served can be prevented by

- Not letting the end sneak up on you. By anticipating the finishing phase, you can close the curtain as an appropriate wrap-up.
- Mentally reviewing your agenda. All bases touched? The other person may have bases to cover as well. Accordingly, ask the interviewee if he or she has any further questions or needs clarification of any points.
- Check for understanding. Before concluding, make sure the other person retains the essential information, agreements, or conclusions that have been reached. Query the other about any matters in doubt and certainly on understanding of key points.

2. *Eliminating needless prolongation.* Consider these remedies:

- Use a clock. Setting a time limit and sticking to it can help you pace yourself with a deadline for the end in mind.
- Sidestepping trivia. "Drivel," says one experienced executive, "has a way of stalling too many interviews." Conversation sometimes has a way of running on. When you sense that talk has gone out of control, stop, assess what you want to cover, and get back on track.
- Check for fatigue or boredom. You can often tell visually when an interviewee is adrift in ennui or too tired to concentrate. Take note: Are the other's eyes wandering, is expression blank? Is he or she still as sharp as at the start? Are your statements being misunderstood? Do you hear, "Please repeat that," more than once?

3. *Tying up loose ends.* Things are left hanging for two reasons: failure to cover points during the talk, or failure to specify follow-up action (who is to do what, when, and how).

Some unfinished business may be easily visible: "We forgot to set a time for our meeting with Engineering." Other matters may not be so simple: "If things don't go as planned, we will have to place an order for new equipment immediately." Behind that simple sentence lies a complicated procedure of observation, analysis, and decision making.

Get help in spotting loose ends. Ask the other person:

- "Anything else we should discuss?"
- "Have we now taken care of all the items on our agenda?"
- "As a result of our decisions, are there other people to be notified, actions to take?"

MISTAKE 25: NOT FOLLOWING THROUGH

You go through every item on the agenda, come up with some excellent decisions and lines of action. You think you're all set. But it's amazing how even experienced executives fail to make the ultimate move and lose out on the payoff. What can happen: decisions and actions agreed on in the interview require follow-up and this essential step is omitted.

Case in Point

Executive Sandra Smith and her assistant Ken Seiko hold a problem-solving meeting to figure out how to improve the layout of equipment in the department. It goes well and the close is mutual congratulations on their success.

Smith puts all their rough sketches in a folder and says, "The new setup is going to get rid of a dozen bugs and bottlenecks. Just changing the location of my desk is going to save me a mile of walking every day. And remember how the copying operation crowds the main doorway? The new spot is going to cut down on the turmoil. I'll show the plans to Lee tomorrow."

But a rush job comes up. She doesn't see her boss the next day, or even next week. When she finally has the time, he isn't available. When the meeting is set up, she stops in to see Ken Seiko. "Did I give you the folder with our layouts? I can't find them." Ken can't, either. They scour both offices. No folder. She says, "I'll try to reproduce them," but her memory isn't good enough, nor is Ken's.

She may be able to duplicate the ideas for the improved layout in the future, but what a waste!

Analysis

The degree of loss felt by Sandra Smith is probably extreme, but it makes the point: Some interviews require follow-up. Not following up promptly and thoroughly may mean, at the very least, losing out on the possible gains. When the implementation of ideas and decisions of your interviews has any degree of complexity, it's important that you organize them as carefully as you would any other extensive activity.

Why is such a damaging oversight relatively common? The reasons are both psychological and procedural.

- Follow-up is seen as "another task," rather than an extension of the interview. Accordingly, new questions arise: Who should take on the assignment? Executive Sandra Smith feels she should

have, but pressure of other duties forced her to put off this "extra job." Perhaps she should have handed it over to Ken.
- Responsibility may be unclear. There may be no logical person to do the follow-up. Seiko thought Smith would do it because she walked off with the sketches, a fair assumption. But nothing was said between them to pin down the responsibility. Seiko forgot about it, and the problem was pushed out of Smith's mind by the crush of other matters.
- The magnitude of the job may be overwhelming. There can be a deterring amount of work in follow-up, or its innovative nature might be fazing. If the subordinate is left with an extensive task, the manager may be derelict in not supplying help or sharing the burden.

Effective Action

Various notes to remember about follow-up planning:

1. *Be aware of the size of the task; it may be deceptive.* For example, you and a subordinate spend a couple of hours working out some details of a new approach to security in the department. You started with the expectation of a few changes but, swept along by an abundance of good ideas, you end up with a big program. You may have bitten off more than you can chew.

This obstacle often sneaks up on managers in problem-solving and planning sessions. You have two options:

- Keep your follow-up tasks in mind during your session. You may decide not to plan too ambitiously or to rule out solutions to problems that are too costly or extensive.
- Use a task force. You needn't limit follow-up to yourself and the other person. If the ideas to be implemented are worthwhile, consider using a task force approach, selecting people and organizing the group from the entire department, or company, if warranted. Standard task force practices, such as freeing people from their regular assignments for their additional duties, can start you rolling.

   Don't overload any one individual, including yourself. Assign and delegate tasks to spread the burden and avoid having one person bottlenecking what has to be done.

2. *Develop a regular follow-up procedure after your interviews.* In

general the question you answer in your planning is, Who will do what, when? Usually there are three "agents" involved: You, the Other Person in the interview, and Third Parties. Here is an example that might involve follow-up requirements generated by a meeting such as that between Sandra Smith and her assistant:

A FOLLOW-THROUGH LIST

You	*Other Person*	*Third Parties*
Brief boss. Describe plan, show sketches, specify what changes will be required, and approximate costs. Talk to treasurer about budgetable items.	Get together with employees involved. Ask for suggestions about moving equipment. Inform heads of neighboring departments.	Secretary to send memos to those who may be affected. Memo to purchasing to get prices for new items required by move.

Usually, follow-up duties are allocated on a can-do basis. Note that the You in the example above takes care of upper-echelon communications, the Other Person works at his or her level, and Third Parties are asked to take on tasks in their own areas of responsibility.

HIRING

MISTAKE 26: MISUSING A CANDIDATE'S RÉSUMÉ

Résumés from job applicants are a basic element in hiring. It can be useful to examine the preinterview phase of résumés, along with their role in the assessment meeting itself.

To executives who hire, résumés may be a means for the discovery of a good prospect or boring forms to skim and discard. Two major reasons why résumés may be discarded are:

- A résumé may be spoiled by poor handwriting, typing, or spelling, with the result that a highly qualified candidate's chance for the job goes into the wastebasket. (There was a time in the 1950s when spelling fell out of favor in grade schools in some areas. Fifteen years later Ph.D. graduates presented dissertations with misspellings typical of high school dropouts.)
- A help-wanted advertisement pulls too well and résumés fill the in-box to overflowing. The executive calls on whoever is available to help and the screening process is turned into a joke, not a very funny one.

Case in Point

"Jessie," her boss tells the receptionist, handing her a batch of résumés, "you have time on your hands. Pick out the good ones." Any Jessie, with the best brain in the world, would have trouble carrying out the assignment. Unfortunately, the example is neither exaggerated nor rare. Screening résumés is a demanding operation. Having it done by untrained, inexperienced, and consequently bored employees can only benefit writers looking for horrible examples in management practice.

Analysis

How can managers eliminate flaws in the résumé process? How does the résumé-reading executive get the most out of his or her time investment? Poorly written, sometimes inappropriately slanted for the job in question, résumés themselves are part of the problem. But a larger part is the mishandling of résumés by management. An examination of what hiring executives actually do makes it possible to highlight the good and discard the bad.

Effective Action

Use the guidelines that follow to assess and sharpen your present résumé handling.

1. *Avoid two practices that lessen the efficiency of screening procedures:*

- Erroneous rejection. The manager sorts through forms, many reflecting less the candidate's abilities than his or her deficiencies as a writer. Impatience sets in, and the simplest solution is to toss out the résumé.

  This negative attitude, either of the hiring executive or a delegated assistant, encourages short shrift, and many promising résumés meet their fate in the wastebasket, unread. The executive is then left with a skimpy assortment from which good candidates may have been eliminated.
- Unfounded acceptance. Not because of naïveté, more likely under the influence of two factors, the executive may react with unjustifiable favor.
  —Need for relief. "This procedure is killing me. Won't fate send me an ideal employee?" The hope: the very next résumé will produce the miracle. One of the executives verified this attitude: "Some of us are decision-shy, and we hesitate to select a

candidate from a packed field. Our fondest hope is that one résumé describes a candidate who is an obvious winner."

—Empathy. Executives are aware of the mindset of the typical job hunter, know the joy that comes with the words, "I got the job!" The awareness probably reflects the executive's own past experience. A soft-hearted (in business a synonym is "soft-headed") reading may cause looser screening that increases the number of useless submissions you handle.

2. *Know the résumé for what it is.* "No one gets a job from a résumé," comments one of our resource group of executives. "All a résumé does, even if it's the best in the world, is to get the applicant an interview." This thought puts a more realistic face on the entire résumé-screening process. Making this fact clear to your screeners should help make them more matter-of-fact in their decisions.

3. *If others assist in the screening, provide adequate preparation.* Here are the points to cover in a briefing:

- Describe the job. If a written set of specifications or a job description exists, have the assistant study them.
- Show the assistant the ads or other publicizing material that bring in the résumés. They are then better able to judge the aptness of the submitted material and develop a more realistic basis on which to assess it.
- Provide a basis for judgment. Put the qualifications in order of importance, pinpoint the knockout factors: "Education isn't too important, but two or more years of drafting in an architect's office is essential."
- Use a rating formula. When the number of résumés is small, a two-category separation (yes or no, retained or discarded) may suffice. But when the volume of résumés is large, a three-category system may be better: yes, no, doubtful. The doubtful category tends to decrease the chance of unwarranted rejection. True, it may force a second or third screening, but for jobs difficult to fill, you may modify priorities and find your hirees in the doubtful group.
- Have a trial run. Before turning the assistant loose, do two things: First, have him or her go through a few résumés and explain their "readings" to you, their negative or positive reactions to the data. Continue until their judgments are in line with yours.
- Maintain control. Suggest that they report back to you after the first hour or so of screening, or stop in yourself to check on progress.

4. *Prepare the interviewees before meeting them.* If it makes sense in your case, send along informational material about the company, the job, and so on. When good people are scarce, when you're under pressure to hire and the company story is favorable, the advance selling strengthens your hand.

5. *Use the candidate's résumé as an agenda for the hiring interview.* Focus on the points relevant to your requirements. Skim in advance. Check the résumé for the candidate whose interview is coming up. Make marginal notes, check items you want to pursue. Generally, your follow-up touches on three key points:

- *Verify.* "Your résumé states that you increased productivity in your department. How was that measured? How big were the increases? (You can ask for unit figures or percentages.) How did your record compare to that of other departments?"
- *Ask "Why?"* Motivation can be revealing: "You left company X after two years for company Y. Why did you do that?"
- *Discuss goals and aspirations.* What the candidate hopes for in his or her future often shapes tomorrow's attitude and performance. You might ask: "Are you interested in continuing your professional studies?" If the answer is affirmative, "Specifically, what areas would you cover? What would you do to pursue this interest?" For a candidate you are eager to win over, you might inject information of the company's support of employee's studies. One executive sometimes asks: "How would getting this job fit into your long-range goals?"

For more on résumés and the hiring process, see Mistake 81.

MISTAKE 27: HIRING FOR YOURSELF ALONE

"No man is an island, entire of itself," said the seventeenth century poet John Donne. His insight applies to managers in their hiring role. Face it. Invisible bonds tie your new hires to others alongside whom they may work or to whom they may report. Even if they are lions and lambs, will they lie down together, or will the blood flow? Ignoring the ties can negate what seemed like a good choice. In some instances the manager must share the decision with a superior or colleagues.

Case in Point

Manager Sam Gage is interviewing for an assistant and finds him in Jack Verben, the third applicant. He feels Verben will complement his own weak and strong points. His skills are excellent, his experience and motivation fine. Gage is about to tell the man he can come to work as soon as he is ready, when he remembers his boss, Tom Palmeri, had asked, "Let me spend a few minutes with your top candidate." It had been said casually, but belatedly, Gage realizes Tom meant what he said. He wonders how Verben would impress Tom. He makes up a little chart in his head comparing his and his boss's probable reactions to Verben:

Quality	Sam Gage	Tom Palmeri
Mild-mannered	Likes	Rubs him wrong way
Relishes details	Likes	Sees it as a mark of small-minded people
Big talker	Dislikes	Prefers the quiet type

Gage decides he'll hold off until he gets Tom into the act.

Analysis

If hired, an applicant is judged twice—in the interview, then on the job. The second judgment is by his boss, as a performer, and by his or her peers, as a person, co-worker and team contributor. Will the newcomer help or spoil things?

A boss may share a subordinate manager's values and judgments or differ with them. It makes sense to consult with your boss on candidate evaluation, certainly when hiring key people, and in many instances this consultation is built into the procedure. If Sam Gage had kept his boss's values in mind, perceptions and outcome in the hiring interview might have been different.

Organizational factors, along with your boss's and staff's views, may apply. How will the candidate fit in with the staff? What will his or her long-run prospects be with the company?

Effective Action

Having others participate in hiring can be a useful procedure but will have varying relevance for different managers. Read the paragraphs that follow in the context of your own circumstances and job relationships. If members of your staff are managers who do hiring, you may want to appraise what follows from your position as boss along with its implications upward to your boss.

1. *Your boss.* The advantages of meshing your own and your boss's views are won in these situations:

- Consider discussing the job and the kind of person that might fill it, job description, recruiting, and so on in the earliest stages.
- Talk to your boss about the kind of person you will be looking for, modify as the conversation may suggest.
- Offer the boss the chance to interview top candidates if it isn't already required. He or she will have to live with the candidate, too.
- Tell the boss of your final choice, before you offer the job.

2. *The candidate's potential colleagues.* Almost as crucial as the boss's views are those of the people with whom the new employee will be working. Consider the same preparatory phases with colleagues as with your boss. Keep their possible preferences in mind. Of course, don't be influenced by their poor judgments or biases, but lend an ear to useful ideas. "Hope you'll get us someone who can do a little artwork. The department needs an illustrator and chart maker," can be an important reminder.

3. *Organizational fit.* Some companies have an image of their ideal employee, and seek to hire those that conform. For example, at one time there was said to be a "banking type," or an "advertising agency type," or IBM or AT&T types. Some companies may "cast against type," as theatrical casting directors sometimes do. The idea is that the unusual matchup may provide above-average, even sensational performance. Determine for yourself, based on your own views and values, how important, if at all, this particular consideration is.

4. *Knockout factors.* Get agreement on qualities that will automatically disqualify job applicants. If you approach the interview with the negatives in mind, as well as a clear picture of the must-have qualities, you are less likely to be forced into a premature choice that could mean a new employee in a job for which he or she lacks a basic requirement. (See Mistake 30, on the knockout factor, for more on this subject.)

If you decide to consult with colleagues, or to have them interview candidates, be sure to equip each with essential information: qualifications, special requirements, key areas of experience and skills to explore. Among other things, a common base from which you and they operate makes it possible to compare perceptions and conclusions. "Get their impressions and evaluations soon after the interview, but allow enough time for them to digest their observations and conclusions," is the advice of a manager who routinely calls on colleagues to participate in hiring procedures.

MISTAKE 28: LETTING STEREOTYPES RUIN YOUR PEOPLE JUDGMENTS

Managers frequently judge people. In hiring you do it continuously, culminating in a final yes or no decision. In every one-on-one encounter, your judgment of people influences what they say, what you hear them say, and what you say to them.

Unfortunately, stereotypes (defined by the dictionary as, "an oversimplified opinion or uncritical judgment as of a person") may influence judgments. In social settings it's unfortunate, in business it can be costly. A person may be hired or promoted inadvisably, or unfairly rejected or held back, because of stereotypic thinking. Stereotyping is bad for the victim, bad for the manager, and if widespread, imparts unnecessary limits and rigidity on the organization in which it holds sway.

Case in Point

"I know you're not hiring right now," Pete Kemp tells his friend Allen Wesley, "but a nephew of mine just graduated from college and I'd appreciate your seeing him. I think you might be able to ease his way into the world of work." Kemp doesn't say, "You might want to find a spot for him." He knows Allen Wesley will understand that.

Nephew Carl Farmer makes an appointment with Mr. Wesley and shows up on the appointed morning. The executive takes one look at the young man and that's it. "Typical college stuffed shirt," Wesley thinks. Indeed, the ex-collegian's shirt seems starched, as does his entire manner. "A rigid type," Wesley concludes, and from there on the interview is perfunctory. The executive has confused Farmer's embarrassment with stiffness. Farmer doesn't like the idea of getting a job on pull. An interviewer not prone to slotting people on sight might have discovered that and been able to discover Farmer's sterling qualities.

Some time later Pete Kemp tells Wesley, "Remember my nephew, Carl Farmer, you saw last month? IBM grabbed him for a creative engineering spot!"

Analysis

In the distant past, stereotypic thinking had survival value. If a creature was a saber-toothed tiger, it didn't make much difference what kind of saber-toothed tiger it was, you just got out of there. Or, if you were after a meal yourself, one rabbit was as good as another, going down the gullet. What makes sense for hunting tigers and rabbits doesn't for hiring people. And yet, the oversimplification is common. One reason is that stereotyping occasionally seems to prove out: For example, some stiff and reserved people are stuffed shirts. But to judge people on the basis of one aspect of appearance or manner leads to erroneous decisions that may have sour repercussions.

Effective Action

Stereotypes haunt society and the business world in many categories. Just listing a few should suggest their fallaciousness and make you aware of the hazard.

Stereotypes Not to Be Put Off By

• *Physical size.* Fat people are happy and jolly, tall people are better leaders than short, and thin ones are mean and miserly.

• *Hair color.* Redheads are flamboyant, brunettes deep and smoldering, and blondes are good-time people.

• *Gender.* Men are macho, women dainty; assertive men are "forceful," while assertive women are "bitchy." (This is one category where many people make up their own stereotypes that are as misleading as anybody else's.)

• *National categories.* No reason to belabor the point; just say the words: Swedes, Italians, French, English, Americans. Each summons up an image by which many are mistakenly judged. Since national stereotypes are often set by citizens of other countries, they usually have a negative tinge.

• *Business types.* "Capitalist" still has the negative aura of the robber-baron days—bloated, greedy, pig-eyed, ruthless. In contrast, the dictionary definition: "A person who has capital, especially invested in business." In the performance-rating situation, managers' judgments may be warped by pigeonholing: An employee is seen as "passive" or a "deadhead," and efforts to excite and motivate are missed. Negative conclusions may stem from appearance: A woman may be seen as "too good-looking" to have a strong professional drive, and so job objectives are set unchallengingly low.

• *Job-candidate types:*

—*Loser.* Individuals who earn an unenviable place in this category because of appearance, unassertiveness, or poor self-presentation. There may be gold hidden behind the dross.

—*Fair-haired boy or girl.* Has the appearance, brains, and charm to make it up the ladder.

—*Eager beaver.* Not much of anything, but strongly motivated.

—*Fur-coat employee.* Usually female, only works to earn enough cash to afford life's little luxuries.

—*Yuppie generation.* People who are just out to feed their personal satisfactions; accordingly, they have no loyalty to the company, can't be bothered with playing by the rules, and will quit and go over to the competition for any increase in benefits.

Here are some ways to avoid stereotypic thinking:

1. *Individualize your judgments.* It's a simple way of evading the booby trap of stereotypic thinking: Consider each person as a complex entity, with strengths and weaknesses. Job assets may be the result of training, experience, or a natural bent that assists in reaching high skill levels. And don't be surprised to find unexpected combinations. The governor of a state may be a portrait painter of professional caliber. A movie actress may be a champion bowler. A systems analyst may be the best auto mechanic in town.

2. *Go deep.* Another way to avoid the evils of seeing people as stereotypes is to learn about them at levels that may not show up in everyday behavior and contacts. One executive relates, "By chance I met our chief warehouse clerk, a man I'd known for years, in a local restaurant. We were both alone and shared a table. After an hour's conversation I discovered that Al was one of the best-read people I'd ever met and ran a discussion group for his church. I attended one of his meetings and he did a terrific job. I'm getting Personnel to consider having him form a similar group for the company." Not all hidden abilities lend themselves to on-the-job application. Some do.

3. *Review your record.* Judgment by stereotype has the strong appeal of seeming to save time and ease the burden of decision making. It's hard to shun the self-image of being the kind of executive who can size up an individual in a glance, the implicit promise of stereotypy.

To check the extent to which you are able to reject this short trip to trouble, answer a brief quiz:

	Yes	No
Do you agree that stereotypes are a threat to accurate appraisal of people? If your answer is no, you may not want to bother with the questions that follow.	☐	☐
Do you hold off your people judgments for a reasonable length of time?	☐	☐
After you have decided that a person is bright, capable, highly motivated, or is undermotivated and sub-par, or whatever, do you test by pinpointed questions aimed to confirm or deny your conclusions?	☐	☐
On the whole, are you satisfied with the judgments you make about people in the course of your interviewing?	☐	☐

In each case, yes is the preferred answer. You may want to rethink no answers, if any, and decide whether those areas indicate a handicap in an important area of executive perceptiveness.

MISTAKE 29: OVEREMPATHIZING

Says George Black, executive vice president of Poppe Tyson, a Lorimar Telepictures Company, "I'm a salesman at heart. If I like the person I'm interviewing, I tend to help him sell me. Unfortunately, it decreases effectiveness." Call it good-heartedness or being a pushover for the other's "personality." Overempathy sufferers have what the dictionary describes as "the capacity for participating in another's feelings." Result: distorted judgments.

Case in Point

Executive Ellen Muldoon is in the market for a department head. She is favorably impressed by the first job candidate she sees. Grace Garcia has a quick and ready smile, is well spoken, and responds to Muldoon's one or two witty sallies with profuse laughter. In short order they seem like old friends.

"I'll get back to you," the executive tells the applicant, and then informs her secretary that she intends to hire Garcia. "I think she's just right. Why waste time looking?" It's not like the executive. Her usual objectivity has been inactivated.

After Garcia has spent three months on the job, Ellen Muldoon develops mixed feelings about her subordinate. Garcia isn't bad in the job, but she isn't quite good enough. The initiative and creative thinking the department needs aren't forthcoming from its new leader. "I really should have seen other candidates, Muldoon tells herself sadly.

The executive is suffering from the syndrome George Black diagnosed in himself and described as "helping him to sell me." In this context the term overempathy seems to be synonymous.

Analysis

Ellen Muldoon has been victimized by her ability to put herself in another's shoes, to so identify with Grace Garcia that the objectivity of her perceptions and judgment have been subverted.

In addition to being led astray by feelings, the abandonment of a sound procedure can heighten the damage. Swept along by her positive responses, Ellen Muldoon makes the mistake of failing to interview other candidates, losing out on the benefits of comparison and increasing her range of choice.

Effective Action

Be aware of your susceptibility to a favorable overreaction to interviewees. To make this awareness less abstract, think about some recent interview sessions or even informal one-on-ones and use the scale below to rate your vulnerability to overempathy. There is nothing scientific in this self-appraisal. It just provides perspective that helps focus on the question.

How objective am I in judging job candidates? To what extent do I avoid overreacting to their charm, personality, and self-selling ploys and evaluate them from my own and the company's standpoint? (Ten is tops.)

☐0 ☐1 ☐2 ☐3 ☐4 ☐5 ☐6 ☐7 ☐8 ☐9 ☐10

If you rated yourself 9 or 10, overempathy is one mistake you don't make. You're home free. A rating of 6 to 8 suggests that some self-monitoring may be needed, and if your gut tells you that you rate a 5 or less, overidentifying with interviewees may create serious problems for you during the hiring process. In any event, whether you think you're a 10 or a 2, it will pay you to adhere to the following guidelines:

1. Spot and dismiss subtle appeals to your personal rather than your professional self (for example: "That snapshot on your desk tells me you have children. I have two kids, the best in the world.").
2. Shrug off blatant offorts to get on your "good side" ("I read that article about you in the local paper. I also started from the wrong side of the tracks . . ."). However, if this fact were tied to superior achievement, you'd be right to judge the candidate as a person of determination and resolve.
3. Identify charm for what it is, a possibly helpful but limited quality, like being well spoken.
4. Distinguish between more or less objective statements of facts— on job performance, achievement, relations to co-workers—and self-description as a world-beater or one who is "exactly right for the job." He or she may be, but you have to make your own judgment.
5. Follow procedures built into interviewing practice that reinforce your objectivity. For example, see all possible candidates. If you do find a gem early, double check and ask for a second interview. Then you can make sure your judgments are based on the entire range of qualifications. In many companies, the personnel department will do this kind of double checking for you by having their own interview with job candidates. Heed their evaluation.

MISTAKE 30: IGNORING THE KNOCKOUT FACTOR

There is a shortcut you can sometimes take in the hiring interview: identifying early on an essential qualification absent from the candidate's repertory. Of course, key qualifications are generally stated in your help-wanted ads. But there can be slipups; or an applicant may try to fake requirements he or she doesn't have.

You don't want to conduct a long interview only to discover at the end that your candidate for head groom, with a lot of experience as a valet, doesn't know one end of a horse from the other.

The earlier you verify the presence or lack of key needs, the more time-efficient your interview can be. But be warned. The knockout-factor concept misapplied can run you into serious trouble.

Case in Point

Years ago, gang foremen had their own version of a knockout rejection. "Let's see your hands," they would say. If your hands were soft, you weren't a good bet to swing a pick or shovel for a ten-hour day. Today, knockout factors are less susceptible to visual identification.

Supervisor Ned Hinman is seeking a replacement for one of his best employees, Claire Towne, about to retire. He is unaware that what he's really after is another Claire. His requisition to Personnel stresses, "Someone strong on self-organization and self-monitoring."

It's a tough qualification, difficult to pin down in recruiting. After some weeks with no luck the personnel director decides to discuss the situation with the supervisor. During the talk, the PD sees the light: "Ned, we're out of focus. Claire got self-organized after ten years of work. Let's look for someone with the potential. What you're after isn't genetic; it comes from on-the-job training."

Analysis

Ability to deal with abstract qualities such as stress-resistance, creativity, and leadership skills must be verified by both direct and indirect probing. Most jobs have knockout factors, but danger lies in misidentification. A manager ran into a legal tangle when he told an applicant, "We need a man for the job."

Traditional knockouts, those used before antidiscrimination laws, now may incur legal penalties. For example, a company and its representatives may be sued for using age, race, national origin, or sex as a reason for not hiring. However, legitimate factors may make an otherwise qualified applicant unsuitable. For example, if the job you offer requires travel and the candidate is unwilling or unable to do so, that may squelch the deal.

Effective Action

A correct application of the knockout concept can save you time and keep your hiring procedures focused on the fit between what an applicant can bring to a job and what is needed. Inept use of the concept may result in money loss and a tarnished reputation for fairness. Here's how to avoid the losses and gain the benefits:

1. *Identify the must-have qualifications of candidates.* Some managers use a comprehensive list derived from a job description or an application form. Usually included are such headings as experience (length, locations, the kind of data contained in a work history) and skills (for a financial assistant, these might include budgeting, preparing an annual report, maintaining records, and so on). From these the crucial items are selected.

Some managers prefer to note the essential qualities. Here is one executive's list for hiring a personnel assistant:

- Minimum of two years' experience working in Personnel
- A knowledge of personnel methods and systems
- Ability to explain and administer personnel policies involving contact with rank and file employees
- Sufficient writing skill to produce a monthly house organ

Managers who want to reinforce their own judgments sometimes discuss such a list with their boss or colleagues. Of course, these must-have items become knockout factors. But in using key qualifications as knockouts,

2. *Be aware of the legal hazards.* In 1964 the federal government passed a Civil Rights Act to insure equality of treatment to all employees in business and organizational life in general. Title VII of the Act prohibits discrimination with respect to race, color, religion, sex, or nationality in specific situations, including hiring and firing. In the intervening years court actions have clarified and enforced penalties. Discrimination against pregnant women or those with related medical conditions is forbidden, unless the work presents a genuine health hazard. The Rehabilitation Act of 1973 requires companies doing business with the federal government to have an affirmative action plan in regard to hiring the handicapped.

For the interviewing executive, this legislation requires a clear understanding of the restrictions on questions asked, decisions made, and action taken in hiring, firing, and setting compensation and policy on raises and promotions. For the same reason that the executive who used age as a reason for not hiring was in trouble, you may not use the qualities stipulated by the civil rights acts as the basis for not hiring an employee. However, aware of the realities of the world of work, the government does permit exceptions.

3. *Understand the BFOQ exception.* Nothing in the civil rights acts requires that you hire someone incapable of doing the job. In other words, race, color, sex, and so on are not acceptable criteria, but ability is. An employer may even discriminate on the basis of religion, sex, or national origin (but not race or color) if one of these factors is a bona fide occupational qualification (BFOQ) necessary to the normal operation of the business. But the employer must prove it.

In a relevant case, an airline that operates between Japan and the United States claimed that being Japanese was a BFOQ for its stewardesses. But the Washington State Board Against Discrimination ruled that what was required was competence in speaking Japanese, not Japanese national origin. A company hiring models for women's fashions could properly claim that femaleness was a BFOQ.

4. *Be aware of the flexibility of the knockout factor.* Practicality suggests that even an element marked as essential may be modified. An executive hiring for a computer programming specialist started out using less than four years' experience as a knockout. After weeks of searching it was discovered that the field was so new, the number of people who could survive that restriction was close to zero. Eventually the hunt turned up a winner who had only two years of experience but was considered the pick of the crop. Similarly, you may have to ease up on some qualifications—education, experience, degree of skill—and try to offset the deficiency by training, closer supervision, and so on.

5. *Ask the "marriage question."* The movies have sensitized us to the drama of that penultimate moment in a marriage ceremony when the officiator intones, "Is there any reason why these two shall not be joined in holy matrimony?" Use the closing moments of what is about to become your final interview (before you forge that more or less eternal bond by pronouncing those fateful words, "You're hired") to review the whole picture. You may have had several interviews. You may even have asked others to interview your final candidates. Perhaps you haven't had the chance to put all the pieces together, the dozen avenues of discussion, the facts learned, the strong and weak points. Do so, by matching what you're getting with what you need, both short range and long. If you still have doubts, as unfair as it may be to the candidate, consider suspending judgment, particularly if there are some possibilities you haven't explored to your satisfaction.

One veteran executive gives herself the benefit of the doubt.

Occasionally I've taken on people that, despite careful interviewing, I'm not sure about. They had a weak point that might have been used as a knockout factor—insufficient proof of initiative or creativity, for example. But then I tell myself, everything I know about this person is in the past. Now use everything learned in the interview to make him or her over into the best employee possible.

She sums up with a final statement: "I try to knock out the knockout factors."

MISTAKE 31: ASKING QUESTIONS THAT ARE NOT RESULT-ORIENTED

The techniques of asking questions have been theorized over, written about, and practiced for centuries. Material by the shovelful is available in management literature, most of it excellent. If there is a weakness, it's in the practical area. To get a helpful perspective on which to hone your questioning methods, examination of some background factors is in order.

There is no disagreement about the importance of the tool. Questions fuel the interview. Well-directed ones, like high octane, speed the way toward your goals. But problems arise over the way in which the tool is wielded.

Case in Point

The happy subordinate manager tells his boss, "T. R., we've got ourselves a great new supervisor for the inspection unit. What a find! She's got exactly the experience and background we need, and excellent educational background as well. Her work history reads almost as though we made it up ourselves."

"Sounds fine, Ted," the executive responds, "as far as it goes. But we agreed that the tough part of that job is not so much the technical end but dealing with the staff and being able to improve procedures. Is she a people person? Is she creative?"

Ted shrivels a bit. "I didn't go into those areas directly, but I imagine she had to be OK to do so well in her other jobs."

"Maybe," the boss says, "maybe. You should have asked questions in those areas to get direct clues."

Analysis

Perhaps Ted is right. His new hire may have all the qualities the job demands. As one authority put it,

> Some people often put the cart before the horse. They frame a question that they like and do not consider the kind of response it might bring. The primary reason for asking a question is to get a response that is usable in some way. This thought should underlie all other decisions concerning asking questions.*

Agreed, then, that the ultimate test of questioning is not output but intake, whether the manager gets all the information for which the interview has been convened. A key element is completeness, making sure that despite satisfaction with answers you have gleaned, there are no major omissions. Shortly you will be offered a method designed to prevent such oversights where it is often needed, the hiring interview.

One of the executives who contributed ideas to this book came up with a kind of universal outline for questioning job candidates. Others liked it and helped develop it further. They named the final product the Whole-Person Approach. Here is the rationale of the concept.

Successful hiring requires a check on the qualities and qualifications of applicants without leaving blind spots. For a job in which requirements are simple, and the skill level relatively undemanding, the manager usually has no problem in planning an adequate interview. But for organizationally vital, key jobs, there are a series of areas that cover the full range of hiring interest. Look at the following list:

Elements in the Whole-Person Approach

Facts	Feelings
Opinions	Values and attitudes
Ideas	Self-image

The executives felt that the basic coverage in hiring tends to be limited to facts—work history and so forth. To fill out the picture of the candidate in anything approaching lifelikeness requires exploration of the other five factors—opinions, ideas, feelings, values and attitudes, and self-image.

Effective Action

The Whole-Person Approach was designed for the hiring interview, but the same principle of devising your questions to satisfy all your areas

---

* C. W. Downs, G. P. Smeyak, and E. Martin, *Professional Interviewing* (New York: Harper & Row, 1980).

of interest in the candidates applies to most interviews. To further describe the Whole-Person Approach in action, use these guides:

1. *Facts.* In the typical hiring session there as many facts to accumulate as are needed to get an accurate picture of the candidate's education, experience, work history, skills, and so on. Many of the facts you need to know are on the résumé. Your questions can further clarify and expand individual items.

2. *Opinions.* "By their fruits ye shall know them," the Bible says. In our sense, opinions are fruits of the mind, and so people's opinions tell us what kind of human plants they are. When we say a person is opinionated we are stating, pejoratively, that a person is bound by beliefs with which we disagree. (If we agreed, we would say he or she is very intelligent.) When a manager in a hiring session asks, "What do you think of Smith?" (the candidate's ex-boss), the question is likely to bring a great deal of useful information:

- How the person relates to authority.
- How well or poorly the person rates the boss as a boss.
- The basis on which he or she rates a boss. For example, if the answer is, "She was very creative but not a strong leader," the interviewer learns that creativity and leadership are two parameters the individual uses to measure superiors. If the candidate responded with, "Very tough, he wanted everyone to stay in line," you can deduce that the speaker doesn't take well to strong discipline.

Similarly, questions on the other factors of the Whole-Person Approach bring you replies from which you can learn about the other's experience and about his or her way of thinking and evaluating. For example:

3. *Ideas.* "In what kinds of situations in your last job did you come up with ideas and suggestions?" That question brings two lines of information, first, about the kinds of problems that stimulate the interviewee, and second, the quality of his or her ideas.

4. *Feelings.* Where does the applicant stand on the friendly-hostile scale? Is the applicant easygoing or rigid? (Remember, there is a rigid good and a rigid bad.) Does he or she like people or prefer them at arm's length? The right questions can draw out expressions of feeling that enlarge your picture of the other: "What's your favorite holiday?" (It's usually Christmas.) Then you can go on to ask why, and so on.

"Describe your previous employer." (You're sure to get emotional coloring in the reply.)

5. *Values and attitudes.* Does the candidate think employees are wage slaves or that working in a job one likes is one of the greatest goods in this life? Is he or she a person who approves of taking chances, thinks heroes are dumb, is open-minded about relationships between people, and so on? Knowing a candidate's values and attitudes may be inconsequential in some jobs, crucial in others.

6. *Self-image.* This can be the most revealing of all the factors. When you know how a person sees himself or herself you get a measure of aspiration, motivation, and the nature of his or her goals. Some questions that touch on self-image: "How do you rate your professional success compared to your goals?" If the individual is in a middle-level job and feels good about it, the implications are different than if the answer shows frustration and the urge to get much further.

There are three phases to the technique of questioning: framing the questions, listening to the responses, and interpreting their meaning in terms of the immediate situation and person you are interviewing.

MISTAKE 32: NOT KNOWING HOW TO SELL AN UNDESIRABLE JOB

You admit to yourself that the job you're hiring for is not very desirable. And yes, you wouldn't want any kid of yours to get stuck with it. But the wheels of industry are kept turning by a host of activities that are poorly paid, monotonous, require irregular hours, may even dirty hands. But, until the robots come along, the work must be done.

Getting these jobs filled is a problem for the managers in charge. And interviewing for them poses tough questions: What do you say about the work? Do you tell the whole truth and frighten off nine out of ten applicants? Or do you gild the (bedraggled) lily and lose the employee after the first day or week, in some cases, the first hour?

Case in Point

Managing editor Grace Schwartz is told by her boss that the company has finally acquired a small competitor, which includes the latter's in-process manuscripts. They discuss personnel needs. "I understand they used outside proofreaders," the boss says. "You will have to hire one right away."

Grace Schwartz gives a groan, not a small and discreet one, but a loud and mournful one. "It's tough to get good proofreaders," she says. "I hired and lost three in the last six months. Unless you're a born proofreader, a small genetic group, it's dull, demanding work."

"Start looking tomorrow," the boss says. "We can't bottleneck ourselves anywhere along the line."

Analysis

Hard-to-fill jobs are a problem, and sometimes even a bad employment situation doesn't make a difference. A major factor, preferences of the individual job seekers, is an unknown. Difficulties vanish if the right person turns up. But you can't sit on your hands and wait. You need a policy and a plan. You have to decide on answers to tough questions: How do you present the job, what do you say, what if anything do you hold back, to get the job filled?

Effective Action

There's a heartening idea that personnel experts pass along to interviewers: "Don't be disheartened by past difficulties, or the horror stories you hear from agencies about how picky jobhunters are. You're not hiring a thousand people, you're looking for just one person." Certainly, it's best to be optimistic. It not only makes you feel better, but believe it or not, it increases your chances of finding someone. Good feeling, like the measles, is infectious. The applicant may catch it. Then:

1. *Opt for honesty.* Incredibly, in these cynical years, honesty can be the best policy, because

- By not overselling, you are less likely to have a quit on your hands when the realities sink in.
- Even if the new employee lingers on, he or she is apt to be resentful of misrepresentation: "My supervisor told me I'd be working with a nice bunch of people. I liked that. But the first hour on the job, I realized I was in a snakepit with a bunch of unfriendly grumps. They don't even say gesundheit when I sneeze. I'm already looking during my lunch hour."

2. *Know which positives to accentuate.* Every job has its good features. Don't underestimate an important one: You. Studies of job satisfaction often show that good supervision, or a considerate boss, or however it's worded, usually places in the top three factors, and it's often first. Here's a typical list:

Factors Influencing Job Satisfaction

Recognition of achievement
Quality of supervision
Interpersonal relations
Security
Company policy and administration
Working conditions
Work itself
Chance for advancement
Growth in job

3. *If you use the warts-and-all approach, let the applicant know it.* When managers give a balanced picture, it helps to say, "The job has good points and drawbacks." For example, "You may have to work alone in the back room once in a while, and occasionally take your lunchtime at irregular hours. But the people around you are easy to get along with. . . ." They will probably take the newcomer out for lunch on the first day. The manager will see to that, and foot the bill as well.

4. *Lead with your chin.* Consider it, anyway. If your job has an obvious wart, you may do better to recognize it than to cover up. One manager says, "I can see that transportation might be a problem. But one of our clerks commutes on the same bus line you would, and the service is pretty good." Putting it on the table shows your candor, and any alleviating factors you can add makes the obstacle less formidable.

5. *Show them.* Unless the workplace and company premises are actually repulsive, it can be a good move to give a clearly interested candidate a tour, certainly the show spots. Introductions to company regulars—you shouldn't have to hire these from central casting, every company has pleasant oldtimers—can seal a deal.

6. *Give good prospects the full treatment.* No matter what the job and its drawbacks, your friendliness, as shown by the time you spend, and a relaxed manner can communicate an "at home" feeling that will color the other's perceptions.

7. *Toss them the ball.* Get the idea across early: "A job is what

you make it." A case will help make the point, especially if immediately relevant: "George Marek, that man at the second desk, has been doing that job for eight years. He's had the chance to move up but seems to like things just as they are."

Give candidates a chance to speak up and ask questions. If you can honestly say, "What happens to you on this job is at least partly in your control," you send the best message possible.

MISTAKE 33: LETTING THE JOB APPLICANT MAKE THE FINAL DECISION

John McCooe, in his position as president of McCooe & Associates, management consultants heavily into executive search, is in a good position to detect the less-obvious hazards in hiring. He indicates that managers may unwittingly abdicate their responsibility in hiring interviews.

"Some people are decision-shy," McCooe avers. "They pray for a candidate to come along and sweep them off their feet. It seldom happens, and even these decision-wary folks must hire the good old way, comparing and evaluating those intimidating intangibles, human skills and qualities."

Case in Point

"I've just hired a new department head," Frank Davis tells his boss triumphantly.

"I thought we agreed I'd help make the final decision."

"Right, Bill, but I'm positive this guy is perfect for the job. As a matter of fact, he did all the talking and really knew all the answers. And after the klutzes I've been seeing, it was music to my ears."

Analysis

Whether Davis has found a rare pearl or a dud is not yet clear. But a serious mistake in technique has been made. If as he reports, the candidate "did all the talking," it's possible that the manager didn't do enough, and the decision will backfire.

Also, it was wrong not to get Bill into the act. In this kind of situation, two heads are often more astute than one. The boss too will have to live with the decision. But the major Davis error lies in turning the interview over to the interviewee. It's not only a violation of principle, but as a practical matter that John McCooe points out, the applicant has manipulated the final decision, literally talked himself into a job, which is not the best situation from the company standpoint.

Effective Action

More is involved here than simply exhorting managers to maintain control of the interview or to be sure to get all relevant queries answered. Consider:

1. *Understand the ambiguity of the hiring interview.* Two factors are in conflict:

- You want the applicant to talk, fully and freely. (Remember the old saw, "You can't learn while you're talking.") True enough, you learn from the other's talk. But in some cases, the volume of verbiage has the purpose of cutting down on any probing you may contemplate.
- You must have your share of conversation time. You need it not only to ask questions, but to control the pace and direction of the interview. Also, you will want to offer facts and persuasions to make the job attractive to promising candidates.

2. *Be aware that false fronts have the potential of overimpressing interviewers.* The interviewee who runs away with the session is likely to be putting on a show, rather than showing you what his or her qualifications are.

"He's too good," an executive tells a colleague to explain why she is suggesting that he go slow in hiring. "I think you have to get past the talk to find out what's below the surface."

3. *"Buy, don't be sold."* That's the advice of one veteran employer. It comes down to how hiring decisions are made. If the candidate, in effect, has hired himself or herself, you may acquire an employee with many obvious virtues but also, one or two hidden vices that will eventually show a losing bottom line.

MISTAKE 34: RUSHING THE HIRING PROCESS

The head of a management consulting firm specializing in executive search nominates "rushing to a final decision" as a major hiring fault. She follows it up with a cogent reminder to her staff and clients, "Hiring is forever."

Case in Point

The ABC Company was seeking a vice-president in charge of personnel. Mr. X, the third candidate, was very impressive—tall, good looking, easy-mannered, clearly a boost of the company image, particularly in a high-visibility job such as personnel VP.

"Grab him," said the president, after glowing reports from two interviewing executives. The top man liked his reputation as a fast decision maker and aimed to maintain it.

Mr. X was grabbed. After he'd been on the job for a few weeks ABC started a belated check of his references and work history. Some of the responses were completely favorable. A few raised questions. His past salary figures seemed incorrect, his reasons for leaving his previous job were unclear. One source suggested "serious differences with superior."

ABC's president, on seeing the file, said, "Get an outfit to do a PEI." PEI is a preemployment investigation, which ABC was undertaking after the fact.

The findings were bad. Mr. X had left his last job under a cloud. His "degree from Princeton" turned out to be two years at a community college. He had a record of passing bad checks in his personal financial dealings. There were some hints of alcoholism.

"Fire him," the president directed the personnel director. "And what," he murmured, "was my hurry to hire him in the first place?"

Analysis

Although Mr. X had been interviewed at length by two senior executives, the final result revealed obvious oversights. It wasn't just a matter of failure to check. A more important and prevalent weakness: depending on the employment interviews to tell all you need know about a candidate. Whatever flaws existed in ABC's hiring process were compounded by hurry.

Effective Action

The one saving grace of a goof like the hiring of Mr. X: You can learn a good deal from it. For example:

1. *Answer a key question: "What's the rush?"* It's not rhetorical. Look for answers. If your hiring reflects undue haste, consider it a danger signal. Seek out the reasons. They are pretty sure to require remedial action.

2. *Be aware of what the interview can't do.* The hiring session can tell you a tremendous amount about applicants, but it can't tell you everything. The interviewer is almost always at the mercy of the interviewee's glibness and prevarication skills. "A really polished liar," says one case-hardened personnel executive, "can always put one—or even two or three—over on an interviewer."

3. *Check work history and background of candidates getting serious consideration.* The higher the level, the more thorough the probe. Let the statement of the head of a firm that does preemployment investigation alert you to possible trouble. According to Jeremiah P. McAward, president of a New York investigating agency, McAward Associates:

> About 25 percent of job candidates can be expected to falsify their answers to some application questions. The most misrepresented area is the individual's employment record. Typical falsifications: The individuals don't hold the jobs described; their salaries were not as high as claimed; major difficulties with superiors are completely covered up.

4. *Recheck the entire process.* If hiring has produced some duds, there is usually some hunt for explanations. The trouble with most reviews is that they tend to focus on one or two people and one or two parts of the chain. In many cases it is the employment interviews that are spotlighted with the greatest suspicion. But from the decision to "look for someone" until the "You're hired" conclusion, several people and procedures have been involved.

Of course, give the screening interview and interviewers special attention as key parts of the process. But preemployment checking methods may be both poor and lax. Many firms find their hiring can improve significantly if they test and strengthen each link in the chain, from job descriptions and recruiting methods to the induction and orientation of the new employees.

MISTAKE 35: HESITATING OVER A TURNDOWN

Hiring can be an edgy procedure. While managers who hire may relish the satisfaction of finding the perfect, or nearly so, candidate and feed on the other's pleasure in winning out, turndowns may hurt them as well as the applicants. Usually there are many more rejections than hires. Can turning away a job seeker be made painless? Perhaps not altogether, but as painless as possible is still a desirable goal for all concerned. There is a lot to gain.

Case in Point

Executive Edith Grenville is hiring and hopes she is finally on the verge of success. Things are going well, and she is almost at the decision point. But she continues questioning, trying to enlarge and sharpen the picture of the candidate.

Instead of making her more positive, the additional information suggests that the applicant lacks the mental skills for the job. Finally she opts for a negative decision and begins to have qualms. She feels the prolonged session has understandably raised the other's hopes. "I'm sorry," she starts, and the interviewee stands up, frowns, and says "Thank you"—could that be a note of sarcasm Grenville hears—and departs abruptly.

The executive feels her conscience twinge. She scolds herself, "Stop being so softheaded." But she wonders what she could have done to ease the blow for the other.

Analysis

With some rejections there is no difficulty. Early on you and the other agree that there's no fit. But where a candidate scores a near miss, the disappointment can be great. Companies that are conscious of public and community relations are particularly aware of the importance of hiring to the organization's image. Fortunately, passed-over candidates can be left with a good impression by perceptive interviewers.

Effective Action

Interviewers who score high in hiring savvy usually incorporate a number of specific elements in their approach. First, note two essential preliminaries. Effective hirers always:

• *Follow company policies and procedures.* Many organizations develop guidelines for those who conduct their hiring interviews. If this is true in your case, be sure to keep updated and toe the line. Discuss in advance with the policy-making echelon any points that are unclear, ambiguous, or not covered. A specific search may involve unusual aspects requiring special treatment.

- *Do nothing to raise false hopes.* Some interviewers, wanting to be friendly and encouraging, overdo it, and an applicant mistakenly assumes that success is at hand.

Besides these two essentials, many good hirers use the following techniques:

1. *Plant warning cues.* Not every hirer uses this device, but those who do say it prevents misunderstanding. Says one,

> This morning I interviewed a likely job candidate, but I quickly realized his educational background was below what our ad specified. Now if further conversation revealed that he had offsetting qualifications, I might have hired him. But to make sure I could continue the interview without overbuilding expectations, I made a point of emphasizing his underqualification. Then, when I decided the fit was poor, I could say so without making it an unpleasant surprise.

2. *Tell the applicant "No dice" shortly after you decide, without seeming to give him or her short shrift.* Veteran executives agree that there is nothing to be gained by pretense. But you can soften the message by a show of warmth, perhaps regret, encouragement, or praise for superior qualifications. And although the sense of your message is "No dice," the phrase has a blunt, unfeeling tone to be avoided. "We're sorry, but . . ." starts you off better.

3. *Handle the "perhaps" candidates carefully.* Question: How do you put people on hold gracefully? Answer: Be candid. If you plan to see other prospects, say so. If you don't want to specify the reason for the delay, you may favor some form of, "We will let you know in a few days," but then you must follow through. If you have to say no, a simple form letter may be suitable and is an appreciated courtesy. If appropriate, a few friendly words of encouragement may be welcome: "We thank you for coming in, and wish you the best of luck in your endeavors."

Two statements to avoid: "We were very favorably impressed by your qualifications . . ." Sounds good, may even be true, but it might cause bitterness: "If you think I'm so good, why didn't you take me on?" Another well-intentioned statement that often misfires is "You should have no trouble finding a position."

4. *If a candidate is still being considered, send a brief note.* State the facts: "Thank you, Mr. Jones, for coming in to see us yesterday. As soon as our interviews are completed, we will notify all those involved."

5. *Say "Don't call us, we'll call you."* It may not but usually does signal a failure. Savvy job seekers take it that way. Managers who do not intend to rule out an applicant would do well to avoid the much-abused cliché, often taken as a brushoff. Some, who feel there is a chance, will phone if they don't hear. Whoever answers these calls should do so with special courtesy. Job hunting sensitizes the hunter.

TERMINATIONS

MISTAKE 36: FAILING TO DISTINGUISH BETWEEN FIRING AND THE EXIT INTERVIEW

"Pick up your pay," the boss says. "You're fired." That was adequate in the horse-and-buggy days, but modern management is more thorough. Usually the company handbook specifies the procedures for both terminating employees and for the exit interview. (Surprisingly, some books on business interviewing slur the difference between them.) Managers who confuse the two procedures run the danger of losing out in both.

Basically, in a termination interview, the employee is told that he or she is fired and usually the reasons for the decision. Some managers offer some reassurance and assistance for the other's professional future, others hold off for the exit session.

The exit interview usually follows shortly. One authority suggests that the exit talk be held within the last two weeks of employment, but preferably not on the last day, which may be devoted to the departing employee's farewells, and so on. In the exit interview the manager probes for weaknesses and strengths of company hiring and supervisory practices, gives the employee information about the last paycheck, and so on.

Case in Point

A single case covers the two meetings:

Firing session. After several months of monitoring Dick Main's performance as a copywriter, Copy Chief Ed Byrnes decides Main is unable to catch on to the agency style and decides termination is the only answer. Friday afternoon he calls Main into the office and tells him he's fired, explains why (after repeated tests and trials the quality of work still wasn't acceptable) and does his best to ease the blow. He concludes by suggesting how the other's strengths might be applied in his job hunting and next job.

Exit interview. Byrnes aims at two objectives:

1. To uncover information that can help the company in its recruiting, hiring, and supervisory procedures. These facts can help assess and improve company policy.

2. To provide Main with the data supplied by Personnel and to make sure that all loose ends of information and obligation are tied up. Here are major items:

- Insurance
- Pensions
- Vacation pay
- Bonuses, overtime
- Termination of employee privileges, clubs
- What is expected in predeparture activity
- The nature of references to be offered
- Pending organizational obligations: library, loans, locker, keys, tools

Byrnes tries to make the parting as pleasant as possible, and tells Dick Main the favorable statements he would make to people checking on references. In addition to other benefits, a constructive sendoff is seen as good public and community relations for the company.

Analysis

Your own company situation determines how you proceed in the separation process. Whether or not you use a two-session approach depends on company practice. In some companies the exit interview is a personnel wrapup of details such as final pay, pension, and insurance status. Smaller companies may merge the two sessions, with the manager conveying essential information in the closing phase of the termination meeting.

Effective Action

Give yourself a refresher by reviewing other aspects of the separation process. Here, four points:

1. Keep in mind the goals of both the termination and exit interviews, include the essential points in your agenda, and work with Personnel and the cashier's office to tie up loose ends.

2. Use your experience as a guide and a measure of the adequacy of your separation procedures. Are the procedures improvable?

3. While you may assess current termination methods, you may want to consult with Personnel and other executives on adequacy of the exit procedure. Are you able to provide feedback? Do you do so? Are there suggestions you could make?

4. Investigate the outplacement possibility. In the course of the interviews, either termination or exit, you may be asked, or even volunteer, the possibility of outplacement assistance for the employee. Outplacement, securing the help of an outside organization to counsel, guide, and otherwise assist an ex-employee in exploring job opportunities, has become a substantial factor in job changing. Some companies offer this help for most people terminated, some offer help to an employee toward whom a special obligation is felt, and some offer no help at all. But in general, managers properly understand the mutual benefit of having the exit meeting end on a friendly note.

MISTAKE 37: MAKING AN ORDEAL OF FIRING

Termination can be one of the most traumatic interviews executives ever face. Here are a few of the reasons:

- *You tell a subordinate that the company no longer needs, wants, or can use him or her. This is never a big ego builder.*
- *The future the firee faces is threatening or at least in doubt. The loss of security is immediate and shocking. You can't help but empathize, for which you pay in discomfort.*
- *The relationship, usually friendly and perhaps of substantial duration, is abruptly damaged. Even if both the executive and subordinate realize the inevitability of the procedure, both are bruised. If the subordinate is particularly resentful or fearful of what lies ahead, the wound is even more severe.*

- *In some cases, the company may seem to be at fault. Unless the original hiring was temporary, the assumption is that it is in perpetuity. Then, perhaps the company has done something wrong, not trained properly, not used the employee's skills to best advantage, and so on.*

As unpleasant as firing may be, managers suffer unduly, usually beyond the realities of the situation. Managers can minimize the discomfort, not only to their own advantage, but for that of the firees as well.

Case in Point

Chris Colaco, new to management, has just discussed with her boss the personnel situation in her department. By careful planning, a layoff has been held down to a single employee. But even that one firing promises to be an ordeal. Chris's boss says, to cheer her up, "It could have been a lot worse. And as you said, the employee hasn't been much of an asset."

True, Jim was a subpar performer, and even if the layoff hadn't been necessary because of budget considerations, he still might have been a candidate for firing. But even this thought holds little comfort. When Colaco was a teenager her father had been laid off, and, next to flood and earthquake, that was the severest blow the household ever had experienced. The family had barely made it through the year it took for Dad to get another job. Facing Jim wasn't going to be easy.

Analysis

Managers suggest many reasons for feeling bad about terminating employees. A partial list includes:

- Empathizing with an upset firee.
- Knowing the economic and family difficulties that may result from the wage earner's loss of income.
- Wondering about your own job security. In some cases, layoffs are a sign of an ailing company. The executive may wonder, "Who's next?" and doesn't exclude himself or herself.
- Regretting missed opportunities to help, by training, counseling, encouraging the employee to make the job more secure.

- And, last but far from least, feeling guilt. Perhaps feeling personal failure, managers may say, "It's partly my fault." It may not be at all, but that irrationality is typical of the syndrome. The guilt factor is important enough to deserve fuller treatment, for which see Mistake 38.

Effective Action

You can make firing less difficult and alleviate some of its traumas by following these steps:

1. *Use existing procedures.* Most companies develop a firing procedure to help managers avoid traps.

- Legal considerations. The antidiscrimination laws cover terminations. An employee who feels he or she has been discriminated against because of race, color, religion, sex, nationality, or physical handicap may sue. Companies have precise instructions for avoiding this possibility. Review these.
- Contractual restrictions. Organizations that have contracts with unions must adhere to agreed-on procedures in firing, such as giving the employee notice, or a specific number of verbal and written warnings. The personnel department includes these factors in the firing process, and should be consulted on any matters of doubt.

2. *Get support for your move.* Often, managers discuss the intention to fire with a superior or personnel. These sources of guidance can further help minimize the friction and provide the information that employees must have and assist in answering specific questions of particular employee concern. For example, employee benefits are usually canceled, and the employee must be informed of his or her status on each.

3. *Make the dismissal interview as constructive as possible.* Avoid recriminations, accusations, or dwelling on opportunities missed. If the employee wants to get a load off his or her chest, be receptive, within limits. Nothing that you or the other might say should suggest that the door is still open, and that the termination is negotiable. Any of those possibilities should have been discussed in the course of making the firing decision.

You should not only show goodwill but should provide useful feedback to employees who are interested. Anything you can do to cheer up the employee, not by pumping up overoptimistic expectations—although you can reinforce and remind the other of experience that will help—but by realistic appraisal of strong points.

Subjects the employee may bring up that suggest a counseling session should be boiled down to questions about information that should be supplied later, probably in the exit interview. Wide-ranging discussions about past work, disagreements, or missed opportunities are inappropriate. Pursuing these may raise false hopes. Final help and information may be communicated in the exit interview (see Mistake 36).

MISTAKE 38: FEELING GUILTY ABOUT FIRING

"Guilt kills me," says a young manager, "when I have to fire."

A colleague responds, "If firing is an evil it's a necessary one. No reason for you to suffer."

"I can't help myself. We're cutting back, and I have to fire Sid Weymouth tomorrow. I'm jittery. I know I won't sleep tonight."

"Weymouth? He won't have much trouble finding another job."

"I know that should make a difference, but it doesn't. I lay no claim to being rational."

There you have Guilt confronted by Reason, and Reason loses. Result: separation interviews are more difficult and less constructive than they might be.

Case in Point

Tess Sperling, colleague, friend, and one of the nicest people manager Ed White knows, comes into Ed's office.

"I guess you called me in to discuss my report," she says.

"No."

"Another assignment?"

White shakes his head, miserable. "We agreed that report was to be a final test. It doesn't cut it, Tess."

She realizes the situation. "You mean I'm fired?"

He nods. "That promotion landed you in the soup instead of the driver's seat. You weren't ready. I told you to turn it down."

"OK, I pushed too hard. I'll take my old job back."

Ed White shakes his head again. "It's against company policy."

Tess stands up. "I'm sure you can put in a good word for me."

"I've been talking myself blue in the face. They say no." Ed White sees the pain in her eyes. While he doesn't wish he were dead, he sincerely wishes it were a bad dream from which he would awake.

Analysis

Of all the reasons for discomfort in the firing interview, guilt is the most prevalent and so deserves this special unit on ways to cope. Not all managers suffer as Ed White does. Firees are not always longtime associates or friends. And some employees don't mind leaving, having other plans elsewhere. But objective reasons don't always dominate feelings. Inside the psyche is a guilt mechanism that may even be triggered by events beyond our control. We punish ourselves nevertheless.

Guilt may be said to have a purpose: punishment for those who do wrong. From that view, it discourages evil and promotes good. But then how explain Ed White? If he had misled or lied to Tess Sperling, he would have had reason to feel uncomfortable. But he had done her no wrong, even tried to help her.

While logic may not apply in an irrational situation, the mind offers relief by rationalizing. The *Dictionary of Psychology** by J. P. Chaplin offers a revealing definition of "rationalization." It is "the process of justifying one's conduct by offering plausible or socially acceptable reasons in place of real reasons."

Effective Action

It's an inescapable part of a manager's job to have to fire subordinates from time to time. (Well, maybe not altogether inescapable. Executives have been known to pass along the firing chore to an assistant or the personnel department.)

Occasionally you hear of an executive who fires by the written word, for example, a memo left on a desk. But such subterfuge can ruin reputations, and at the very least, raises questions of a manager's TI, toughness index. However, there are alleviations for the guilt reaction:

1. *Consider degrees of guilt.* Sid Weymouth is being let go because of operational retrenchment and his boss takes it hard. But guilt isn't

* J. P. Chaplin, *Dictionary of Psychology* (New York: Dell, 1982).

a uniform reaction. For example, it can vary with the cause of firing. The amount can be estimated roughly:

Reason for Separation	*Amount of Guilt*
Retrenchment	High (the employee may be loyal and a good worker)
Subpar performance	Low to medium (your relationship with the person is a factor)
Discipline (disobedience, safety violations)	Low
Serious misconduct (theft, armed assault on job)	None

2. *Be aware of faking feelings.* Some executives are pleased that they feel bad about firing. It suggests they are people of sensitivity. For those who play this trick, you have just been exposed. Take yourself to a mirror and say, "It's unworthy of you. Cease and desist."

3. *Backtrack.* Review the events that led to the firing decision. Don't bug yourself by such quibbles as, "I could have done more," or, "I'm partly to blame." Is the subordinate the major villain in the piece? Did he or she shirk responsibility, neglect to make needed reforms, fail to learn from failure? Yes answers mean the termination was in the cards, justice was done. So get off your own back.

4. *Face the realities:*

- Some firings are necessary, even desirable. Remind yourself of this fact, keep feeding it into the mental hopper till it waters down the guilt. That's what rationalization is for.
- You may have taken steps to help the individual and prevent the firing decision. Each step should be a strong guilt alleviant.
- Don't be unduly influenced by negative reactions from the firee. If you are, your sympathies are being used to make you an emotional hostage. Let the rightness of the decision and the knowledge that you played fair purge your conscience.

In the case of layoffs, when the employee is blameless, a traditional alleviant is to make extra effort to help the employee find another job. Management may step in, offering outplacement help, either internal or by an outside service, with the side effect of lessening of the manager's negative reaction.

Special Note: To those executives who think this segment is unnecessary, even mawkish, my respectful apologies. But for those not of your number, the opening statement that, "Guilt kills me when I have to fire," is a widely-suffered experience, though perhaps here overstated. For those who hold it, the remedies prescribed can prevent premature grey hair, ulcers, and sleeplessness.

MISTAKE 39: SOURING THE TERMINATION SESSION

Termination interviews, improperly conducted, may inflict discomfort on both employee and executive. It's not easy to tell a person who may be a good and loyal employee, one you have worked with and perhaps liked, "You're fired." Understandably you try to soften the blow. It's a commendable effort and will be more successful if you avoid phrases that not only fail to soothe but may actually enrage.

Case in Point

Manager Lila French tells Claire Rand that the company will shortly conclude the project on which she worked. Her job is finished and unfortunately no transfers are available.

Noting the other's shock, French says, "I'm sure you don't have to worry. You won't have any trouble getting another job."

"There's always trouble," Rand responds sourly.

Analysis

It's understandable—humane, considerate—for an executive to try to temper the trauma of separation. Various things can be done to achieve this worthwhile end. But what doesn't work is anything that is saccharine, however well intentioned. You can help by being realistic, making clear your sympathy without overdoing it, and avoiding assurances that embitter, as in the French-Rand case.

Effective Action

A group of executives were asked for their nominations for statements to avoid in a termination meeting. Their responses, and the possible reactions to them:

What You Say	*Reading the Firee's Mind*
"Now this is what I'd do if I were you."	*If you were me, you'd be throttling my boss—you.*
"All of us think you are a swell person."	*An interesting way to show it.*
"In the long run, you will benefit. . . ."*	*In the short run, my family and I will live on beans.*
"There's probably a great new job waiting for you out there."	*On the moon.*
"Trust me."	*I did, and see where I am.*

The point of the reactions above is that for upset employees on their way out, bland phrases backfire. The following tips may work better:

1. *Face up to your own feelings.* The fact is, sugary assurances are often for the benefit of those who give them. Temper your compulsion to use phony encouragements. At worst, the decision to fire had to be made, or you wouldn't have made it. At best, it is truly not the end of the world, and might even put the other in a more compatible job situation.

2. *Give the reason for termination fairly but firmly.* Explain why it is unavoidable: The person's job has been eliminated, business has fallen off so that retrenchment is necessary, and so on. If the employee's poor performance is the reason, this is not the time to raise that ghost. "Things haven't worked out. . . ." is an acceptable statement.

3. *Make it clear that the firing decision is irreversible.* Overcome any attempt to reopen the issue. But

4. *Offer all reasonable help, both in the termination session and the exit interview.* If the employee raises questions about such things as pension rights, unused vacation time, and so on, if you don't have the answers, arrange to get them. Feel free to listen to any gripes or accusations the other may voice, as long as it constitutes getting a load off the chest, and you can keep it in that realm. Make the distinction between the relief of complaining and the pain of opening old wounds. Only the first is constructive.

MISTAKE 40: DISREGARDING THE SIX THOU-SHALT-NOTS IN FIRING

Of all interviews the dismissal may be the most explosive. You have two censors standing behind you, ready to second-guess and punish you if you violate their tenets. The first is company policy, dictating firing procedures. The second is government antidiscrimination laws, threatening reprisal for what may be seen as violations. It's important that managers know the taboos of firing, in addition to the law and company policy.

Case in Point

Despite five years as manager, Stephanie Alden has had little experience in firing. The day arrives when she must fire, and she is determined to perform the task in a calm, businesslike manner.

The grapevine beats her to the punch. Ella Greene comes unannounced into her office, closes the door, and says, "You're not going to fire me. I support a sick husband and two kids. . . ."

The next half hour is the worst of Alden's entire working experience. She finds herself, in turn, being sympathetic, making suggestions for Ella Greene's future, trying to minimize the difficulties the employee will face, counseling her to hope for the best, and, at the continued imploring and tears of the other, eventually reduced to saying she will try to get her boss to reverse the decision.

Analysis

This last move of Alden's is inexcusable. If indeed Ella Greene were to face extreme hardship, this fact should have been taken into account in the discussion of the separation decision.

In termination interviews, both executive and subordinate may feel stress. It's up to the former to anticipate and prepare for problems. In some cases the employee is content to leave. In cases like Ella Greene's, the manager must be savvy enough to stick to her guns, regardless of the incoming flak.

Effective Action

Gain confidence from the knowledge that there are things you can say and do to minimize the possible trauma. By all means, examine these sources of amelioration for the employee and use them as needed. To strengthen your hand further, avoid statements that, however well intended, serve only to harpoon you and upset the employee. For example:

1. *Don't beat about the bush.* The first minutes or even seconds of the termination meeting should set the tone. Blow no uncertain trumpets. The employee should understand from the first that a decision has been made and cannot be reversed. From there on, you try to be as supportive as possible.

2. *Don't permit argument.* Cut off any attempt of the other person to engage you in the rights or wrongs, the justice or injustice of the decision. For your part, don't be tempted to repeat explanations to justify actions in the past.

The subordinate may ask the reasons for the termination. Decide in advance how to handle this question. In most cases you give the actual reasons: "We're cutting down on staff," "The job you were doing is being eliminated," and so on. If the reason is detrimental to the employee—for example, the inability of a probationer to perform to standard—you may use a face-saving euphemism: "I guess having to memorize all those stock numbers was too difficult. . . ."

Don't hesitate to be direct if necessary: "You were given five warnings, that's two more than is required, and your attendance still didn't improve." Your statements should be as factual and inarguable as possible.

3. *Don't be fatuous* (which the dictionary defines as "complacently foolish"). "It's all for the best," says one well-meaning but not too astute manager. It may be as he says, but for the employee sitting there feeling rejected, the words will have a bitter ring.

4. *Don't commiserate.* An occasional well-meaning manager, in an understandable attempt to make the other feel better and less alone, tries to establish a community of feeling. In this effort come such statements as, "I know just how you feel." ("Oh, you do, do you?" thinks the dejected individual, "Liar!") Another attempt to avoid: Faulting the company. "It's a lousy place to work" may make the manager seem a victim also, but an unemployed victim is in a different category from an employed one, a truth that will be crystal clear to the other.

5. *Don't look back with nostalgia.* "We certainly had some good times on the job. . . ." You probably did, but the firing interview may not be the appropriate context for such fond memories. Save them, if you like, for the exit interview. Friendly but firm is the best tone for the termination meeting.

6. *Consider the law.* Stay away from any discussion of "Why you

were fired" that impinges in the slightest on the antidiscrimination laws or that may be even remotely libelous.

In both cases, avoidance and circumspection are recommended. And it's not quite as simple as, "Watch your words." Statements may be misunderstood or twisted enough to become the basis for legal action by the employee. For example: Employee X is terminated for stealing company property. However, that conclusion is based on circumstantial evidence, and the incident was not reported to the police.

During the exit meeting the manager, in passing, mentions that he will not put the crime on the record.

"What crime?" the employee asks. "You're accusing me of being a thief! You never proved anything."

The manager realizes he has put his foot firmly into his mouth. The case against the employee is shaky, in the legal sense. If the manager is lucky, the employee will be content to let matters rest. If not, a slander suit may be threatened.

Similarly, managers should be careful about the slander hazard in responding to employers checking on references. In the previous example, the manager might have told an inquiring would-be employer, "We fired that individual for dishonesty." Then there really could be trouble. The former employee might sue, with the argument that the slanderous statement prevented procurement of a job. Further, there was now a third-party witness, the potential employer, who could make his case.

TEN ACROSS-THE-BOARD HAZARDS

MISTAKE 41: SLIGHTING THE ART OF ELICITATION

Consider interviewing as the art of elicitation—drawing out information, opinions, expression of feelings from your interviewee—and your opportunities and techniques take on a new and useful meaning. There are two ways in which eliciting applies:

- *Getting specific responses to questions*
- *Enriching ongoing communication*

In both these, applying the elicitation concept can heighten your level of expectation and your chances of realizing it.

Case in Point

"I couldn't get the guy to open up," a junior executive gripes to a colleague. "I hit him with every question I could think of, and all I got was one-word answers and I-don't-knows." His approach is strong on input. He apparently considers questions as a weapon for beating information out of people. He gets an F in elicitation.

Analysis

The young manager's failure demonstrates the limited utility of direct questions. We tend to rely on them because they seem simple and surefire. But even the simplest question may not get a satisfactory answer. Consider a street study conducted by a sociology student. He has two colleagues dress in shabby clothes. Each is stationed at corners approximately similar in pedestrian traffic.

"Got a quarter you can spare?" asks one.

"Help out a happy tramp?" queries the other.

At the end of the trial, the happy tramp amasses three times as much as his opposite number. Although they have both posed a question, the spirit and nature of the appeal favors the second panhandler. It's the interviewing version of, "You can catch more flies with honey than with vinegar."

Effective Action

Note the lessons in eliciting that the example suggests:

1. *Consider motivation.* You increase the responsiveness of the other person when the reaction you want flatters the individual's self-image. Clearly, the pedestrians liked seeing themselves as "helping a happy tramp" better than having a quarter to spare.

In a performance review situation, the manager gets a better choice of task from a subordinate by saying, "Of the three jobs, which is the one that will make you feel best?" And the subordinate chooses, as her boss hoped she would, the one that was most challenging and provided the best learning experience.

2. *Act positive rather than negative.* Proposals, situations, and actions put in a constructive context will get more cooperation and enthusiasm, than neutral or negative-sounding ones.

3. *Make it easy to respond.* Help the person along, both in thinking through a response and in giving it. "What I mean by challenging," a manager explains, "is an assignment that is tough enough to stretch you, but not so difficult as to pose too great a chance of failure." Clarifications, explanations, even definitions of words, can help the other person's understanding. And the manager who says, "If you mean you would like the latitude to plan your own schedule, I think that's fine," assists the subordinate in making a clear statement on which they can agree.

4. *Threaten.* Vinegar sometimes succeeds where honey doesn't. The manager must sometimes apply pressure to achieve essential goals: "This is the second time," a department head tells her assistant, "that you

have failed to bring in information I requested. The work here is too important for that to happen. A third miss will mean penalties."

To keep the communication flowing, consider these further guides to elicitation technique.

5. *Set an appropriate pace.* Don't let the conversation drag, and don't let it proceed quickly at the expense of understanding and losing rapport.

6. *Register satisfaction with progress.* "We're really getting somewhere," the manager in a planning session tells his subordinate. It gives them both a boost, and the meeting rolls merrily along.

7. *Listen.* And equally important,

8. *Show you are listening.* These signs help:

- A nod
- A smile, plus a minimized nod
- An intent expression, gaze focused on the other
- Praise and encouragement of what's being said

The broader aspects of eliciting should also be remembered. A comfortable meeting place, low-tension atmosphere, an established rapport, all materially assist progress. And for the tough communication blocks—when an interviewee has a reason for not responding—remember the tools, such as leveling, building rapport, and getting the interview off to a good start (see Mistake 13), to keep the ice broken.

MISTAKE 42: SUCCUMBING TO THE LURE OF THE STRESS INTERVIEW

At one time, the idea to "break people down" in order to get information in a hiring interview had wide acceptance. The aim was to crack an outward calm and force the interviewee to blurt out things that otherwise might not be revealed. Also, it was seen as a test of how individuals might react to job stress. These ends were supposed to justify the means.

Of course, there are degrees of stress. An interview may be an ordeal to a nervous person even with a bland interviewer. There is an acceptable level of stress that may be used. Some executives routinely include in their hiring, usually in the closing phase, a period of blunt questioning on revealing issues: "How much autonomy do you feel works best for you?" (Answers might range from, "To the full extent of my authority," to, "It depends on the kind of person

I report to.") "Where do you stand on the matter of job versus home responsibilities?" This kind of probing is about the acceptable limit. Beyond that comes the old blood-and-guts approach that now has few adherents. But managers can benefit from knowledge of the bad old ways in fine-tuning their own repertory of methods.

Case in Point

There was once an executive named John Raven who believed in stress interviewing. "It's surefire," he tells colleagues. "You get what you want and fast." He dismisses any arguments as to the method's flaws or unethicality.

After ten years with the company he gets a call from Hal Kipp, the CEO. "Come on down to celebrate an occasion." Raven arrives at the boss's office, expectant and grinning. He believes the big raise he has hoped for is finally at hand.

He sits across the desk from the boss. "You may not remember, Hal," he says, "but it was on this day, eight years ago, that I interviewed you for your first job here."

"I've never forgotten," the other said. "You gave me a rough time. There was that chair with the shaky legs. . . ."

John joins in, laughing, "And the phone! I asked Myrtle to call me every five minutes. And the water bottle! I guess you thought I spilled it on you by accident—"

The Big Boss stops him. "I recall every detail, John. I've never forgotten the discomfort and humiliation. But I want to talk about something more timely. You interviewed a young woman yesterday. She happens to be my son's wife but uses her maiden name professionally. I offered to place her on the staff, but she wanted to get by on her own. After her interview she came in to see me. Seems you still use your stress techniques. Ann said your cigar smoke almost choked her, and your intimidating manner made her wonder what kind of a company this was. You decided to hire her, but she told me she turned you down because she didn't want to be on the same payroll with a person like you. The company has lost the services of a capable person with a fine potential."

The executive rose. "John, I'm firing you. I should have done it long ago. Your work has been mediocre, natural for a person who clings to obsolete ways. See Jack Hall in Personnel. He'll go through the separation procedure with you."

Analysis

As the Raven-Kipp case suggests, excessive stress can create wounds that heal slowly. Another caution: Using stress as a test of the candidate's adaptability is based on the false premise that you can measure a person's ability to withstand job stress by seeing how well he or she copes with stress interview methods. Industrial psychologist Dr. Mortimer Feinberg has said, "The person who caves in under pressure interviewing might eat up stress on the job, and vice versa. The one who comes though with flying colors may be able to do so because he or she sees the interview situation as a kind of make-believe."

Tracey Etelson, CEO of Special Service Freight Company, of Bridgewater, New Jersey, makes the positive point: "I don't believe in interviewing by intimidation," she says. "The more at ease and comfortable people are, the more you can learn about them."

Effective Action

Avoid the stress approach as you would any outdated, loses-more-than-it-gains method.

1. *Be clear on the practices barred in contemporary interviewing.* In general, these are aimed to upset or mislead. A short list gives you the idea. Items from the interviewing junkheap: bullying; creating physical discomfort, such as sitting the person in a cold room, in a draft, or next to a heat source like a radiator or hot-air vent; ignoring him or her intentionally, as a test of patience (too long a period suggests lack of assertiveness). There are known cases in which an interviewer suggested a friendly drink, and took one as an example, then set out to inebriate the individual. This and any other moves intended to artificially break down resistance are definitely unethical.

2. *Consider acceptable methods that create not so much stress as alertness.* Senior Vice President Terry M. Gruggen of the Minneapolis office of Bozell, Jacobs, Kenyon & Eckhardt says he uses pressure tactics in the final stages of hiring that are neither abrasive nor abusive. For example,

> I ask the candidate to tell me the three things he or she liked best about the previous job. Then I ask incisive questions, intending to get below the surface with the person: "You say one of your greatest days was when you beat out a competitor for a promotion. Why?

How did you feel about the loser? Any compassion? What did you do about those feelings?

Gruggen says he does the same with an area that usually is even more sensitive and revealing. He asks, "What are the three worst things that happened in your last job?" He proceeds to probe these, trying to get the person to level both for his or her own benefit and to advance the goals of the meeting.

3. *Remember, the person who uses manipulative stress procedures is toying with the interviewee's psyche, the equivalent of playing God.* While the technique may have some utility for a qualified psychologist, it can be dangerous in the hands of a nonprofessional.

4. *Identify your own motivation.* If you find yourself wanting to grab the interviewee and shake a fact or an admission from him or her, or apply techniques like those listed under Point 1, STOP. You are probably in a bind that requires your answering three questions:

- What is there in the present situation that frustrates me?
- What is it I want to learn from the other person?
- What other approaches, what line of questioning have a better chance of producing useful answers?

Informal investigation can add further to your evaluation of stress techniques. Consider: Why do some managers, whether interviewing a job seeker, settling an argument between subordinates, or conducting a performance review, feel tempted to turn the screws?

Talk to colleagues whose techniques you feel reflect the stress approach, or, equally important, individuals who have been at the receiving end. Get their opinions of the experience and your insights can be still further enriched.

MISTAKE 43: ALLOWING CHAOS IN A PROBLEM-SOLVING INTERVIEW

You meet with a subordinate, your boss, or a colleague to solve a problem. The agenda of the meeting, when well planned, can proceed with a minimum of time and effort waste, and a maximized result. But failure and frustration are the payoffs if the interview, instead of developing under the guidance of a prepared interviewer, consists of erratic and uncontrolled verbal and mental groping.

Case in Point

"We've got to get to the bottom of this pilferage problem," department head Len Kahn tells his assistant, Mary Landis. The losses are becoming intolerable."

Landis has fast reflexes. "Let's sit down right now and see if we can't figure out what's happening."

Kahn, impressed by the other's get-with-itness, agrees. They start off like twin express trains, but soon run into blockage. They don't have the records of the depredations and try to get by with general impressions of the what, how, when, and who. Finally Mary Landis says, "I guess I made a dumb suggestion. We need input from the supervisors and some of the old-time employees. We'll also need the stock records. Then we'll be able to talk about the problem."

Analysis

Of all kinds of interviews, problem solving lends itself most readily to structure. In some cases, problems may be probed by two people, a manager and a subordinate, executive and his or her assistant. But, as in the Kahn-Landis case, input from others is necessary, the meeting requires additional people. Some experts call this procedure a group interview, because many of the attributes of one-on-one interview techniques apply.

Effective Action

The agenda for a problem-solving interview runs a natural course. When you and your co-solver—subordinate, colleague, or whoever—seek a solution, consider adapting the sequence of points that follow as a framework on which to build your discussion:

1. *What are the symptoms?* You know, or suspect, you have a problem the same way you know you have a cold. The signs tell you: you cough, you feel slightly feverish, and a box of tissues vanishes like the morning mists. Pin down the facts. If the reject percentage of a major product has risen dramatically, you know you've got a problem.

2. *Why is it a problem?* It may be cost, inconvenience, complaints

from employees. A phenomenon may be unusual, but if there is no unacceptable consequence, no problem.

3. *What kind of problem is it?* At this stage you're looking for a general category. In the reject situation, you may not know which of the following possibilities apply: Is it a poor piece of equipment? Untrained operators? People getting careless? Some individuals registering antimanagement hostility? Inspectors modifying the standards?

4. *Do you have specific identification?* This step moves you from the general to the particular. You narrow down the possibilities to the one or ones that cause the difficulty. In the reject case, you may find that some of the machines producing the parts are out of adjustment, or it may be that summer replacements haven't been sufficiently trained.

5. *What actions can eliminate the cause?* It's been said that a problem defined is a problem half solved. True. And often, the other half of the solution lies in implementation. How will you go about applying the cure? What action is needed, who will take it? How often?

6. *Is there enough control?* To apply a cure and have it stick requires attention over a period of time.

7. *Have you planned?* Arranging for both implementation and continuing control is the last part of your interview, and may be the longest. To do justice to this phase requires your attention and the cooperation of your subordinate to agenda items such as:

- Costs
- Time considerations—scheduling, deadlines, and so forth
- Human resources—do you have the people required (and do they have the time to apply) to undertake assignments?
- Equipment
- Suitable site or facilities
- Agreement, approval from others—your boss, service or other departments
- Active cooperation from those responsible for jurisdictions you will be entering. This could range from maintenance to security, off-hour coverage, and such

- Add your own: _____

MISTAKE 44: BELIEVING THAT FRIENDSHIP ON THE JOB IS AN UNMITIGATED GOOD

What! you may exclaim. Friendship a hazard? What can the author be thinking of? Well, let him explain.

Having the person across the desk be a friend may be helpful, but the reverse may be true. Just identify the reason for the proximity: a hiring interview, a firing situation, a case where the other has a bitter complaint about a company policy you can do nothing about, and you see the potential difficulties.

Friendship may turn an interview situation into a confrontational crisis. When the executive and a subordinate are friends—that includes the somewhat ambiguous designation, business friend—what takes place in the interview becomes suspect to others and may be an ordeal for the principals.

Case in Point

Manager Cal Abbott is trying to end a feud between his longtime friend Alex Vesey and another subordinate. The quarrel involves nothing more than a disagreement over who should control the scheduling of the office copier. But that is all it takes to make both men almost violent. Abbott knows he's got to come down hard on the feudists. But he just says, "Al, you're going to have to settle this thing," and his friend is on his feet, enraged. "I'm going to have to settle it! Why, that guy has falsified records and even recruited people from my own department to take his side! As a friend (he uses the frightening word) Cal, you know I'm not lying."

Cal Abbott knows Alex is not lying, but he's not telling the truth either. What he's doing is exaggerating the facts. Actually, the honors and dishonors are about even between the opponents. And Abbott's position is not made easier, knowing the whole office is watching, ready to jump on any decision that reeks of favoritism.

Analysis

What are the obligations and prohibitions of friendship between interviewer and interviewee? To disregard the friendship, make believe it doesn't exist, is neither logical nor possible, unless the executive takes the ultimate step and terminates the friendship on the spot. But to let oneself be influenced by a warm relationship with the other is equally unacceptable. To pick your way between these two reefs requires a hard look at what friendship on the work scene means, and specifically, how to deal with it in the interview.

Effective Action

Temporarily suspend your ideas about the responsibilities of friendship versus those you have toward yourself and company. See to what extent you can embrace the guidelines that follow, if and when you find yourself facing friends who expect you to hire them, reverse a firing decision, side with them in a complaint or quarrel, let them off easy in a performance review, and so on.

1. *Clarify the difference between friendliness and friendship.* There is a helpful distinction between the two words:

- Friendship involves special feelings toward a select few.
- Friendliness implies a warm and sympathetic attitude that may be shown to all.

You can offer friendliness widely. But, as a person in authority, you may have to bend over backward to avoid the appearance of favoritism.

2. *Publicize your "no favoritism" policy.* "All friendship ends here," a foreman of a molding department would intone, on entering his department. It was always good for a laugh, but also made a point.

There are more subtle ways to show you don't favor friends. One of the most persuasive is to make decisions that are clearly fair. And if you should get a complaint, be in a position to justify your actions.

3. *In a feud situation, make the interview a threesome.* Avoid one-on-ones when you're an arbitrator, as in the Abbott-Vesey case. Or, if it is desirable to interview individually, give each equal time and tell the antagonists you expect to get together with both in a three-way session.

4. *Put your cards on the table.* "Dan," says an executive, about to start a career review, "we both realize that our friendship creates a complication. I want you to know that without demeaning it, I hope to make our talk helpful and satisfying to you, as well as others in the department." If appropriate, explain decisions that are suspect. "I'm sending Paula to the planning meeting as the department's representative because of her special experience with employment practices."

5. *Be prepared for the ultimate test.* You may face your friend in a situation that pits him or her against other loyalties you have—to your organization, to your own conscience. Feelings may be put to the most painful test. For example, the person you are to fire pleads, in the name of your past relationship, to undo an irrevocable decision.

Or, in a raise or promotion interview, your subordinate makes no secret of his or her expectation to get a favorable decision that in your mind is not deserved.

One seasoned interviewer says, "Two rules protect me from the ravages of guilt and regret. First, I make sure in my own mind not only that my action is fair, but that I can justify it to the other. And second, I try to present my side of things." When asked how he does that, the manager explains, "Once I had to fire a person I was very close to. He finally asked to stay on for a year or two, to get him to early retirement. I said, 'Don't you think I've already tried that? I've been to the front office half a dozen times, trying to change things. It's just not in the cards. . . .' "

Business friendships have one aspect that buffers the occasional harsh realities. Both you and the other person understand the business values and attitudes from which harsh decisions may flow. A good friendship can withstand the greatest strains if both parties feel the reasonableness of the decisions or actions taken and that the relationship has not been violated.

MISTAKE 45: GETTING FOILED BY THE "SECRET" INTERVIEW

The concealment may not be intentional, but failure to inform those who may have a stake in the interview can cause trouble. Some individuals (your boss, colleagues, others) should know about the interview in advance for three possible reasons:

1. *It's in their area of competence and authority, and not informing them may seem a slight or affront.*
2. *They may have information that bears on the subject. For example, if you are interviewing for engineers in your department, mentioning it to another manager who has experience in similar quests may uncover useful information.*
3. *They may be involved in follow-up action, so prior knowledge will find them prepared.*

Case in Point

In a fact-finding interview with a member of the cosmetic company's R&D staff, manager Sue Winters comes up with a novel way to apply face makeup. The gadget could give a tremendous boost to the company's new line. She tells no one about this at subsequent meetings. She wants to develop the device on her own. She spends several months refining the invention, using different shapes and materials. Finally she has a satisfactory version. Soon she's in her boss's office with the exciting discovery, complete with models.

The boss smiles sorrowfully. "I admire your enterprise, Sue," she says, "but we had that idea ten years ago. We began to produce it and were sued for patent infringement. It cost us a hundred thousand dollars in direct costs and twice as much in indirect. You talked to Tim Kane in R&D? He's too young to have known about that. You should have checked with me. . . ."

Analysis

Some interviews need not be announced and indeed may be secret. For example, a founder's fortieth anniversary celebration required the person in charge to interview everyone from caterers to entertainers off the premises to maintain the element of surprise.

However, the idea that so-and-so "wouldn't be interested," even though the meeting is in his or her field, can lead to trouble that starts with, "I should have been informed," and goes on to argument and hurt feelings.

Effective Action

To inform or not to inform others of an interview is not always clearcut. In some cases there is no question. If you are conducting a termination interview, you're pretty certain your boss should know about it. But in borderline cases, the decision to inform or not is a matter for considered judgment.

Watch out for a special angle. The reason and need for notifying others may arise during the interview and could not have been foreseen. For example, in an interview to evaluate a cost-saving suggestion, your subordinate unexpectedly admits that it originated with another manager. It would be wise, as soon as possible, to let your colleague know, so that any proprietary rights or his evaluation of the idea can shape your judgment.

These points can guide you:

1. Consider informing others if the subject is in another's area of authority or expertise (money matter with the treasurer, safety with the safety director, and so on).

2. Consider notification if the interviewee has a special relationship to others: "Fred, I thought you'd like to know that I am talking to Pete Glasser about that new assistant supervisor's job. I believe you were his first boss. . . ."

3. Even if there are people you'd rather didn't know about the interview—for example, in the case above, the manager might not want Fred to know that he was considering Pete Glasser for a promotion— it might be unwise not to tell him. The news gets around, and he may earn Fred's resentment. It makes more sense to show consideration to others than to keep them in the dark on a matter they are likely to hear about anyway.

4. If you want a meeting to be secret, as might be the case if you are interviewing a subordinate for an assignment that must be kept under wraps,

- Change the place and time. Consider getting together away from the office, after or before hours. If this is not practical, use a cover story, such as disguising the real subject of the discussion. This kind of action should be undertaken only upon your considered judgment. If it goes wrong, the embarrassment may be out of proportion to the deed.
- Reinforce possible leak points. Caution the interviewee and any others privy to the action of its confidential nature.

MISTAKE 46: IGNORING THE GROUP INTERVIEW

Two or even three or four people facing an interviewee simultaneously can pool their perceptions and opinions to good advantage. The group interview is useful in hiring and other personnel-evaluation functions. It should not be confused with. series interviewing, in which a job candidate may be seen by two or more managers in succession.

You get a better feel for the strengths and limitations of group interviewing when three points are clarified:

1. Group interviewing is suitable when assessing job candidates or appraising personnel for promotions or assignments when the stakes are high. Hiring for the lower echelons does not justify mobilizing the somewhat ponderous group operation. But in filling key positions or making key assignments when the choice is critical, shared responsibility and pooled capabilities can yield worthwhile benefits.

2. Each participant must understand the broad picture—the job or assignment, its needs, some idea of qualifications sought. Getting several people into a joint endeavor without this information means more trouble rather than less.

3. Not much guidance is available for those unfamiliar with group technique. Though it is not uncommon, particularly in large companies, there is not much literature on the subject. Examination of several books on interviewing find them without any coverage at all. But this dearth of material shouldn't discourage you. Skill in one-on-one interviewing provides a good foundation, although it's essential that you be clear on the differences.

A unique benefit of the group session is that it duplicates two major elements of the manager's job, and so becomes a test of ability for the management candidate:

- *Performance under pressure. Additional strain that stems from facing more than one interviewer may be felt by the candidate. But unlike the stress interview, in which stress elements are introduced artificially, facing two or more interviewers may be unusual, but is not unnatural.*
- *Coping with multiple demands. Typical of management activity is the need to be alert to a range of interests at any given time. The candidate whose attention tends to be linear, who cannot keep a number of balls in the air at once, who is fazed by the several faces across the table, isn't likely to manage well. On the positive side, the applicant who takes the group in stride has demonstrated an important qualification: the ability to retain composure despite tension.*

Case in Point

"How about," Ben Avery's boss says, "having Len and Grace sit in with you on the meetings of the three finalists? Not that I don't trust your judgment. But I imagine you yourself would want the benefit of their participation. This isn't an easy hire."

"Good idea," Avery responds, but isn't as pleased as he sounds.

Yet he agrees it's a key job, and he doesn't mind spreading the responsibility around.

Next day Ben Avery introduces the first candidate to his two colleagues. The session runs for an hour and a half. When Avery comes back to the conference room after shepherding the candidate to the elevator, Grace Magnin says, "What do you think?"

"We did a lousy job, but the guy did very well."

Len LeGrand says, "I agree. He kept the interview on course while we floundered. Ben, why did you let me go on and on with that quibble with you over his college achievements? Even while I was doing it, I realized his five years of work experience was the vital factor."

"We'll do better next session," Ben Avery says.

Analysis

The case confirms the point that managers in a group interview may have trouble getting by on their regular interviewing experience alone. The incident of the cross conversation between Avery and his colleague, not possible in a regular interview, found the former taken by surprise. While it's possible for a group interview to move along reasonably well when it is a first for panel members, some preparation makes all the difference.

Effective Action

The preparation of panel members is best done in two phases: briefing on the subject matter of the session and agreement on "rules" for the interview itself.

Preparation

1. *Briefing.* The manager with primary responsibility for the operation, whether it's hiring, or otherwise, takes on the briefing honors. The relevant facts and circumstances, updated, should be communicated sufficiently in advance so that any questions can be taken care of. Any documents connected with the interview (résumés, letters of reference, or in a promotion, work and achievement records) should be passed along.

Make a point of stressing the qualifications that are central to your search, the particular difficulties of fit between candidate and the nature of the job. Admit to your own biases or weaknesses that they may be able to be offset: "I've been on this search for so long, I tend to lower my guard and take a claim for a fact. Come in on any fudging of actual achievement."

2. *Rules for the session.* Not too much detail. You don't want to over instruct panel members. Their experience in small group meetings will give them a sense of rules of order. Remind them not to raise points among themselves or pose arguments that may be taken up later, outside the interview.

Critique

A special advantage of group interviewing shows up in the meeting of the panel to share findings and conclusions. In this session the manager can do something absent from one-on-one interviewing. He or she can raise questions that linger on despite the interview: "Do you think his ability to communicate, his fluency, would be adequate in big-customer contact? Does he have sufficient presence?"

You can discuss areas of doubt, get perceptions and opinions confirmed or contradicted. Major problem: adjusting differences. Of course, you will anticipate these disagreements of various kinds and at various levels of perception and opinion. It's the comparison and modifying of different viewpoints that is a major benefit of the group interview.

MISTAKE 47: DOING THE DON'TS AND NOT DOING THE DO'S IN COUNSELING

The counseling interview is still controversial despite its long history. The so-called Hawthorne Experiments conducted at the Hawthorne plant of Western Electric by WE executives and management experts from Harvard in the 1930s studied the human factor in work. In that effort, it was found that the peace of mind and ability to perform of employees upset by personal problems could be restored by counseling from their immediate superiors or staff professionals.

Few question the theory of personnel counseling. Experience by others following the Hawthorne lead show that it can help. Generally, it's the application that comes under fire.

Case in Point

Senior accountant Lily Vale comes in late and visibly upset and confronts office manager Fred Zerbe. "Fred, I may have to be out for a while. I'm having trouble at home."

Zerbe closes the door and waves her to a chair. "Let's talk." He gives her time to compose herself, then, "You're obviously distressed. What's wrong?"

"I guess you know that Larry and I have been having problems. Yesterday he packed up and left to live with a girlfriend. The kids are only six and eight. . . ."

Zerbe nods thoughtfully. "I can imagine the problems. Lily, you know I will help as much as I can. What can I do right now?"

Vale says she might be able to hold things together if her work hours could be adjusted, and she could arrange for child care. Fred Zerbe helps her plan new starting and quitting hours. He tells her about company help: "The personnel office has all kinds of lists, from baby-sitters to agencies for marital difficulties. Just remember, we'll do all we can. Chin up. Let me know if there's anything else."

She stands up. "Thanks, Fred." Some of the tension has drained away.

Analysis

As brief as the case is, note that all the basic elements of counseling are present:

- An employee has a personal problem that threatens her work situation.
- The employee comes to her manager with the problem. (In some cases the manager takes the initiative if he or she suspects trouble and performance has fallen off.)
- The manager offers support and practical assistance.
- The manager assures employee of his interest and willingness to help.

Most managers would agree that the Vale-Zerbe case is a good example of how useful a counseling relationship with employees can be. "See how much better off Lily Vale is with her boss's helpful hand. His efforts not only ease her personal problems, but the company retains the services of a productive employee."

Others would point to seeds for trouble: Lily Vale may now lean on her boss for support of all kinds. Worst of all, they might say, is the commitment by Zerbe to future help. "It's likely to be taken advantage of," they will warn. Some other objections can be made. You judge their aptness:

- Managers are not equipped to counsel. (With or without training, some are better at it than others.)
- Counseling by immediate superiors conflicts with the basic relationship between boss and employee. (It does tend to add another dimension. Good or bad? You decide.)

Counselees may complain of being misguided or of having benefits promised that don't appear. (In their eagerness to help, some managers may promise more than they deliver, obviously a bad practice.) Counseling may hold some pitfalls for managers:

- The interviews cut into the manager's work time. (Can happen. It's up to the manager to avoid overcommitment.)
- The insight into employees' personal lives may be a disturbing factor, destroying the manager's objectivity. (This may result either from seeing an employee either in a bad light or an attractive one, injecting an emotional element that may warp feelings and judgment. Wariness and a rein on runaway feelings are needed to keep matters under control.)

These are certainly strong arguments, but many organizations assert that they actually derive the benefits described by the pioneers back in the 1930s. Lester R. Bittel of James Madison University's School of Business lists the personal-problem areas that counseling has benefited:

Absenteeism	Accident-proneness
Alcoholism	Anxiety
Compulsive work effort	Drug abuse
Emotional problems	Continuing hostility

Effective Action

The field today shows a range of counseling practices. Some company policies approve of counseling within reasonable limits, others try to discourage it. The procounseling view asserts that managers who don't counsel shirk a responsibility. The anti's ask, "What responsibility?" Counseling and the arguments for and against it could fill a book, indeed have filled many. (See the brief bibliography at the end of this unit.) For coverage here, recommendations are in the form of key Do's and Don'ts.

The Do's in Counseling

1. Know your organization's policy on counseling. If you have any doubts on limits, discuss these with your boss.

2. Counsel as needed, neither more nor less. The limits are determined by the character of the subordinate and the nature of the problem.

3. Distinguish between the two counseling styles, which differ in technique, implication, and results:

- *Directive*—a preplanned line of questions designed to cover all points considered relevant to the situation at hand.
- *Nondirective*—an unstructured conversation between executive and subordinate. The manager takes few initiatives, leaves it to the other to guide the talk, and occasionally seeks to elicit clarifications, examples, and explanations.

4. Show interest and caring in the subordinate's situation and for his or her feelings.

5. Probe enough to learn what's wrong. If the employee resists, stop short of a depth that is overly personal or painful.

6. Offer options, not opinions. A subordinate asks, "Can you suggest a doctor for my wife's eye problem?"

It may seem like an innocent-enough question, but a specific answer should be avoided. If you say, "Dr. Smith," and subsequently there are difficulties or dissatisfactions, you face the, "You-told-me-to-do-it" accusation. When the services of a doctor, lawyer, or financial adviser are required, instead of a single name offer a source of referral and leave the final choice to your subordinate.

7. Help the counselee clarify and accept his or her own feelings. Understand that the best counseling helps employees realize their problems and solutions. It's been said, "Don't try to put yourself into the other's shoes, but to put them in their shoes."

The Don'ts in Counseling

1. Don't undertake counseling unless:

- The employee accepts it. You are not likely to hear, "Let's have a counseling talk," but the other will imply some kind of problem he or she would like to discuss.
- His or her behavior suggests that there is a problem: a depressed mood, signs of disquiet, and especially unsatisfactory performance.

If you initiate the talk and the other denies having any difficulties, limit your discussion to his or her poor performance.

2. Don't be judgmental.

3. Don't overcounsel. Avoid long intensive sessions that take up too much time and energy for both of you, or too many sessions that put you in the professional counselor category, in clear conflict with your main responsibilities.

4. Don't play God or psychiatrist.

5. Don't make the employee's problem yours. At all times, the other must understand that the most you are offering is assistance. The burden must rest fully on his or her shoulders. To fail in this can lead to damaging consequences to you because you get stuck with a responsibility you should not have, and the other has shaken off a responsibility that he or she must accept.

6. Don't try to change the employee. If that's the only thing that will help, a professional is called for. You may tentatively suggest that the other see a professional, but if it's resisted, don't push. Repetition later may be more effective.

7. Don't argue. If you argue, you're in a partisan stance, likely to put the counselee on the defensive, an undesirable attitude.

8. Don't make the decisions. It's the other's problem, and he or she must make the final judgments and plan the courses of action that spring from them.

Recommended Reading

Belkin, Gary S. *Counseling: Directions in Theory and Practice.* Dubuque, Iowa: Kendall/Hunt, 1976.

Black, Kathleen. *Short-Term Counseling: Theory and Practice.* Reading, Mass.: Addison-Wesley, 1982.

Dickman, J. Fred, et al. *Counseling the Troubled Person in Industry: A Guide to the Organization, Implementation, and Evaluation of Employee Assistance Programs.* Springfield, Ill.: Charles C. Thomas, 1985.

Dickson, W. J., and F. J. Roethlisberger. *Counseling in an Organization.* Cambridge, Mass.: Harvard University Press, 1966.

Levy, Seymour. *A Guide to Counseling: Developing Employees Through Performance Reviews.* Larchmont, N.Y.: Martin M. Bruce, 1976.

Miner, John B. *People Problems: The Executive's Answer Book.* New York: Random House, 1985.

Myers, Donald W., ed. *Employee Problem Prevention and Counseling: A Guide for Professionals.* Westport, Conn.: Quorum Books, 1985.

Purkey, William W., and John J. Schmidt. *The Inviting Relationship: An Expanded Perspective for Professional Counseling.* Englewood Cliffs, N.J.: Prentice-Hall, 1987.

Wilson, Howard. *Counseling Employees.* Irvine, Calif.: Administrative Research Associates, 1973.

MISTAKE 48: MISHANDLING THE COURTESY INTERVIEW

Managers are sometimes requested by a friend, relative or colleague, to see a Miss Smith or Mr. Jones, usually a friend or relative of the person asking. The request may be followed by, "He needs a job badly," or "She's graduating from college, and you could help her clarify her career goals."

The hope is that you can use your experience and influence to get them a job in your own company, to provide leads to other job prospects, or to assist in starting or untangling a career.

These meetings are called courtesy interviews because often you can offer nothing more than the solace of a half-hour's conversation and encouragement. Some executives consider the request an imposition. Certainly for the time-pressured manager, meeting with a stranger as a favor seems out of line. At any rate, the manager faces a dilemma: "To do, or not to do. . . ."

Both for professional and humane reasons, most executives do. Many good things have come from such interviews: the seekers have gotten help that materially improved their situation. For the executive came the satisfaction of helping others, no mean benefit.

Case in Point

A neighbor of Wilma Carlson's asks if she would mind talking to her nephew Les Greenleaf. "He's just in from the West Coast and trying to get his foot into the job market."

Carlson, head of advertising for a land development company, hesitates. It's the second such request she's had recently, and she doesn't feel she can do much, but with kids graduating and jobs scarce, she doesn't feel too good about adding another item to her To-Do list. Nevertheless, she says, "Tell him to call me for an appointment." She hopes she doesn't regret it.

Without realizing it, she has developed a negative mindset: "hoping that she doesn't regret it" is clearly not a positive start. She's annoyed at two things: first, that she's been asked a favor, and second, the possible waste of her time. Unless Les is an exceptional young man, the going doesn't augur well and doesn't work out too well. Note the complications:

Wilma Carlson keeps her visitor waiting while she prolongs a phone call unnecessarily. Revenge for Greenleaf's imposition? She'd stoutly deny it, but it probably is.

She comes out and after mutual greetings she says, "My office is a mess, let's talk here," and seeks a pair of armchairs in the corner of the reception room. Her visitor would have to be naïve not to get a message: "I'll get rid of him in a hurry."

She asks perfunctory questions in a perfunctory tone of voice, and accepts his answers with little reaction. One might say she's being painfully honest. She doesn't find Les Greenleaf's situation interesting. He is an average young man, and she has decided she can't be of help. But she is considerate enough to give him an upbeat sendoff:

"Thanks for stopping in. If I can think of anything, I'll let you know through your Aunt Meryl. Don't be discouraged. It's a big city, and opportunity is where you make it. You're sure to find something after a while."

"How did it go?" Aunt Meryl asks that evening.

"It didn't, partly my fault. I guess I should have been more charming and assertive. But I felt like apologizing for keeping her awake several times."

Moral: Managers whose hearts aren't in it should keep their courtesy interviewing to a minimum. They will offend fewer people and waste less time, their own and the visitor's.

Analysis

The courtesy interview falls into that grey area of the executive's social obligation, a contribution to the community at large. Others feel it's an imposition. You decide where, between these extremes, your own attitude lies.

Despite what Wilma Carlson has decided, many executives reject the request. Others, deciding against a turndown, divert the job careerist to the company's personnel department, or to a subordinate, even one of doubtful ability in this area on the principle that something is better than nothing.

The request may be considered a social service sometimes expected of managers, a philanthropy to the community at large. Even if all that is offered is encouragement, it can be an appreciated beneficence. There's a glum side. Executives have put themselves out for an individual to little avail. Leads are offered that are not followed. Or, a connection has led to a job and the return has been dead silence from the beneficiary. Gratitude? Try the dictionary.

Effective Action

There are two phases to the courtesy interview situation. The first is how to respond to the initial request, the second concerns the interview itself.

1. *Adopt a policy.* Decide how you will handle the request. One executive has a flexible approach: "If I'm asked by someone to whom I feel some obligation—a colleague, friend, or relative—I usually agree to a meeting. I recently became 'too busy' when an acquaintance, for the third time in as many months, asked me to see someone."

Another executive judges on an individual basis, the person asking, the executive's present schedule, and so forth. "If I have the time, I don't mind. Such contacts keep me in touch with an important aspect of business life."

You have four choices: (1) decide firmly against the courtesy visit; (2) agree to all reasonable requests; (3) judge each request on its merits; or (4) arrange for the caller to see someone in personnel or a colleague or subordinate able to give guidance.

2. *Develop an agenda.* Some executives freewheel these interviews, relying on their experience and savvy to sort out the net of questions and statements and end constructively. Consider developing an agenda within two limits:

- Don't put yourself out unreasonably. Managers, favorably impressed by the caller, or aware of opportunities for them, have done everything from suggesting leads that meant good jobs to providing travel expenses for the person to follow up. But be fair to yourself. Avoid activity that leaves you thinking, "How did I get into this mess?"
- Protect callers from disappointment and even resentment because you've wasted their time. Let them know at the outset that you may be able to do little to help.

Then, here's what you can talk about:

- What's on their mind? What are they after? ("Very important," says one manager, "to get their ideas first, otherwise you run the risk of going off in a useless direction.")
- What are their goals? What would be an ideal job? What work have they done that they enjoyed? What have they disliked doing?
- What have they themselves done to reach their goals? To what extent did their efforts pay off? What was lacking?
- How can you help?
- Suggest some things you think might produce results. What do they think about them?
- If appropriate, have the person list what he or she now plans to do, and you note any actions you think may assist.

Your tone of voice and demeanor are vital parts of the interview. Be encouraging, even enthusiastic, if appropriate. Warn against dead ends that the other may view as ripe opportunities.

A mistake to avoid: It happens, and it's ridiculous when it does. The executive gives what he or she considers good advice. The other voices doubts or rejects it, and the executive is put in the position of arguing for the idea. You are the expert. If the person understands your advice, leave it to him or her to accept it or not. One executive, having her visitor turn down three suggestions in a row smiled, stood up, and said, "I guess I'm not able to help you. Sorry. I do wish you all the luck in the world." End of interview.

Encouragement can nourish the soul. Don't stint, but also don't condone efforts that are unlikely to pay off.

MISTAKE 49: BECOMING ENSNARED BY THE AD LIB INTERVIEW

Manager Bob Goralski's interviewing is being undercut by his self-image. He sees himself as fast on his feet, able to improvise, particularly in verbal situations. Seldom caught flat-footed, conversationally speaking, he likes to improvise his interviews as he goes along. This practice has one virtue—spontaneity—and three drawbacks—he rambles, he overlooks major points, and his interviews too often fail to produce satisfactory results.

A less impromptu approach would yield more for his time investment. He misses out on better results because he hasn't planned for them. Because of his self-image as a freewheeler, he feels uncomfortable bound in by an agenda.

Case in Point

Let's spell out more details of Bob Goralski's situation. He feels so practiced in interviewing that he can do sessions in his sleep. And lulled into self-satisfaction by that belief, he remains unaware that his "freedom" prevents him from getting to the bottom of key matters. For example:

A feud has broken out between two groups in his department. One group is against what it sees as excessive overtime; the other thinks the more overtime the better. Goralski phones Ritchie Hall, a subordinate, occasional beer buddy, and member of the "less overtime" faction.

"Ritchie," Bob Goralski says, "come on down. I want to discuss this overtime problem."

With Hall across the desk, Goralski starts off with, "This whole thing is ridiculous. We should be able to settle it without too much trouble. Just fill me in on the major points."

Ritchie Hall proceeds to spout for twenty minutes. Goralski interjects an occasional question. The picture that emerges is that those who want overtime are a lot of money-grubbing employees whose home lives are unsatisfactory. "And," Hall concludes, "they don't want the company to hire more people. They're afraid that would weaken their job security."

"OK," says Goralski, "I have a good idea of the problem."

Analysis

With his propensity for winging it, Bob Goralski believes he has gotten all he needs for his investigation. But, he has heard only half the argument, and he has omitted a major step, prethinking his interview with Hall to insure covering the full dimension of the problem.

The self-appointed Monarch of the Meeting hasn't used two of the professional interviewer's basic tools: (1) a clarification of objectives; and (2) lining up key questions aimed to develop the subject.

With only a minimum of thought he would have realized that he needed information Ritchie probably couldn't provide:

- How much overtime is involved?
- What is the size of the respective groups? (It would make a difference whether they were evenly matched or one was considerably larger than the other.)
- Which operations are affected?
- What solutions other than changing overtime practices could solve the problem?
- What are the cost considerations?

There is something to be said for the informal approach. Some exchanges can be brief: "How's the Dow at noon?" a broker asks her colleague. "Up ten points." End of interview.

The off-the-cuff methodology is suitable when the subject is limited, the list of objectives short. But planning has a utility sometimes overlooked: It helps you develop the full scope of a situation and to identify all relevant objectives.

Effective Action

To enrich interview results:

1. *Understand what planning accomplishes.* The ad libber depends on a "string" pattern to develop an interview. He or she starts at one end of the string and keeps going until the other end is reached. But the outline of many subjects requires branching: you go along for a while, veer off on a productive tangent, return to the main subject, and so on. Some of these worthwhile branches may not come up in an unplanned session. But the process of thinking in the abstract—preplanning—causes relevant matters to come to mind.

An interviewer finds that thinking about a subject and questions to explore it lead to related questions. For example: You plan a problem-solving interview with a colleague on the security of your two side-by-side departments. Once you start on the subject, you list a number of questions: What are the problems? What does the record show are the worst ones? How did the lapses in security come about? What is the experience of other departments? Who can we consult for advice on specific preventives? Now you can start your interview with a broader and stronger approach.

2. *Don't accept the dictum of those who say preplanning is the recourse of the inexperienced and insecure.* Planned sessions will pay off better than those that depend on facile language and impulse to bull it through.

Two advantages do favor the ad libber: flexibility and spontaneity. Both are desirable. Adding these to a well-planned interview gives you the best of the two possible worlds.

3. *Review your interview results.* The quiz below will provide a rough estimate of how you are doing. Keep in mind your more recent interviews in answering each question. The more accurate your replies, the more useful your rating.

HOW SUCCESSFUL ARE YOUR INTERVIEWS?

	Always	Some-times	Never
1. I achieve all the goals of my interviews.	☐	☐	☐
2. After an interview, I never have to strike my brow and groan, "I should have gone into that during the session."	☐	☐	☐
3. I take the time to write out notes for everything but the shortest interviews.	☐	☐	☐
4. In preparing for an interview, I note points to cover; key questions to ask; goals to accomplish.	☐ ☐ ☐	☐ ☐ ☐	☐ ☐ ☐
.5. In difficult interviews it's wise to confer with the interviewee in advance to get agreement on agenda, objectives, and points to discuss.	☐	☐	☐
6. I am aware of the mistake of holding an interview when a memo would suffice.	☐	☐	☐
7. I hold two or more interviews when a single meeting would run too long or interfere with other important schedules.	☐	☐	☐
8. I believe that 5 minutes of preplanning is better than one hour of low-yield interviewing.	☐	☐	☐

[*This quiz is not so much an accurate appraisal tool as it is a device for focusing on key result-getting checkpoints. Nevertheless, scoring your responses may be helpful. Scoring: Give yourself 10 points for each Always, 6 for each Sometimes, and 0 for each Never.*

90–100. You're a strong result-getter.

90 to 80. You may be missing out on some aspects of planning. Check on the points you checked less than 10.

Below 80. You might profit from rereading this unit and rethinking your interview preparation.]

MISTAKE 50: IGNORING THE DARK SIDE OF OPENNESS

We live in an era when openness between people is "good," restricted communication "bad." This view holds for relationships in general, between husband and wife, couples, family, and friends. But how about interviewer and interviewee? Should you always be completely candid with the other? For example, in a performance discussion, should you tell the subordinate that he has slipped badly even though you believe it would be wiser to minimize the decline and put your emphasis on encouragement? In hiring, should you paint a picture of your company, warts and all, even though some of the warts are pretty bad (cash flow problems, poor prospects for advancement) and risk losing a good prospect?

The point of view advanced here is that openness is fine, up to a point. After that it becomes damaging. You must know the limits and acceptable substitutes for openness.

Case in Point

Ben Larmer is seething: "Why can't I have that promotion? You agree that I'm the most capable person on the staff. I've even stepped in to fill your shoes, kept the department going when you were away."

Manager Walter Kane is silent, but his impassivity hides a racing brain. How can he do justice by this capable young man? Within limits Ben is qualified to take over when Kane's own promotion comes along. Now that it's only a few months away, the pressure to make a decision is increasing. But Kane has discussed Ben Larmer's promotion several times with his boss and it has concluded with the other sounding a strong negative: "He can run the department, but a key part of your job is dealing with customers, and Larmer just rubs people the wrong way." From the boss's tone the manager knew it was final.

Now Kane hesitates, then, "I'll level with you, Ben. Your promotion has been discussed in the front office. It's the feeling there, and I agree, that you have trouble dealing with people. That's a knockout factor. I suspect they'll hire outside."

"Do that," Larmer says. "I quit," and marches off.

Kane realizes he has goofed. He should have been able to break the news without pushing Larmer over the edge, pointed out other opportunities in the company, suggested ways for Larmer to polish off the rough edges and qualify for a management job in the future.

Analysis

In interviewing, whether it's hiring, firing, or encouraging a failing employee, telling the truth, the whole truth, and nothing but the truth may be inadvisable. Like a food concentrate, it must be watered down to be palatable.

There are times in managerial life when you must view candor with the same wariness as you would a pit of vipers. You help yourself and the other person by figuring out what to substitute when the whole truth cannot or should not be told.

Effective Action

A major difficulty with openness: you are in the delicate area of ethics and individual sensitivity. Your values and attitude will make some actions palatable, others less so. Other executives might feel and act differently. Here are the kinds of considerations you must make:

1. *Understand that you're on your own.* To tell the truth or not, as a general proposition, is not the issue. Your course becomes clearer when you realize that what is involved is a case by case judgment. Two points:

- Usually, in an interview with you doing the interviewing, your grasp of the situation will be better than anyone else's. As a result, you are able to weigh the factors, concrete and abstract, better than anybody else.
- Expect to make judgments with which others may disagree. It's always easy to second-guess, it's the first-guessers who have it tough. Don't be impressed by opponents who come on strong. They often do so because they don't know the nuances as you do, and they feel freer to make sweeping, but not necessarily better, judgments.

2. *Clarify your decision.* Since a lot may be at stake, give decisions you must make the time needed to untangle the kinks. For example, should you, in the course of reviewing a subordinate's performance, tell him that his or her aspirations are far beyond what you think can be accomplished? Match his abilities against what is needed. Aren't there things he might do to improve his chances? Knowing the person as you do, do you think a dose of the truth, slightly modified, would be better than well-meant encouragement?

You may have to make the conscious decision not to confront the individual with the truth as you see it. But you usually must give some answer.

3. *Seek a substitute for the truth.* You may not want to play God,

but in some situations executives must come pretty close to it. The fact of your authority occasionally forces you to deliver judgments or take actions that will change a person's future. The mere fact of hiring someone, giving a subordinate a raise, or refusing one, unavoidably molds the individual's life. Granted, you want your pronouncements to help rather than hinder, certainly not to be destructive.

4. *Select alternatives.* When the truth is inadvisable, you must make other choices.

"The white lie," asserts on executive, "is absolutely indispensable in business, as it is in social dialogue. Using it expertly not only solves immediate difficulties but preserves hope, self-respect, and future prospects for others."

When you intend something less than the truth, here are some courses open to you:

- *Evade.* "Are you satisfied with my report?" a subordinate asks, and her boss says, "It's an improvement over the previous one." The truthful answer would call for an expression of disappointment, but the manager sees no benefit from that.
- *Toss the ball back.* "Don't you agree," asks an employee in a feud-settling interview, "that George was wrong to give orders to my employee without asking my permission?" The boss knows it was wrong, but it was only one of a string of actions in the battle between two power-hungry junior managers. So the answer delivered is, "Was it any worse than your borrowing his copier without permission? But let's get away from old wounds. . . ."
- *Embrace the euphemism.* In some situations, the truth is inadvisable. Fortunately, language offers an assist in which you present a fact so as to minimize the hurt or damage. Management has a special vocabulary for letting people off the hook, easing feelings, helping them save face. It is euphemistic language, which is defined by the dictionary as, "substitution of a mild or roundabout expression for another felt to be too blunt or painful."

For example, in a firing interview the employee asks, "Will you be telling people that I'm being fired because I made such a mess of things?"

The boss responds, "I've already sent a notice of your leaving to the house-organ editor. It states that you're quitting the company for family reasons that will take you out of state."

A manager is in the not-so-happy situation of having to tell an employee of many years who has been slipping that he will be demoted.

He says, "I'm explaining that you were asked to assume your new assignment because we wanted to take advantage of your special knowledge of our customers and their needs."

There's an old saying, "Tell the truth and shame the Devil." A contemporary parallel: "Tell a painful truth unnecessarily and punish your conscience—unnecessarily."

PART II

Mining the Hidden Gold in Listening

Interviewing involves two activities. One is speaking, the other listening. The speaking element is accepted by most executives as the area in which training is most needed. Training sessions aim to fine-tune such speaking factors as tone, pace, incisiveness, selection of types of questions, and so on. Listening gets some attention and is pushed with vigor by some trainers, but it is seldom taken as seriously by the students. They don't really believe it requires the same kind of serious regard as the speaking part.

Mr. and Mrs. Executive Talk Shop at Home

"What are you reading, Sylvia?"

"The Harvard Business Review. Good article on listening."

No response from hubby.

"Ed, that subject should be right up your alley."

"I don't expect to be insulted by my own wife," Ed responds and stalks out of the living room.

The reason for Ed's departure explains why listening is one of the most improvable of all interviewing skills. Ed thinks he knows all there is to know about listening. What he doesn't know could fill a book.

Listening vs. Listening in the Interview

Ed thinks his indignation is justified. He resents Sylvia's implication that there is more to listening than he already knows. After all, he's been doing it since birth.

Apparently Ed's tête-à-têtes at home don't go too well. But at work, particularly when not catching the subtleties means missing the essence of what's being said, he just gets by. Listening at the professional level, as in business, is more demanding and requires a wider range of techniques than does everyday listening. More depends on it.

One obstacle has been well identified: novice managers believe that hearing and listening are the same thing. One piscatorialminded executive contradicts that. She says, "The difference between hearing and listening is the same as between throwing a line into a stream and catching a fish." Another: "Most people don't listen to half of what they hear."

The units that follow focus on the mistakes that deprive managers of the full benefit of professional listening. Unified as they are, they offer cumulative effectiveness, a concentration of checkpoints for reviewing your present listening practices.

MISTAKE 51: NOT REALIZING WHAT IT TAKES TO LISTEN

"Listening, real listening," says Bert Holtje, of James Peter Associates, a communications firm of Tenafly, New Jersey, "requires a great investment of energy. If it is done conscientiously, an interviewer might be as exhausted as a runner out to beat a four-minute mile."

Case in Point

Junior executive Russ Chavez has just interviewed a job candidate. He stops in to give Al Dale his report.

"What do you think?" the boss asks.

"She's a good prospect," Russ says. "Well spoken."

"Fine. What about her experience? I noticed her résumé seemed a bit skimpy on that."

"Good experience."

"What about her last couple of jobs?"

"I forget the details. I have the impression of her doing quite well."

"Impression?" the boss says.

Analysis

You might question whether Russ's fudged reply means that he's a poor listener, has a weak memory, or did a terrible job of asking questions. The former seems most likely because a good listener knows when it happens that what he or she is hearing is low-grade information.

Professional listening, at the level at which managers practice it in interviewing, is a precise skill. It is more demanding because more depends on it. Impressions may be formed by listening, and may be useful, but not when hard information is required.

Effective Action

It helps to know the full range of factors that contribute to listening. The component skills that constitute listening vary in two ways: first, in the ability of individuals to use them; and second, in the importance they have with respect to any given interview.

• *Concentration.* An effort is required to focus one's attention on what the interviewee is doing to communicate his or her message. This involves not only what is said, but the other nonverbal cues.

• *Matching pace.* The listener must match the movement of his or her attention with the pace of the speaker. To lag behind, for instance, thinking about an idea just presented, may mean losing something of importance in the words immediately following.

• *Continuing analysis.* It is necessary to evaluate and organize what you hear in such a way that you understand the thrust of what is being said. "Now she has explained her purpose in researching color effectiveness on customer buying," a listening executive tells herself in getting a marketing analysis from a subordinate. "Next, she should report what she found out," and she listens for that.

The mental activity that keeps relating what is being said to what has been said gives continuity to what's heard. It helps answer such key questions as: What was said? What does it mean? Does it make sense? How does it compare with expectations? What should be said next?

• *Periodic evaluation.* As you listen to an interviewee's "presentation," whether it's in a hiring session, performance review, or a negotiation, there are points—they may be pauses in the conversation—in which you take a reading of where the speaker is. You seek answers to, "How is the interview going? How is it shaping up? Does it have unity? Is it credible? Realistic? Useful? Are we achieving our interview objectives?"

• *Body language.* Is the listener "seeing" the other's nonverbal communications, body posture, facial expressions, and so on. (See the Index on this subject.)

• *ESP.* There is a level of communication that involves not so much the ears and eyes, but the listener's ability to sense, by ESP—extrasensory perception—what the other is communicating, either intentionally or otherwise. (See Mistake 86.)

Finally, for the professional listener, there is a recourse that can further extend the effectiveness of his or her skill. You can better the quality of the signals you get from the other person. Mistake 56 can help eliminate some obstacles in your path.

MISTAKE 52: NOT IDENTIFYING THE THREE INFORMATION SOURCES

Several reasons for imperfect listening are mentioned in Counseling in an Organization, *by two leaders of the Hawthorne Experiments,*

William J. Dickson and F. J. Roethlisberger. The authors state that, in the interview situation, three sources contribute to what can be learned:

1. *What the person wants to say*
2. *What the person doesn't want to say*
3. *What the person cannot say without help.**

Ordinary listening gets you what you want in the first category. More is needed to benefit from the other two.

Case in Point

Purchasing agent Frank DiRenzo is pleased to learn of a supplier for the kind of paper his paper company requires. The grade is not common, and if shortages occur, it's safer to have a backup to fill the gap. He phones and a field representative comes in, eager to get a starting order.

DiRenzo and the rep talk at length, and prospects look fine. But DiRenzo eventually realizes that the other steers away from any statements about the size of his company or its capacity to supply in the quantity needed. Questions about firm delivery dates get grudging answers. The interview ends with DiRenzo asking for samples. But he has already concluded that there's something fishy about the supplier. Perhaps it has no manufacturing facilities and is trying to do business as a middleman.

Analysis

The case shows in action the three information bases that Dickson and Roethlisberger describe. The field representative talks freely about the things that promote his sale. He evades completely the information that would end the negotiation. And the answers that DiRenzo is able to coax out of him don't help his case, but apparently he feels they don't ruin it.

* W. J. Dickson and F. J. Roethlisberger, *Counseling in an Organization* (Cambridge, Mass.: Harvard University Press, 1966).

Effective Action

The three types of information—that willingly given, that held back, and that requiring your help in expressing—apply to the entire range of interviews, whether in hiring or negotiation, performance review, or counseling. The type of information the other is willing to give is generally no problem. It is the other two areas that need your special attention.

1. *What the other doesn't want to talk about.* You may not get direct information, but there are things you can infer. For example, you ask a job candidate, "Just what did you do in your first job with the X company?" The answer is vague, and the candidate concludes by saying, "After all, that was three years ago," as though that put it well out of memory's reach. What could you speculate about the non-answers? Possibly:

- That the entry job was so low-status, the other feels he or she would hurt his chances by revealing it.
- Something about the job, the pay, the nature of the work, the other thinks would tarnish his or her image.

2. *What the other needs help in expressing.* This is often an excellent source of meaningful information. However, this category, unlike the first, may not be unfavorable to the interviewee. There are other, perfectly understandable and acceptable reasons for the interviewee's hesitation:

- The subject may be too personal.
- The subject may involve other people in a negative way.
- There is an element of shame or guilt attached.

To assist your interviewee to talk about subjects that are not secret, confidential, or unmentionable but are difficult for him or her to broach, try:

- Reassurance. In effect, you ask for the other's trust. You may say, "You know me well enough to be sure that whatever the problem is, you can depend on my good judgment to deal with it in an acceptable way.

- Confidentiality. This goes one step beyond the commitment in the previous paragraph. Here you are saying that you will not pass the information along to anybody else under any circumstances. You may understand, correctly, that the word "confidentiality" is somewhat ambiguous. To make your meaning clear, you may want to spell out your meaning (total secrecy or whatever).

• Understanding. An interviewee who is reluctant to talk because of its personal or embarrassing nature may drop the barrier if you suggest that you don't intend to judge or blame: "I don't know what your problem is, but I can tell you that over the years I have people confide all kinds of things. I'm neither a judge nor a policeman. My only interest is helping you, and no matter what the difficulty, if I can I will."

Often, this is a situation in which persistence pays. Don't be put off by a first refusal. Repeat your offer of help, and it may be accepted at the second, fifth, or tenth repetition. Most people want understanding and help more than they want to be silent.

MISTAKE 53: NOT KNOWING WHAT TO LISTEN FOR

In your interviews there are as many dynamics as there are combinations of subjects and individuals. As a practical matter, this means your listening targets may change from one interview to the next. It's not only that the subjects vary, but the points of your interest may change. It helps your listening to know the specific information in which you are interested.

Case in Point

Phyllis Green is conducting a series of performance evaluation meetings with her staff:

Greg Toomey. He's a solid contributer. Green's conversation focuses on how he's doing with projects he has developed for himself and what his new ideas are for the next quarter.

Jane Jones. She is new to the job. With her, Green focuses on how she is adjusting and tries to spot obstacles impeding progress.

Analysis

The process requires not only asking questions but concentrating on the key aspects. If Phyllis Green were taking notes, she would list Toomey's new projects and probe to get details. In Jones's case, she would note the pros and cons relating to the newcomer's adjustment. Meaningful listening gets to the meat of things.

Think of an interview as having many aspects. They are not of equal importance. You have to select those that are of greatest relevance to present and future interests.

In his book, *Human Listening,* Carl Weaver* lists the range of directions on which attention may focus:

To get main ideas
To hear the facts
To make valid inferences
To get the central theme
To retain pertinent content
To identify the main and supporting ideas
To perceive differences between similarly worded statements
To identify correct English usage
To use contextual clues to determine "word meanings"
To comprehend oral instructions
To hear details
To hear difficult material
To adjust to the speaker
To listen under bad conditions
To resist the influence of emotion laden words and arguments
To take notes
To structuralize a speech
To prevent the facts from interfering with hearing the main idea
To improve concentration by use of special techniques
To hear the speaker's words
To develop curiosity
To follow directions
To judge relevancy
To recognize topic sentences and to associate each topic sentence
    with some previous bit of knowledge
To recognize what the speaker wants the listener to do
To understand how words can create a mood
To understand connotative meanings
To predict what will happen next
To understand denotative meanings
To identify speaker attitudes
To get meaning from imagery

* Carl Weaver, *Human Listening* (Indianapolis: Bobbs-Merrill, 1972), pp. 9–10.

To notice sequences of ideas and details
To check for the accuracy of new information
To avoid the effects of projection
To evaluate and apply material presented
To introspect and analyze one's own listening disabilities
To judge validity and adequacy of main ideas
To discriminate between fact and fancy
To judge whether the speaker has accomplished his or her purpose
To recognize self-contradictions by the speaker
To be aware of persuasive devices used by the speaker

Effective Action

To use the technique of focusing your listening on desired aspects of the interviewee's conversation:

1. *Preselect if necessary.* In some instances, as in the Case in Point, you are pretty sure in advance what angles you are most interested in. In a hiring situation, for example, you know the priorities of the qualifications required. Make notes that will help you stay on target.

2. *Pinpoint your questions.* The Weaver list gives you a graphic idea of how sharply focused your listening can be. The sharper the questions, the easier it will be for you to select the essential information you are after.

3. *Evaluate direction.* In the course of the interview, take stock. Are you getting the kind of information you need? Sufficient quantity? Satisfactory quality?

4. *Stay flexible.* No matter how clear-cut your listening objectives are at the outset, the dynamics of the meeting may substantially alter your views on what is important. A revelation from the other, a piece of information that changes a situation drastically, probably will alter needs. Be prepared to shift your approach and your listening focus.

Remember the fluidity possible in the interview. Preconceived ideas may be invalidated, what seemed important may become irrelevant, and windows may open on new and promising territory. Finally, what you get from the meeting depends on the precision of your listening. The way you listen can actually change the nature and quality of what the other communicates.

MISTAKE 54: FAILING TO LISTEN FOR MEANING

The interviewer strives for two major objectives. One is to understand meaning—the sense, the ideas, the intent of the interviewee's words.

When a subordinate explains his absence by telling you, "My wife was ill and I had to get her to a doctor at once," the meaning is clear (its credibility is another matter). The other purpose is to grasp the feeling content (subject of Mistake 55). Some fortunate people comprehend both meaning and feeling readily. Some are better at one than the other. The manager may miss out to the degree that either of the two elements escape him or her. The effective listener often can pick up information the speaker doesn't intend to convey.

Case in Point

Charlie Dalton comes into Managing Editor Henrietta Clay's office to report on how the new proofreader is making out. He begins by describing the assignments he has given.

"OK, Charlie," Clay says, "bottom line. How is he doing?"

"Not well," the assistant says. "He's slow and still misses a lot of errors."

Henrietta, being a good listener, hears an interesting message. While the words portray a negative result, she is surprised at an undertone of satisfaction in Charlie's voice. Why, she wonders, is he pleased that the newcomer is doing poorly? She suspects the answer. Charlie is the one male on a four-person staff. He would like it to stay that way, and the new proofreader is seen as a competitor. Henrietta Clay will have to look into the situation itself to get the undistorted picture.

Analysis

The Clay-Dalton case illustrates how meaning is modified by feeling. Much of what you typically hear is factual and nonemotional. But feelings like anger, fear, protest, or combativeness can be important aspects of a message and modify its intent.

Another modifier of the meaning of an interviewee's messages, and one that is crucial to your understanding of meaning: Not everyone is a great communicator. Many are poor communicators. Faults include botched thinking, incoherence, poor choice of words. When these malfunctions of message-sending occur, the problem of listening for meaning becomes compounded. Logically, to improve your ear for meaning requires a familiarity with the kinds of things you hear that require special interpretation.

Effective Action

The following key factors affect what you hear in interviews. They can help you review your ability to listen for meaning:

1. *Faulty sending.* "I listened to him for fifteen minutes," a junior executive tells his boss, "and didn't understand a word he said." Not everyone can readily put thoughts into words on all occasions. Most are adequate; many do a so-so job. Remember this possibility when the message isn't coming through clearly.

2. *Personality factor.* The interviewee's personality influences the message, and you may have to recast what you hear. For example, you're in progress reviews with two subordinates:

Optimist: "The work's really moving. It will be tough, but I'm hoping we'll meet the deadline." He has a history of failing to meet such commitments. His "hope" had better be monitored.

Pessimist: "We're doing reasonably well. If we're lucky, we might just make the deadline." He or she often performs better than expected. Check progress, prepare for a pleasant surprise.

3. *Subtleties of language.* "I'll never learn to speak English properly," asserts an executive from abroad, brought in for indoctrination at the home office. "Different words sound alike, and the same word can have more than one meaning." People for whom English is the mother tongue accept its irregularities unthinkingly. The fact that B-O-W can mean half a dog's greeting, a fancy configuration of a ribbon, a violinist's tool, a bending of the body, and an ancient weapon is accepted as a matter of course.

Word choice may trap even the well educated. Here is executive Carrie Vernez trying to straighten out a disagreement:

Supervisor: "He was loafing on the job."

Subordinate: "I was resting. We all need a breather now and then."

"Synonyms are often not synonymous," is the way one language instructor puts it. Vernez will have to decide which of the two words most accurately describes the employee's behavior.

And there is another complication: "You're always ordering me around," a subordinate complains to his boss. The boss responds, "Of course I give you orders. That's my job, and it's yours to follow them."

The two senses of the verb "to order" are the difference between denotation and connotation. In the subordinate's usage, "ordering" connotes bullying, the supervisor is saying that the word denotes an instruction or directive.

4. *Misuse of words.* Occasionally an interviewee throws you off track by using a word or phrase incorrectly. One executive says:

> I was interviewing a college graduate who claimed experience in office methods gained in summer jobs. I asked whether he had a knowledge of order-processing methods. "Oh yes," he said, "I have a great dearth of experience in that." You don't hang a person for thinking "dearth" means "a sufficiency" instead of "a lack" but you don't hire him, either.

5. *Context.* You only have to read the political columns in a newspaper to see how often people accuse one another of "quoting out of context." And it can be true, as one manager discovered when he phoned a previous employer of a job candidate:

"Jess Grace's résumé quotes you as stating he is good at handling details. Correct?"

"I said that, but he left out an important part of the context. If I remember correctly, I said, 'He is good at handling details when closely supervised.' "

Also, the context in which an event takes place may influence the meaning of the words used to describe it. In an information-gathering interview the manager hears, "Patrick panicked. If he hadn't been so quick to pull the fire-alarm lever. . . ."

"Panicked?" Patrick responds. "If those firemen hadn't arrived when they did, we'd have ten times as much damage." The manager will have to do some more digging to determine which opinion is more accurate. Certainly, the threat of fire would justify precipitate behavior that might otherwise suggest loss of control.

6. *Selective listening.* One executive says, "I suit my degree of concentration to the importance of what is being said." Makes sense. It would be incongruous to hang on every word of a subordinate discussing with almost total ignorance his ideas about a new hiring policy.

A physical factor may exert an unconscious and certainly undesirable influence on listening. Fatigue may diminish the sharp edge you need. Managers who walk into an interview tired are sure to lose out on comprehension.

7. *Listening between the lines.* Your knowledge of a subordinate's

language habits, the kinds of things he or she says and doesn't say, the very words used, puts you in a position to interpret what is meant. One subordinate says, "Sure I did that job." You know it's been done and done well. Another says the identical words, but from him they only mean the task has been performed. How well is a second consideration you must verify.

8. *Checking understanding.* You don't have to analyze every statement made in an interview. However, where meaning is crucial, you may want to double-check, possibly questioning others, until the meaning is clear and unequivocal.

MISTAKE 55: FAILING TO LISTEN FOR FEELING

What you hear from the other person in the course of an interview is always intended to convey meaning. But communication may also have an emotional aspect, an always important, sometimes crucial part of the message. For example, an interviewee may feel angry and want to conceal it. But she can't hide the edge in her voice. Detecting emotions, suppressed or otherwise, is necessary for the listener to understand the message fully.

Case in Point

Executive Georgia Myers is in an assignment meeting with Gene Willis. She describes a task for which she feels Willis is now ready. "How would you like that to be your next job?"

The subordinate hesitates. "Fine. Should keep me awake nights." His laugh is less than hearty, his expression grim.

The strained quality of the other's laugh tells the manager the crack about losing sleep is not altogether made in jest. Myers thinks, "He's just going along, he really isn't excited by the challenge." She decides to make the assignment, anyway. Kill or cure. If Willis finishes up in good shape, she'll be persuaded that he is capable of further growth. If not, she will have to rethink just what his potential is, and what she should do about his future situation. The good thing is, she has listened carefully and heard his uneasiness over the assignment, so her decision is made knowingly.

Analysis

Listening for feeling requires listening not only with the ears, but with the eyes. And sometimes what your eyes see contradicts what your ears hear. Then you have to probe for the real message.

The whole range of interviews fosters emotional responses. Uncertainty, trepidation, rage, or frustration may come through. There are two aspects to understanding the feelings:

- Their implications in the context of the interview.
- Your own emotional responses. Emotions are infectious but not necessarily in a direct way. You may become angry with a subordinate who registers anger. You may also be annoyed, puzzled, or frightened. What you do about your own feelings is an important factor in guiding the conversation.

As a professional listener, you must deal with both aspects.

Effective Action

Some major considerations for dealing with the feeling factor:

1. *Sensitize yourself.* Tune in on the emotional content of the other's communication. "Do I detect a note of uncertainty in what he is saying? Why? What does it signify?"

And you may have to remind yourself to listen to your own feelings. Just as emotions may be expressed by the interviewee, you may have feelings, even strong ones, that remain unfocused in your consciousness. You may have to search them out. For example, ask yourself, "How do I feel about Hal's hostility toward me? Am I to blame for it? Should I accept it as justifiable and try to improve things gradually, or confront him and help him see the light?" What you do will affect your one-on-ones thereafter.

2. *"Read" emotional content.* Sensing the other's feelings may require sharpened perceptiveness on your part. Emotions overlap, and you may have to probe for clear identity. Is it anger? Resentment? Frustration? The degree of feeling is also an important aspect of what it implies. If an interviewee seems slightly ill at ease, that's one thing, but great discomfort is another.

3. *Decode body language.* Look for the signs. It can be simple to identify feelings that the interviewee expresses with his or her body, facial expressions, and gestures. In the Georgia Myers case, a strained laugh was the tipoff to Gene Willis's false front, behind which she sensed resistance and grudging acceptance.

Hidden emotions can be detected in two ways:

- Falsity. The interviewee's overt behavior is artificial, intended to cover up anxiety or other feelings. "People sometimes put on an act of nonchalance or heartiness," says a personnel executive. "I always take phony behavior as a bad sign and make my questioning more intensive."
- Physical cues. "Cigarette smoking is bad for job seekers aside from health reasons," avers one manager. "You get doubtful assertions, delivered with an impassive expression, but the hand that holds the cigarette visibly trembles. Something is bothering them."

Familiarity with body language can pay off in two ways for interviewers:

- It is usually "spoken" unconsciously, which explains why it can be so revealing.
- It can be used knowingly by the sophisticated individual, either interviewer or interviewee, to send a separate message, or to reinforce what is expressed verbally.

One mistake to avoid: Don't accept the "readings" suggested by the early popularizers. When the body-language concepts first began to infiltrate public consciousness, there was an attempt to make it a quick-fix mind-reading technique. For example: A person who slumped in a chair could be labeled as "withdrawn and passive." Why not tired or apprehensive? Individuals sitting with their knees together supposedly revealed hidden sexual problems. Why did it not mean wearing tight skirts or signaling a man's preference to have his feet splayed out?

Two guides to help you avoid misreadings:

- *Think of the context.* Instead of the idea that certain body expressions mean thus and so, consider the individual, consider the circumstances of your interview, as cues for interpretation.
- *Consider the traditional vocabulary.* That the body expresses feeling is no recent finding. Our cave-dwelling ancestors knew that when a rival bared his teeth it was an expression of anger, and a smile and nod had a friendly meaning. In the average case, if you focus on the expression, see it in action, you can determine meaning based on traditional vocabulary.

One of the better uses of body language: To spot discrepancies between what is said and what the body expresses. For example, you are telling a job candidate about company policies. She seems to be hanging on your every word, but she idly taps her pen on the desk. If you deduce that she is either chafing at your long-windedness or is bothered by the feeling, "I'm not even sure I want this job," or, "I doubt that it will be offered," descriptions of company policy may seem premature.

4. *Help the other express feelings.* An executive says, "I once told a subordinate in an advancement-counseling session, 'It's all right not to like me. I have my reservations about you, too. But let's not permit negative feelings to interfere with the business at hand.' We got along much better after that."

Accepting feelings can clear the air. Encouraging candor can save a lot of time and prevent confused feelings.

5. *Decide about the feelings.* The manager who accepted the dislike of a subordinate is to be commended. However, the manager who detects negative feelings may accept them, but they may warrant further consideration. An employee who doesn't admire his or her boss may be tops in the department, but resentment, bitterness, and envy are likely to be handicaps. The manager should consider the long-range consequences of destabilizing emotions. If they only affect the one who harbors them, and he or she can function satisfactorily, the difficulty may be minor. But subsequent complications suggest that the manager may have to deal with them as a work problem.

6. *Confront ambivalence.* Modern psychiatry has revealed the puzzling fact of conflicting emotions, love-hate, admiration-envy, and so on. It can be a problem in on-the-job relationships.

Ambivalence is one of the complications you may face in listening for feelings. A subordinate in a performance review may be both eager and reluctant to tackle a demanding assignment. He or she may be tempted by the rewards of success and just as strongly deterred by the consequences of failure.

The dictionary defines ambivalence as "simultaneous attraction toward and repulsion from an object, person, or action." If you come up against such feeling in a subordinate, and it becomes a problem, these points may help:

- Try to identify the emotions. There are many combinations. In addition to those already mentioned, there is anger/fearfulness, desire for freedom to act/dependency, and so on. Careful listening in the context out of the interview can help you decide what's involved.
- Relate the feelings to practical causes. Remember the prohibition against playing psychiatrist. Don't look for primal explanations,

don't attempt cures. The roots may be bigger than the tree. But perhaps you can identify and modify specific factors. For example, if a subordinate develops dependency feelings that repeatedly show up in performance reviews, encouragement and judicious supervision may eventually disengage his or her clinging.

As powerful as feelings can be, it's also surprising how they can sometimes change overnight. Usually it's not because the feelings themselves have been doctored, but because the basic situation has been changed. Is an employee feuding with her boss? Have attempts to improve the relationship failed? A transfer may be the best move.

MISTAKE 56: NOT TRYING TO IMPROVE WHAT YOU HEAR

The good news about listening is that you are not stuck with what you are hearing; the speaker's output is not a given. You can modify what the other says and how he or she says it. In other words, you need not be victimized by the interviewee's speech inadequacies. Even if the other is fluent and a clear thinker, you can still shape what is said into more useful messages.

Case in Point

Manager Wilma Hill realizes, after several meetings with Gary Dennis, a new employee, that reporting on how he is doing is not one of his strong points. She decides on a practical step. She makes up a reporting form on which he can record day-to-day,

> *Job*—What? Time spent? Amount accomplished?
> *Problems*—What were they? How handled? Preventives? Help needed?
> *Suggestions*—How can procedures be improved? What is needed to implement them?
> *Any comments?*

Hill finds the written report form provides structure and points of departure for progress interviews.

Analysis

Structuring an interview, as Wilma Hill was able to do, is one of several ways to improve the interviewee's contribution. Her daily report form prevented rambling and incoherence. Other inadequacies in the interviewee's "sending" cover a range of elements for which you may provide assists.

Effective Action

Consider these assists addressed to various aspects of the interviewee's performance:

1. *Preparation.* Giving the other a good idea of the meeting agenda can mean fewer "I-don't-know-but-I'll-find-out's." Documents on which the discussion will focus can also be asked for in advance.

2. *Physical placement.* In general, you arrange seating to promote good eye contact, comfort, and so on. Now take into account factors that may help individuals. One person may have an eye sensitivity that means facing a window will cause discomfort. Tallness or shortness may influence your choice of chair for the other, and so on. If the person is to take notes, provide the paper rest and lighting that will help the process.

3. *Turning up the sound.* This may be for you, the other, or both. If you've noticed the interviewee's voice drops below audible levels, get your chairs closer together. Or, ask at the outset that he or she raise the sound level: "Amy, the acoustics here are pretty poor. Let's both talk a bit louder."

4. *Atmosphere.* "It's desirable to have a relaxed climate," cautions one executive, "but too much slack makes the conversation slow down and digress. The trick, as I see it, is to make it comfortable and brisk." Different types of meetings fare better in one climate rather than another. The pace and drive of a two-person brainstorming session, described by one executive as "punchy" may be more productive than one that is mellow. But mellowness may be the exact note you want to strike in a farewell meeting you're having with an old friend about to retire.

An executive panel member said, "I once thought that you could only work indirectly to boost interview results. But I overlooked the most productive move of all, stimulating the mind and spirit of the interviewee. I feel it's possible to improve the quality and quantity of what the other person brings to the meeting." His ideas are reflected in the next paragraphs.

5. *Improving the flow.* The psychologist B. F. Skinner's concept of

positive reinforcement, of rewarding the behavior you want to get, underlies the techniques available to you for improving the interviewee's contribution.

Seasoned journalists or feature-story writers who base their writings on what others say develop an eliciting toolkit that gets people talking and increases their fluency and willingness to communicate. Some of their techniques:

- Make them feel special. One seasoned interviewer picks out a quality in job candidates that he feels sets him or her apart: "Of all the people I've talked to so far, you seem to be able to give me the clearest picture of your experience. . . ."
- Encourage verbally. Praising the interviewee (honestly, of course) for a relevant superiority can invigorate his or her performance: "I certainly appreciate the initiative you showed in coping with that breakdown situation." "It must have taken a lot of courage to risk going into a professional area in which you had so little training."
- Encourage by body language. Interviewers who master this technique are especially successful with interviewees who are tense or anxious. In effect, they urge on the other person with facial expressions and gestures. For example, one expert sits rather close to the interviewee, facing him or her directly, gazing as though in complete fascination, nodding at the end of each statement or comment the other made, smiling in appreciation, laughing out loud at a bit of light humor the interviewee assays. The effectiveness of the method seems to result not only from the stimulation of the encouragement but the interviewee's sense that the interviewer is "with him," that a rapport is established.
- Help the other think. Some people freeze up in the interview situation. Aside from thawing efforts based on a friendly and encouraging manner, the interviewer may facilitate the other's thought processes. For example, listen to an executive in a performance review with a subordinate department head:

  "You say you got your task force to improve its effectiveness by rotating leadership among its members. That increased their participation in guiding the work. Fascinating! Could you do the same thing with their own individual tasks—let them plan their work, for instance?"

  The exchange between the two became a productive give-and-take that sent the department head off with a headful of new ideas and the executive left with the feeling that he had had the best performance review of his career.

The trick seems to be not so much giving the other new ideas, as stimulating his or her own. In helping others express themselves, the aim is not to put words in their mouths, but to stimulate them to do better what they do only adequately and to do superbly what they do well.

MISTAKE 57: NOT REALIZING THE FRAGILITY OF FACTS

"It's a plain fact," your assistant tells you, meaning he has just stated an irrefutable truth. But facts can be complex rather than plain, flimsy rather than monolithic. In your interviewing role you know that facts are important building blocks in every type of session. But they can be ambiguous, incomplete, and misleading. You must know their limitations to use them effectively.

Case in Point

Manager Ralph Lamston is determined to get to the bottom of the increasing pilferage in his department. He arranges interviews with his key people, starts the talks, keeps careful notes.

Soon the manager feels he is lost in a fact factory. The probing yields a flood of assertions, among which he tries to separate facts from comments, opinions, and suspicions. He has considerable evidence— suggestive whispers, half-seen figures skulking around after hours, maintenance and even security people who could be wrongdoers. The picture that begins to emerge is murky. He ends up with half a dozen suspects but no leads that pinpoint one or more perpetrators. Like many detectives, fictional or real, Lamston eventually comes to a dead end: lots of facts, no hard proof.

Analysis

The word "fact" itself creates a mental block. Most of us have been conditioned to believe that if we "have the facts" we possess all that's needed to make a decision, solve a problem, plan a program. But quantity can't make up for lack of quality. What kind of facts are needed? And what about the ones we sometimes would like to have (for example, how strongly work motivated an employee is) but despite many career interviews, managers still can't tell.

Relevance is a crucial quality of a given fact but may be confounded by degree: How relevant? Two employees are up for promotion. One speaks French, a favorable factor because the company is on the verge of merging with a French firm, but the other has more experience. Which fact deserves more weight in the decision?

Effective Action

Here are some guidelines for picking your way around the hazards of dealing with facts:

1. Don't let facts blind you to objectives. Fact-gathering tends to become an end in itself. That way lies time waste and futility.

2. Be specific about what you want to know, precede your interviews with a list of the facts you're after. To make sure you're on target, spell it out in writing.

3. Distinguish between facts and implications or inferences. A "fact" may be one only by implication. For example: "The stolen watch was found in Jane's drawer," an assistant tells the boss. Ipso facto, Jane is a thief, right? Wrong. "Stolen watch found in Jane's drawer," is a fact. That Jane is a thief in an inference, and possibly untrue. Stolen items have been planted in lockers and drawers by vengeful enemies.

4. Learn to identify the four subverters of fact:

- Liars. These come in several varieties, from the psychopath to the self-seeker. Pay attention to the motivation of doubtful sources.
- Misperceivers. You see the scene in TV police shows. In the lineup: "He's the one, second on the left," a witness says. Turns out he's a cop. The suspect is at the other end of the line. Our senses often trick us.
- False facts offered with the best of intentions. This is the "tell them what they want to hear" fallacy. Another related subverter is the person who corroborates what someone else has said just to get on the bandwagon. He or she wants to be with the crowd.
- Tellers of half-truths. "I worked for the XYZ Company for about five years." The "worked for XYZ" is a fact, but the "about" phrase is off by three years. This type of half-truthing is common; some individuals do it routinely. In the XYZ instance, the partial

lie might make a more favorable impression, but some people distort even when it means little. "I waited at the cashier's desk in the cafeteria for ten minutes," when it was about five. Ten has more impact.

5. Remember that facts can be temporary. Here's how Ralph Waldo Emerson put it in an essay: "Time dissipates to shining ether the solid angularity of facts."

History may be viewed as the continuing process of replacing one set of facts by another. It's true of your company also. We once believed that the earth was the center of the universe, just as management may believe its organization will always be tops in its field or will retain its market share, regardless of demographic shifts.

6. Organize a fact task force for important searches. For example, if your interviews require considerable information on which to proceed, let's say a marketing problem, consider preparing for the meetings by appointing an appropriate group to do the fact-finding. You may also want the same type of group to assist in dealing with the information collected, for which note the two points that follow:

7. Process factual information. The facts you gather may have to be organized or assessed to be useful. Tips:

- Evaluate. You can do this by starting with a sorting procedure. For example, in rating facts for relevance, one executive applies the same three-way system she uses for her in-box: OK, NG, ?. Those that are clearly helpful or clearly of no use get the first two designations. The ? is a doubtful label, for facts that may be worth a second look.
- Collect and compare. The Russian pioneer in conditioning, Ivan Petrovich Pavlov, advised, "Learn, compare, collect the facts." The last two terms may be switched, that is, you collect facts then compare them, learning more about each by the comparison. Pavlov's basic principle of working with a group of facts to increase your understanding has the value of forming an overall picture, as in a jigsaw puzzle.

8. Know when to quit. In individual interviews, you may have to decide when to end the fact hunt. How much is enough?

- When you have enough facts to make a decision.
- When you feel the well has run dry. You can't extend the effort in scraping the barrel bottom indefinitely. You may have to take a risk, act on incomplete data.

• When the interviewee shows signs of fatigue, or you do.

If the objectives of the interview warrant continuing despite the three tests immediately above, you may decide to press on despite the difficulties. If so, change horses. Sometimes your interview runs down, as does the flow of information. Take a break, change your seating, open a window, move to another office, schedule another meeting in an hour's time.

Many a hesitant interviewee, hung up between telling the truth and lying, has been nudged in the direction of rectitude by Mark Twain. His dictum: "Always tell the truth, and then you have less to remember." You may not want to pass this bit of wit along to the other, but if you think it loud enough, he or she may get the drift.

MISTAKE 58: FAILING TO TAKE NOTES

Take notes? Not in every interview, of course, but for some a record is essential. The challenge is to make the process as painless as possible, which is a function of your decisions as to who takes the notes, how it's done, and so on.

Note-taking of itself can help improve the quality of the interview process. The interviewee, aware that "it's for the record," is likely to winnow his or her words and highlight what's important.

Case in Point

The CEO of a management consulting firm dropped in on one of his department heads. What was intended as a casual chat suddenly generated an idea for a new area of service. The planning interview—for that is what it had developed into—went on for three hours. When they finished they had come up with several exciting prospects.

Right after lunch the CEO was back: "Gina, what was that slogan you suggested?" The department head repeated it. "No, that isn't the way it went." Other questions arose, and they realized with great frustration that important elements in their meeting had gotten lost. Memory alone couldn't retain key elements.

Analysis

A record of an interview retains in permanent form all crucial developments. Some managers say that the process of note-taking also helps the development of the session. How? When you take notes, you tend to zero in on the meat of what's being said. If the "meat" is skimpy, the conversation needs enrichment. It may not be too late to make it so by sharper probing.

This Mistake is in Part II on Listening because note-taking is a listening function. The note-taker must listen in specific ways to highlight what occurs and so provide a structured, analytical view of the proceedings.

Some executives reject note-taking or recording their sessions because they feel:

- They are unnecessary. "I never look at the notes I've taken," says one, "so why bother?" That's a valid objection, and can be a knockout factor.
- They're a nuisance. "They interfere with the progress of the interview," says a manager. This sounds more persuasive than it is.

Note-taking must be for a purpose, and as the Case suggests, when a record can be helpful, not having it can be an annoying loss.

Effective Action

Recording an interview may be done in various ways. Here are some questions to ask yourself.

1. Who should take the notes? You may do the note-taking yourself or hand the task to the other. The choice depends on a number of considerations:

- Who will be less distracted by the double duty (usually the interviewer)? Who is better at it? Who needs the information?
- What purpose will the notes serve? As a reminder, a permanent record, the basis for a memo to others?
- Who will hold on to the record? If you keep your own notes, they can be vestigial and suffice as memory joggers; if for someone else, they should be readable by that person (legible handwriting) and extensive enough to be understandable in the future, when memory fades. Explanatory comments will also add to comprehension.

2. Hand versus machine? Would a tape recorder serve your purposes better than handwritten notes? Here is a brief comparison.

Taking Notes by Hand	*Using a Tape Recorder*
• They can be selective, stress important elements, ignore the incidental.	• You get a total record. But this may be unnecessary and not easy to access for specific material.
• It may distract the note-taker, interfere with his or participation in the session.	• The equipment may intrude: To "mike" the discussion may start a hunt for the right kind of microphone, power source, and so on.
• You highlight only key data for easy referral.	• Running the equipment may be an inconvenience.

Aside from the considerations charted above, a decision will be influenced by personal preferences and the physical circumstances of the interview site.

Videotape? "For key interviews, or when a visual record may be important, I use video." With advancing technology, this practice may proliferate.

3. Third-party notes? "For me," says one executive, "the most efficient note-taking is done by my secretary. When I'm in a one-on-one session with a colleague, subordinate, supplier and so on, and want a record, my secretary, who is experienced and expert, comes in and I explain how extensive the notes should be, what aspects are especially important, and so on."

Further discussion with the executive brought out these additional advantages of third-party note-taking:

- The interviewer can add comments to the record: "Note that Al had the summer season in mind in making that suggestion," thus adding a context when necessary.
- The note-taker can add observations: "Place for the anniversary party: last year's site NG. Start search for replacement early."

To be most useful, notes should be streamlined. In some cases, only key words or phrases need be written down. In all cases, if you don't take on the job, brief the person who will. Directions should help reject the unnecessary, select the items to record. In giving the specifics, it helps to explain the rationale.

The kicker in the pro and con on notes is that you may not know in advance what will arise. Rule: when in doubt, do.

PART III

Handling the Problem Interviewees

Most people you interview cooperate. They accept the objectives you set and follow your lead toward them. They respond to your questions, ask their own, and the interview runs its natural course. Occasionally, an individual may become argumentative, stubborn, discursive, inattentive, even hostile. These are usually temporary obstacles and shortly fade away.

However, there are some individuals whose behavior is a continuing complication and may baffle the most experienced interviewer. In research in the field, executives described their en-

counters with problem interviewees and offered prescriptions for coping with them. The 13 Mistakes that follow represent a gallery of interviewees whose personality creates difficulties.

When you examine these cases as a group, an important principle of interviewing emerges: Dealing with deviant behavior requires that you examine the reasons for it, in a practical sense rather than in terms of depth psychology. There is seldom one explanation or one remedy. For example, the interviewee is close-mouthed, inattentive, hostile. If first efforts to get him or her on track fail, you must determine why he or she clams up, why attention wanders, why he or she seems to teeter on the point of rage. Is it lack of interest in the subject, preoccupation with other matters, resistance to your authority? Countermeasures vary, depending on cause.

The recommendations in the pages that follow conform to this need to determine and deal with cause.

MISTAKE 59: LETTING YOURSELF BE CONNED BY A PROFESSIONAL INTERVIEWEE

Professional interviewees (PIs) typically show up as job candidates. Usually their appearance is impressive. They don't miss a trick, providing themselves with attire, hair style, and so on, appropriate for the job. The more experienced PIs even slant their dress and grooming to specific industries and companies. If interviewed at IBM, they dress in what they think is the approved IBM style. If it's a far-out advertising agency, they try to match hairdos and apparel of staff members. These pretenders have learned through the experience of many job interviews the kinds of images that are irresistible to interviewers. And basically, being good actors or actresses, they try to please.

Case in Point

Here is a PI doing his thing. Rod Walters doesn't ordinarily wear glasses, but he gets himself fitted with a pair to look studious in applying for a job as a systems analyst in a pharmaceutical house.

His résumé is a masterpiece of construction. He barely has the qualifications required, so he fudges those that are doubtful. And he takes the trouble to find a friend of a friend who works for a drug manufacturer, studies up on the state of the industry and accumulates a number of throwaway lines that suggest intimate knowledge of the business.

Rod Walters's skill lies in representing himself as a model employee. He glows with the virtues that employers drool over: "When Mr. Smith was out sick for two months, I became acting head of the department. It might have been a coincidence (humility always looks good) but in those two months, production jumped by 4 percent." And, "I really hated to leave my last employers. They did everything possible to keep me, but I felt I couldn't really achieve my potential in an organization with that kind of family management." Note the slickness of the presentation, complete with a business-wise vocabulary: "achieve my potential," "family management."

Analysis

It's easier to play the PI than you might think. Most people these days understand the qualities that are attractive to employers: loyalty, dedication to one's work, being a team player, being result-oriented and highly motivated. Phrases like these build an image that can be irresistible. Talk to people in Personnel and you learn that "professional intervieweeism" is a tactic that has been spreading. The most effective PIs are those who have a reasonable package of qualifications. One reason is that they are rapid job-changers, as you would expect, since their performance is usually marginal. They exaggerate key qualities to make a mediocre record sparkle.

Successful PIs, which means those hired for jobs for which they barely qualify, have interesting work histories. They start off well, picking up as quickly as they can company politics, sources of power, the information that will help them progress, not so much by ability but by personal favor. Frequently they work themselves into jobs that become sinecures. And happily ensconced, they pull down salaries, sometimes large ones, that they don't deserve and only lose when some observant manager realizes the company is being had.

Effective Action

The critical moment in your dealings with Professional Interviewees is the one where they sit across your desk and busily set about throwing gold dust in your eyes. Here's how to keep them off your company's roster:

1. *Identify them.* Once you look, the signs are clear. Look for the candidate who tries to take over the interview. Such candidates can't spin their webs if all they do is answer your questions. The PI is relaxed, knowledgeable, and personable. A major hazard: make sure you don't confuse the PI with the RQP, that is, the Really Qualified Person. Here's how to separate the real thing from the phony:

2. *Check credentials.* Examine key statements on the résumé and made during the interview. Any assertion of outstanding performance, such as, "I was able to increase output in my department 10 percent each of the five years I was in charge," should be probed. You will probably talk to former employers eventually. However, during the interview, ask such questions as, "Exactly how did you do this? What was your boss's reaction? What about the morale of the people in your department during this push for increased productivity?" Pick up inconsistencies or information that seems exaggerated and explore these further.

3. *Double-check all references.* The PI may not be above rehearsing

the individual you will talk to. This may be a bit of extortion the employer is willing to pay to get rid of him or her. Watch out for meaningless clichés: "He/she was well liked"; "He/she did a good job"; "He/she knew how to get along with people." Facts, examples (and ask about failures) are more helpful than opinions.

4. *Stand back and take a long look.* Despite the bright picture of skills and performance, do you think this person could make a satisfactory employee? One executive says, "I interviewed a perfect applicant this morning. He had good answers for every question. I didn't hire him. He was too good."

The trouble with PIs is that basically, they are seldom well trained and unlikely to perform well. If they could, they wouldn't have to bother putting on a show.

MISTAKE 60: BEING SILENCED BY THE CLAM

Some interviewees you will meet are described as "quiet," or "reserved," or "private people." Trouble is, when you face them, they may be so "quiet" that they become nonparticipants and your interview comes to a halt, as ineffective as clapping with one hand. They are unresponsive or answer briefly when longer answers would be helpful, use nods for yes, shakes of the head for no, and make your own head ache with frustration. How do you get the clam to open up?

Case in Point

For the third time, manager Don Nyquist asks Marilyn Dawkins, only on the staff for a few weeks, "How can I help you?"

Dawkins finally comes out with, "I would like my desk moved."

"Why?"

Dawkins looks thoughtful, as though the possibility that she would have to explain her request is a total surprise.

The manager explains, "It would help me decide what to do if I knew your reason."

The subordinate tries to respond, but doesn't quite make it.

Nyquist suspects some shocking reason for the other's reticence. He says, "I'm sorry Marilyn, but I really must know more."

This time the response comes in only a few seconds. "He's messy."

"Who is?"

"Jerry. Jerry Tobin."

"Why is that a problem?"

"He sits at the next desk."

Don Nyquist is resigned to groping along, although his patience is wearing thin. "What do you mean by messy?"

"He eats at his desk." The manager's silence signals to the subordinate that more information is required. "Yesterday he upset a cup of soup and it splattered on my chair." Again Nyquist doesn't respond. "And he likes garlic. Enough to make me sick to my stomach." Still nothing from Nyquist. "I can't do my work."

Tired but triumphant, the manager feels he now has enough information to go by. He says, "I'll talk to Jerry. If he's been having lunch at his desk, I'll remind him that we'd rather people use the rec room for eating."

Dawkins gets up and turning at the door, startles the boss with her verbosity: "Thanks."

Analysis

Conversation comes more readily to some people than to others. Nyquist had one factor going for him: Marilyn Dawkins wanted something. If Nyquist had initiated the interview, it's possible that it would have lasted even longer. Clams don't open easily, and as the Case illustrates, the manager may have to push and probe.

Effective Action

You must learn what lies behind the close-mouthedness in order to proceed.

1. Consider the possible explanations for the employee's behavior and the appropriate action for each:

- It's a character or behavioral trait. This seems to explain Marilyn Dawkins's difficulties. Don's approach is suitable: patience, simple uncomplicated questions, and silence—more precisely, an air of expectancy that tells the interviewee to speak up.
- He or she is frozen by the interview situation. Not the cat, but intimidation may have gotten his or her tongue. Some element of the situation, perhaps its confrontational aspect, seems threat-

ening. If this is what you're up against, try for relaxation. For example, "Tom, let's be less formal (even if it hasn't been) and just chat for a while." Use a simple lead-in: "When did you first feel there was something wrong?"

- The interviewee may be hostile. This may arise from the interview subject, for example, the interviewee resents a disciplinary session in which he or she feels completely innocent. Or, the resentment may be directed at the manager for a past event, such as a turndown of a request for a favor or special privilege. If hostility is your diagnosis, make an effort to dissipate it. Consider stating your feeling: "Harriet, I imagine you're still upset because I couldn't go along with your request for a leave of absence. . . ."
- He or she is threatened by the subject. Recommendation: Ask a direct question: "Does it bother you to talk about reasons for poor morale in the department? Remember, I won't ask you to name any names. And I'm sure you know you can trust me when I say there will be complete confidentiality."

If this reassurance doesn't increase the conversation flow, perhaps his or her own culpability is at stake. In this case, ask, "Are you bothered personally by our subject?" To deepen the probe, specify the particulars of the situation.

Other less likely possibilities, but not to be ruled out:

- An unseen third presence. Nothing spooky, but the other may be held back by a colleague's stake in the discussion. Or, some current incident, possibly a disagreement with you, may chill things.
- He or she feels unqualified to discuss the matter at hand. For example, you're talking to a subordinate about getting better cooperation on new safety rules. You're looking for practical answers, and she thinks you're asking for abstract principles to form a policy. Change your approach, focus on something with which she is familiar: "Jane, you've had a lot of experience with safety practices. What do you think is causing this outbreak of slipping and tripping accidents?"
- You're up against a slow thinker, and he or she literally doesn't have enough time to come up with answers. Put this possibility to the test: "Bob, how would it be if we pin down some specific questions now, and you think about them over the next few days and we'll get together again next week?"

- Add your own: _____

2. Verify. Whatever your diagnosis of the clam's difficulty in speaking up, check it out. For example, in a case of a real or fancied injustice, it would be wise if the manager added, "Am I right in feeling that's a problem for us now?" If the answer is positive, then deal with that revelation before continuing. If negative, then make it clear that you want to get to the cause of the blockage. You will know when you have hit the mark if the tension dissipates and the level of responsiveness improves.

If verification is positive, ease back into the business at hand.

Don't mistake clams for people who are out of it for more complicated reasons: the subject of the analysis in Mistake 63.

MISTAKE 61: BEING BUFFALOED BY THE UNTRUTHFUL INTERVIEWEE

The truth comes in one simple form, but untruth masquerades in many: evasions, misrepresentations, fabrications, half truths, sins of omission. Every type of interview can be subverted by false statements. The job applicant who inflates his or her educational achievement, the subordinate in a performance review who concocts self-serving reasons for failure, the supplier who offers a purchasing executive falsified records of his product's maintenance costs, all guarantee a faulty interview. Your search for facts and figures must be made proof against the intentional falsehood. A review of methods to lie-proof your interviews can prevent embarrassment in crucial matters.

Case in Point

Sam Vargas, managing editor of a business publication, gets a call from an annoyed psychologist just interviewed by the magazine's new young reporter. The psychologist says, "You told me your reporter had an advanced degree in industrial psychology. I doubt it. She's a smooth talker but didn't understand half of what I said and wasn't up on the literature. You wasted my time. I advise you not to print anything without checking back with me."

The manager calls Personnel: "Bill, did we verify the new reporter's educational credits?" he asks the director.

"As I recall, she said she had a M.A. in industrial psychology."

"That's what she said. Did you check?"

"Not yet. I'll do it now." Shortly the call comes back. "They say she attended the university but dropped out after two years."

Confronted by the information, the reporter confesses, adding, "I thought I could learn what I needed to know on the job."

"Not on the salary we're paying," the manager says.

Analysis

The untruthful interviewee is a constant threat and can cause damaging loss, especially in hiring situations. In a panel discussion at an annual meeting of the American Psychological Association, a report revealed that one third of job applicants lie about their experience, and a similar percentage falsify educational achievement. Some studies report even higher rates, which seem to fluctuate with the ups and downs of the job market.

In any type of interview, it is wise to check on key information you're given, particularly that on which decisions hinge.

Effective Action

How do you recognize the truth? Fortunately, the problem for managers is pragmatic rather than abstract. Six procedures can improve the level of truthfulness you get:

1. *Warning.* When you are about to ask a question that you feel might pose a problem or tempt the other person to lie, precede it by a matter-of-fact statement: "It's a regular procedure of ours to check on employment history to make sure there has been no mix-up in the facts and figures."

2. *Source check.* A division head is exploring procedures in a department with considerable shrinkage of its supplies. He asks the supervisor whether all cabinet and storage doors are kept locked. "All the time," supervisor replies. That evening after work the executive goes down to the department and finds three out of the fifteen doors are unlocked. Now he has a more realistic idea of what's happening.

3. *Documentary proof.* A supervisor checking a habitual absentee's record is told by the man, "I've had an intestinal virus for the past month, I've been in and out of the hospital."

"Bring in the hospital records," the supervisor asks. Next day a document from the hospital, plus a note from the doctor verifies the subordinate's story. "Sorry about your illness," the supervisor says. "Now that you're back to normal, I will hope for perfect attendance. Be sure to let me know if you have to be out for any reason."

4. *The cross-check.* Manager Ned Martin is forced to lay off a good worker who Security tells him was found in possession of cocaine. "You've got to fire her," head of Security tells him. He does. Marina S. turns up at the exit interview angry rather than contrite. "I'm getting a raw deal," she tells Ned Martin.

"I understand the material was found in your locker."

"It was, but I'm not the only one who has a key."

"One of your colleagues said he saw you putting the package into the locker."

"Some witness. He's the guy who has the other key. I haven't used that locker in months. But listen, I was ready to quit anyhow! This place is getting too raunchy for me."

After several meetings with Security, employees verified Marina's story. Finally, Martin was able to persuade her to stay, and the offender simplified matters by vanishing from the scene.

The example is an interesting double illustration of cross-checking evidence because it shows it can be wrong as well as right. In a complicated situation you may have to interview several people to get a story straight.

5. *The trap.* You've seen the scene in the movies a dozen times. The Private Eye says, "So you were in the 17th Infantry Brigade. You must have known Red Thompson. He was the most popular sergeant in the outfit."

"Oh, sure, Sergeant Thompson. He bunked next to me . . ."

You guessed it. There never was a Sergeant Thompson, at least in the 17th Brigade, and the detective has caught his quarry.

Perhaps aping the practices of real or movie detectives isn't the wisest move you can make. But if you have no other recourse, and you have reason to suspect the veracity of your interviewee, you might try a genteel version of the trap. One manager uses it to check on work history when he suspects it's been falsified:

"What safety measures did your department use to handle Mixture X?" he asks a job applicant who claims to have worked for a company producing a somewhat hazardous chemical.

"We used every protection known to man," the man responds. "Every inch of the factory floor was protected with sprinklers or automatic showers. The site had been picked because it was across the street from the county fire house. If we had trouble, we just opened up the gates and the fire equipment was there in less than a minute."

The manager correctly decided he had gotten the truth.

6. *A human lie detector.* The polygraph is not the perfect machine, even though it fills a recognized need. However, the human being can do a fairly good job of sitting across from an interviewee and determining whether or not he or she is getting the truth. The skill lies in focusing on check points:

- Eyes. A person imparting information that may get or lose him a job suddenly accompanies his words with a barrage of eye blinks. It's often a giveaway. Another sign: averted gaze, not being able to have his eyes meet yours.
- Body movement. Shifting about and squirming from a usually truthful individual may be a sign of discomfort at distorting the truth—especially if it occurs during a crucial moment in the conversation. Another possibility: rigidity. The person who has been more or less relaxed and suddenly stiffens his or her body may be having difficulty stating the truth.
- Facial expression. Visible tension or grimness may signal departure from truthfulness. Particularly note the lips. If they harden and the mouth is visibly tightened, the likelihood favors deception.

Finally, watch out for the accomplished liar. Some people can tell a lie with a straighter face than they can tell the truth. Your familiarity with the person, or a background check that shows unexplained gaps or questionable facts, may mean you're in the company of a person who has made lying a tool for problem-solving and progress.

MISTAKE 62: GIVING IN TO THE CHARMER

Charm is usually an asset to the person who has it and a pleasure to those exposed to it. In our culture it tends to be more a social than a business phenomenon. Few people ever put "lots of charm" on a résumé, although it might suit some service jobs. However, an interviewee who radiates charm is likely to puzzle more than please. The reason is that in the interview situation, it may be a manipulative device rather than the artless expression of a pleasant personality.

One model agency owner says, "The charmer can win your heart, but the heart is a notoriously bad decision maker." The manager unduly influenced by a winning manner may be the loser:

hire the wrong person, have it become a halo effect factor in judging performance, even, heaven forbid, lead to giving an undeserved raise. However, don't expect the recommendations that follow to suggest the equivalent of, "How to kill a butterfly." The aim is to enjoy the charmer and defang the charm.

Case in Point

Executive Mae Clark, vice president of Human Resources in a large insurance company, hires scores of people in a given year. She is alert to candidates with winning ways:

"Just yesterday," she says, "I interviewed a candidate for an assistant manager's job. After five minutes, he lost me. He was too pleasant, too agreeable. My high-scoring points are experience and ability. To me, employees who do their jobs well are as charming as they can get."

Analysis

Mae Clark is a good example of a decision maker operating from a poor premise. Nothing is wrong with favoring experience and job abilities. However, it's neither logical nor desirable to treat charm as if it were a bad case of body odor.

Effective Action

Once you put charm in its proper place in the working world, specifically in the interview context, it becomes more tangible and better handled. Key guidelines:

1. *Remember that charm is largely a subjective quality.* Mr. Smith interviews a receptionist applicant and states that he is favorably impressed by her good appearance, bright manner, and "considerable charm." Ms. Jones, also in on the hiring, doesn't disagree with her colleague's first two observations, but, "Charm, Sam?" she says. "I'd say big blue eyes and long lashes." The quality depends on who is measuring it and seems subject to bias according to gender among other things. Granted, too much is too much. Its use as an ingratiating tool may suggest a paucity of other more relevant attributes. But while it should be identified in an interview, as any other behavior—tension,

candor, responsiveness—don't condemn it automatically. For some jobs, it can be a reason for hiring.

2. *Dissect the quality.* A group of executives were asked to identify the behavior that they consider charming. Here are some of the traits that are included on their list:

The Ingredients of Charm

Warm smile
Pleasant tone of voice
Stimulating conversationalist
Friendliness
Physical attraction
Willingness to please (agreeableness)
Sense of humor (fun)
Tendency to flirt (of women with men)
Tendency to flatter (of men with women)
Sunny disposition
Upbeat manner
Intelligence
Big bright eyes (of women)
Muscles (of men)
Good rapport

The consensus was that an individual who had any four or more of the attributes qualified for the charm label. The value of the list is that it can help you identify the elements you feel create that indefinable quality called charm. Go through the items, strike out those that don't fit your concept. Next, add any not listed. Now you're better able to assess the quality.

3. *Consider the extent to which a person's charm, or lack of it, influences your decisions.* The difficulty in answering the question lies in its subjectivity. We do many things without conscious thought. For example, we sneeze and automatically reach for a handkerchief. The act is direct yet usually instinctive. Your decisions in interview situations, such as to reject a job candidate or rate a subordinate's performance, may similarly have a sizable unconscious component. A quiz to help you with this question will be found ahead. Meanwhile, as a basis for comparison, approximate your answer:

☐ Not at all
☐ A little
☐ Strongly influenced

4. *Think about what to do when you feel yourself slipping.* Says one executive,

> Sometimes, when I assess a person, especially in important situations, I make a conscious effort to pull back from the contact, mentally, and clear my mind of factors that are irrelevant. Whether you call it fighting off the halo effect or charm control, this second-guessing before making a commitment almost always pays off. It has confirmed some inclinations and reversed others.

Don't necessarily emulate the executive. But do check back on past "people" decisions. If you find more poor ones than you like, the second-look analysis above might be helpful.

5. *Express your negative reaction indirectly.* One of the faults with charm in the business world is that it can be manipulative. Accordingly, it can be turned on or off by the charmer at will. If you feel the gentle tentacles of the manipulator tugging at you, should you confront the person and, in effect, say "Knock it off?" It's an option you have but generally is not recommended. Your manner, being businesslike and visibly uncharmed, makes the point in a less embarrassing way.

6. *Be careful using your own charm.* You are the possessor of a number of the items on the Charm List, perhaps all. Should you use your personality to persuade, dissuade, cajole, or win a favor from those you confront in one-on-one situations?

- Yes, if you can project a manner that evades phoniness or insincerity. There is no reason to suggest that people "shouldn't be manipulative." That is often a basic in negotiation.
- What is charm and what isn't is a matter of degree and kind. Efforts that are all charm and no substance are inadvisable. Transparent phoniness is usually obvious and puts people off. The person who depends on phony tactics in negotiation weakens overall effectiveness.

The quiz that follows can stimulate your thinking and self-assessment on this provocative subject. Answer the questions as accurately as possible. They represent choices between influenced and objective choices. A score suggests how susceptible to undue influence you may be.

Rating Your Charm Control

1. *Whom do you hire?* You are interviewing applicants for a personal assistant. Which of the two finalists would win?

Sandy is clean-cut, direct-speaking, pleasant, about forty. Her qualifications are solid. You have the impression of a strong team player.

Bernie is in his early thirties, physically attractive, and interested in the kinds of things you are—movies, theater, participation sports. There is an erratic work history based on moves about the country and the intimation of marital troubles, now settled. You have a strong feeling of rapport and visions of pleasant lunches together, perhaps an occasional drink after dinner, laced with pleasant conversation.

Whom do you hire? ☐ Sandy or ☐ Bernie.

2. *Whom do you fire?* You and your boss decide that you must cut one person from your staff. Should it be Pat or Chris?

Pat has been on the job for six years, is a good worker, and tends to be a loner. On the occasions when you have worked closely together you have been impressed by a well-organized approach and the ability to solve problems. You suspect some undeveloped potential. But you're put off by a personal detachment and you interpret that as a faint personal dislike for you on Pat's part.

Chris isn't as good in the job as Pat, but there is a strong feeling of friendliness and respect toward you. From time to time you have to talk to Chris about performance faults, absenteeism, and missed deadlines. You eventually discover whenever there is a reprimand in the wind, Chris recalls that you both come from the same hometown, and the good old days at Tilton High become the center of the discussion. You find it difficult to fault Chris. You keep hoping there wil be some improvement in performance.

You decide to fire ☐ Pat or ☐ Chris.

3. *Whom do you promote?* Your boss tells you the news you've been waiting for: "They're kicking me upstairs," she says, "so I guess I'm going to repeat the same with you. But that means you're going to have to choose someone to fill your shoes. Better do it quickly, so we don't have to mark time for a training period." You have two candidates:

Jac. He's a natural leader, but his loyalty and dedication to the cause of good performance are uncertain. You suspect that self-improvement isn't a top priority, but it's been intimated that Jac yearns for power and wants to move up. There are a lot of outside interests, but you can't fault Jac on those. He's lured you out to nature walks and sightseeing about the city, and those afternoons have created personal respect and liking. You think that a strong pep talk before handing over the promotion might bring about a change in attitude.

Allie. She's a natural contender who has been picking up the savvy to take on your job from the beginning. She is not so quick a learner, but once a lesson is mastered, it is applied well. You have no doubt that the department's performance would not suffer with Allie in charge.

You decide to promote ☐ Allie or ☐ Jac.

Your rating: There's no question as to which of the two choices is the charmer, which the other. To remove all doubt: the better choices, the noncharmers, are 1. Sandy, 2. Pat, 3. Allie. If you chose two out of three or all three, your judgment is fortified against the blandishments of personal charm and favors more utilitarian qualities.

If you are surprised by your choices and their implications, you've learned something interesting about yourself. If your selections were the "better" ones and don't surprise you, your self-appraisal in Point 3 holds up and the quiz has reinforced the accuracy of your self-image.

MISTAKE 63: BEING BAFFLED BY A NONPERSON

He or she is present in body but not mind. This individual goes beyond the clam. It's not that he or she is close-mouthed; all circuits seem turned off. You're not even sure he or she is receiving you. And you're left talking, questioning, communicating with body language, all wasted.

Case in Point

Department head Guy Ferris is puzzled by Joan Boyle's behavior. Ordinarily easy to talk to and to get along with, she is almost completely unresponsive in their meeting to discuss progress of her current assignment. "She seemed really into it," Ferris reminds himself. "Why is she playing dead?"

The manager tries to kid her out of her mood: "Come on, Joan, loosen up. Have you taken a vow of silence since we last talked?"

The other shakes her head.

"Trouble at home?"

Boyle shakes her head again, then says, "Sort of."

The manager nods, and wisely, waits.

The subordinate sighs and says, "I might as well get it out." She hesitates, smiles wanly and says, "Last night I told my boyfriend I was pregnant and this morning he moved out. I guess," she adds, trying to lighten her mood for her own benefit as much as for Ferris, "you could say I lost one of my two babies."

Analysis

The silent interviewee (see Mistake 60) is an enigma you must resolve, whether unresponsiveness is a personal characteristic or, as in the case above, a departure from normal behavior. It's up to the manager to proceed with tact and caution, as Guy Ferris has done, since the problem is likely to be personal, perhaps upsetting.

Effective Action

Five reasons explain the person who is, to all intents and purposes, out of it. Find out which, and you will know what to do:

1. *Preoccupation.* His or her mental focus is elsewhere. While business is supposed to take precedence over other matters—you know, "Business before pleasure"—heavy personal matters may cancel out the old saying, as in Joan Boyle's situation. In this instance you don't have a problem as an interviewer but as an employer. The individual may need professional help.

2. *Lack of interest.* The subject may leave him or her unwilling to participate. If various gambits fail to get attention, ask a direct question that goes to the heart of the matter: "Would you like to join a task force to investigate office security?" If a negative answer is acceptable and that's what you get, bring the meeting to a time-saving close. A "Yes," or "I'm not sure," suggests you explore further. Key move: Encourage participation by relating the subject to his or her interest in ways the other may be unaware of.

3. *Nervousness or fear.* Mental stress may destroy the other's ability to concentrate.

- Note the other's body language. Signs of uneasiness may be evident, such as frequent shifting of the body, foot-tapping, disinclination to meet your gaze.
- Listen to voice quality. Tension shows up in a thin, strained tone. If you detect tension, ask: "Is something bothering you?" If the other responds in any way that is not negative, get his or her mind solidly back in the here-and-now by standing up, pacing, speaking forcefully.

4. *Deficiency.* His or her concentration span may be short, a hand-

icap if the interview has slipped into long and discursive patterns. Try a new approach:

- Keep it simple. If you're discussing a problem, stick to basics, use a vocabulary that should pose no difficulty.
- Keep it short. Cover major points, save the details for another time.
- Clarify and repeat. If you're discussing an equipment problem, specify key aspects. If the other's expression reflects doubt, go over the point again.
- Check for understanding: "Claire, would you feed that back to me? What is our new suggested procedure for qualifying a customer?" (in connection with field selling)

5. *Outside interference.* Cause for inattentiveness may lie outside the meeting room. Check by direct questions:

"Dan, I'm not sure we're on the same wavelength. Are we?"

"You're not really answering my question. Is there anything that's distracting you?"

- Add your own questions: _____

MISTAKE 64: ACCEDING TO THE INTERRUPTER

Psychologists say that people who break in on others' conversation may be unable to permit others to run things. It's their bid to take over. This may be one possibility, but whatever his or her reason, the interrupter can be a prime disrupter. Of course, a certain small amount is part of normal conversation. You say, "Our meeting with B.J. is next Wednesday, and—" "Thursday," your subordinate exclaims, and you thank her. That's a constructive break-in. But many varieties do damage to the pace and purpose of the interview, and you should be prepared to take counteraction.

The skill of some interrupters is startling. You pause a moment for any reason, the floor is yanked out from under you, and you're listening to words that flow along like a runaway river.

Case in Point

Lila Rychalski is a new manager who promised herself that when she became boss she'd treat subordinates with the consideration she had wanted. She finally becomes supervisor of a small accounting group. In an informational session about a new procedure with subordinate Tim Leverett, she finds herself stopped by premature questions and objections.

"Let me lay it all out, Tim," Rychalski suggests, "then you can have your say."

"But I have a better idea," Tim interjects.

"Better than what?" the department head asks. "You haven't heard the new method."

"This is a real inspiration," Tim persists, and reluctantly the manager gives in to the other's enthusiasm. Half an hour later Tim has described his idea and Rychalski has pointed out a dozen flaws.

Time runs out, and she sets a day for another meeting. Wryly she hears herself thanking Tim for his "participation."

Lesson learned: Control of the interview makes more sense than excessive courtesy to the interviewee.

Analysis

Unless you have all the time in the world, you can't afford to permit digressions. Flexibility yes, good-guying it for some fancied equalitarian principle, no.

Interrupters not only break in to disagree but also to agree with you. Or, they have an example for a point you've just made. They are at their worst when they start a line that blocks your agenda. Even at best you are taken off course. If you fail to act, the interview gets deep-sixed. Recognizing what's happening and why helps you repel the invaders.

Effective Action

The person who stops you in mid-discourse may do so for a variety of reasons. If he or she registers disagreement or protest, you have a person who may be more a dissenter than one with a compulsion to take over the conversation. You must often make from-the-hip decisions that distinguish a break-in artist who is to be squelched from one who should be permitted to speak.

Psychologists offer several characterizations of the interrupter's personality.

1. A control seeker. The individual may be power-hungry and sees

in the interview situation a chance to usurp the privilege of your authority and become ruler for a time. Two approaches are available. Select the one that is more appropriate, depending on your assessment of the situation:

- Reclaim your prerogative. You can make it harsh or gentle:
  Harsh: "Gary, this is the third time you've interrupted, and we haven't got the time to waste. Please don't do it again. If at the end of our session you have any questions or suggestions, I'll entertain them briefly."
  Gentle: "Hank, I know you're eager to make your contribution, and ordinarily that would be welcome, but we've got to wrap this up in a hurry. If I leave any loose ends, please send me a memo with any comments you care to make."
- Assuage his or her power hunger. In some cases, managers find it beneficial to satisfy a subordinate's power cravings. You can do it both in and out of the interview situation. In your sessions, permit him or her to have a say if and when it's convenient. Outside, you have a whole range of assignments and delegations to satisfy his desire to run things in constructive ways.

2. A nonlistener. He or she cannot accept the feeling of passivity that listening requires. Accordingly, the purpose in interrupting is to enjoy the feeling of action, indeed, of being at the center of things, while you look on. Best treatment: Be tolerant within reason. But don't hesitate to interrupt the floor-grabber if what you hear is long-winded, wandering, or beside the point. If the interference takes place a second or third time, communicate a sense not of haste but rapid pace in keeping with a topheavy work schedule, yours if not the other's.

3. A dissenter. A problem-solving interview or one aimed at producing ideas, is made to order, or disorder, for the interviewee whose stance is to take issue with you.

But don't turn him or her off. Be patient, credit the other with having something worthwhile to say. Even if what you hear is opposed to your own ideas, let the other state and defend the view. Dissent is one way to proliferate and improve ideas. Be content to keep the other within reasonable limits, both of time and subject matter. But if what you hear is off track, don't hesitate to say, "That's interesting but not relevant. Let's get back to . . ." and pick up from there.

4. Someone with a purposeless addiction. For some, interruption is a kind of speech reflex, almost a tic. One form is the person (if you've never known one you may doubt that this person exists) who

talks along with you and finishes your sentences before you can. In such cases, don't make your conversation an exchange, a verbal give-and-take. Streamline the interview to a series of statements by you, to give directives, get answers to questions, and so on. You demonstrate that you're in charge and expect to continue to be.

    5. Add your own: _____

MISTAKE 65: BEING STYMIED BY AN EVADER

You can't pin some people down. Your questions don't get straight responses; rephrase the question, and you get no more satisfaction. Eventually you get the idea: The interviewee doesn't want to be locked in. Even ask a question requiring a yes or no and you get a maybe. It is behavior seen in fact-gathering interviews, those devoted to problem analysis, and in hiring, particularly when the applicant has something to hide.

    Manager versus Evader is a common battle of wits, a Ping-Pong exchange in which the manager phrases questions to elicit information, and the other person shoots them down, not with relevant replies but with obfuscations. You have to learn how to deal with this behavior or you're likely to be hung up when important matters are at issue.

Case in Point

In a critique of a subordinate's work, Ralph Lee asks George Haley why a visual prepared for a presentation used Fahrenheit instead of Celsius units. Haley realizes it was a stupid oversight but not one he wants to confess. He says, "What's wrong with Fahrenheit?"

    "Nothing's wrong with Fahrenheit, but considering our Swedish clients—"

    "I didn't think it made any difference."

    "If you thought at all, you should have checked with me. Why didn't you?"

    "You were out to lunch." No reason not to put the boss on the defensive.

    "Why didn't you catch me when I got back?"

    "I didn't want to waste time. You said it was a rush job . . ." and so it goes.

    Thinking back to the original question, Ralph Lee realizes the subordinate's ploys. Instead of further conversation Lee simply should have said, "Do it over in Celsius."

Analysis

George Haley is employing the cover-up technique of evasion. In such cases, your best bet is always to go back to the original question and keep hammering away. Example: "You were given an assignment and told to drop everything else. Why didn't you follow orders?" And a final statement might be, "Don't let this ever happen again."

As frustrating as the cover-up evader can be, another type of evader should be mentioned at once and dismissed. This is the capricious individual who may think it's amusing to buck the system (which in this case means you) and starts a verbal version of hide and seek. This manifestation, however irritating, is likely to be temporary. Do the equivalent of administering a good shake—"This is not the time to get playful. Let's have straight talk." If that doesn't work and the matter is serious, bring the weight of authority to the rescue.

Effective Action

Here are other causes of evasion and suggestions for action:

1. *Insecurity.* To an insecure individual direct answers or firm statements seem like traps. Once committed, the feeling is, he or she is prey to fault-finding and censure. This behavior has roots in unpleasant experiences in the distant past, where an opinion or an assertion brought punishment often out of all proportion to the crime.

The insecure evader tries to live by an old safety principle, "Never stick your neck out." In dealing with this attitude, three moves can help:

- Minimize the issue. The evader typically exaggerates the critical nature of things. Calm his or her fears: "No matter what the answer is, there's not too much involved. Let me ask you again. . . ."
- Stress the importance of straight answers. "I must know exactly what was said to the people at Superior. Once I know, I'll be able to deal with them."
- Demand correct answers as your right. It may not be a simple

idea to get across, but in the unwritten contract between manager and subordinate, direct and honest dealings are implicit. One executive says that in this kind of situation he has said, "I expect straight answers from everyone here and expect to give them. I won't make an exception in your case."

2. *Lack of trust.* When wariness is due to suspicion and fear of unjust punishment, mistrust sparks the evasion. Winning trust from subordinates isn't a one-shot act. But managers who have a reputation for honest and considerate dealings seldom have to suffer the evasive interviewee. If you can remind the subordinate of your unblemished record, the appeal, "Trust me," may get the answers you seek.

3. *Guilt.* Crime on the job ranges from the petty, which managers usually try to deal with themselves, to that which warrants police intervention. The focus here is on the former variety.

A session called to get to the bottom of an act of vandalism or petty theft is likely to find the interviewee in the evasive mode, especially if he or she is guilty. If there is no willingness to confess, evasion is all you'll get.

You've probably seen movies featuring a confrontation between a suspect and investigator, the criminal and the law. Sometimes it takes two police officers, one playing good cop, the other bad cop, to pry the truth from the perpetrator. In spy stories, even torture doesn't do it. How can you proceed?

What will work and what won't depends on the situation and the nature of the other person. Don't play detective. You must stay within the limits of your management prerogatives without aping a member of the police force. You still have sufficient latitude to probe for the facts.

Consider these possibilities:

- Hard evidence. If the employee has been found with the symbolic smoking gun—hand in the petty cash box, an attaché case crammed with small, expensive company instruments—stress the fact, and ask for an admission: "Why did you do it?" Despite evasions and denials, repeat the question, or try to get the answer by changing your verbal approach.
- Circumstantial evidence. If there is doubt, confront him or her with the evidence and ask for an explanation. "You were seen at the cabinet during the lunch period. Why were you there?"

Whatever the answer, other than an admission, bear down, keep probing. Eventually, you may have to check some answers with others.

If you finally determine guilt, the question of disciplinary action should reflect company policy. In other words, you may have to consult with other executives to decide. If you come to a dead end, you may have to live with an unresolved mystery. It happens in the best of companies.

A psychological factor intensifies the frustration of dealing with the evader. From your earliest years you are conditioned to give and get reasonable answers to questions. When this procedure is undercut by evasion, the "minicosm" of your world is shaken. By keeping the situation in perspective, suppressing your explosion reflex, you lessen the annoyance without lessening your ability to put the evader on the straight and narrow path of direct response.

MISTAKE 66: BEING VICTIMIZED BY THE NONSTOP TALKER

A person who talks too much may have a place in the universe but it isn't in the interview room. A verbal overflow, even if some of it is on target, produces boredom, wasted time, or confusion.

Of course, you could end the flow by saying, "We'll stop for now," and signal for the other's exit by standing up. However, you might not want to terminate for several reasons, all good:

- *Pride. You don't want to be left with a feeling of defeat in a situation you should be able to handle easily.*
- *Expediency. The subject of the interview may be important enough to warrant staying with it.*
- *Panning for gold. There may be enough of value in the verbal flood to justify salvaging the useful from the dross.*

Case in Point

Executive Bette Landry looks at her desk calendar and is reminded that Trevor MacDonald is coming in right after lunch to discuss a record-keeping problem. "Watch him like a hawk," she reminds herself. "Give him an opening and the session is shot." Despite the self-administered warning, Landry is lulled into complacency after about ten minutes of smooth sailing.

"I believe if you take up the matter of new shelves with Bright in maintenance, you should be ready to install the new system. . . ." and there goes the ball game.

"That's what you might think," MacDonald says, "and maybe your experience is different from mine or the other supervisors, but you might be interested to know that maintenance is the most fouled-up department in the company. Let me tell you. . . ." and he does, while the clock hands race.

"OK," Landry finally breaks in for the third time, "I get the picture. I'll send the requisition to Bright and I'll phone him as well."

"Wish you luck," MacDonald says, "but when the front office got stymied for two weeks—"

"Right," Landry says, "I'll watch the way it goes."

Analysis

The nonstop talker may be a subordinate you know well. Something sets him or her off, and questions come in explicit detail, answers ramble, suggestions stretch on and on. You get endless pros and cons on minor points, amplifications are themselves amplified. You could save yourself by interjecting, "What you're saying sounds interesting, but let's save it for another time."

But the flow may not be too easy to stop because you are up against a compulsive speaker. Some people are made uncomfortable by their own silence. For them, talking satisfies a deep need. If the compulsion is strong enough, you must convert the interview into a two-way give-and-take and keep it under tight rein. It's unlikely that a job applicant whose résumé suggests a good work record would be off the normal length-of-conversation scale. Indeed, for the job candidate, excessive verbosity could be a knockout factor.

Effective Action

Most interviewees can be kept within acceptable limits by actions like these:

1. Transfer some of the interview content to writing. "Your explanation sounds interesting. Please put it in writing for me."

2. Switch the interviewee to someone else: "Instead of telling me about that, see if you can get some time with Al Braun systems and run it past him for a reaction."

3. Avoid open-ended questions, such as "Give me your ideas about improving our record-keeping." Instead, ask specific questions: "Would we would have to replace our present filing cabinets?" The more yes or no questions you can ask, the better.

4. Jump on irrelevant monologue: "I must interrupt you. What you're saying has no bearing on your performance on the Canada project. Let's stick to the point."

5. Trim the other's answers by requests like these:

"Give me a short version."
"Omit the details. Just give me the basic idea."
"Please simplify that for me."
"Our time is running out. Let's move ahead more quickly."

Or, terminate: "We're running too long. Send me a memo that makes the other points you want me to know about."

Learn from previous encounters. With those whose long-windedness inflates the interview out of proportion, ask yourself, "Do I need an interview at all?" A letter, memo, report, even a group meeting might be more suitable media for the nonstop talker.

MISTAKE 67: BEING DAZZLED OR DISAPPOINTED BY THE PERSON WHO OVERPREPARES

This interviewee is like the previous one, the nonstop talker, in that he or she too is given to excess verbiage. Unlike the nonstopper, however, the overpreparer tends to overflow only when preparation is called for. Analysis of the two types indicates differences in motivation and in dealing with them.

Case in Point

Executive complaining to spouse: "Getting into a one-to-one with Art Lucas is a nuisance. He sits in my office reading his notes, and an hour can pass and I don't hear a single spontaneous word." Another executive has a different complaint: "Gail comes into our planning sessions so well prepared—I should say overprepared—that I have to struggle to keep up with her flood of facts, opinions, arguments, and ideas. It may be her way of bucking for a promotion. I'm beginning to think it's my job she's after."

You can gain substantial benefits from examining what over-preparers do, why they do it, and the consequences thereof. These individuals may be revealing a good deal more about themselves and about you than you might think.

Analysis

Subordinates who come to an interview loaded with data, questions, and solutions are a phenomenon worth examining. They may be averse to thinking spontaneously or want to control the conversation. Whatever the reasons, they usually contribute worthwhile information.

Effective Action

Here are some explanations of the overpreparer:

1. He or she is insecure. Psychiatrists are familiar with this phenomenon in their own practice: Says one, "I have a patient who has never come into a session without a notebook in which he has listed all the questions and subjects he wants to discuss. That might be normal for an older person with a poor memory, but for him it suggests doubt of his ability to think clearly under what he considers the stress of the consulting room."

Your subordinates may also feel they're protecting themselves against the need to "think on their feet" in a stressful situation. For them preparation removes some of the threat of the unknown represented by an open agenda.

2. The person thinks it's what you want. It may be a holdover from school days, where homework was routine and students were supposed to come in with all the answers. Or, it could be you. Unintentionally, some executives give cues—a frown at an "I don't know" or a smile at a detailed answer to a question they didn't expect an interviewee to know. Consider the possibility.

3. He or she wants to impress. The subordinate may be out to look good, so he or she devotes time to prethinking the interview session, aiming to blow the boss's mind by a command of the subject, and/or to demonstrate a strong interest in the job, and possibly a raise.

4. The person views the interview situation as an opportunity to be seen and heard. This may be exemplary and shows initiative. But it may also suggest a subordinate's desire to be appreciated, in short, it's a bid for attention and approval.

5. He or she is implying criticism. The action suggests that the manager may not listen to and recognize the subordinate's ideas or contribution in the course of the regular work day. The interview fireworks are a bid for attention not otherwise obtainable.

6. He or she likes the subject. You can often expect extra effort if a subject has special appeal. The subordinate may harbor such affinities without you're being aware of them. When they stand revealed by extensive preparation for a discussion with you, you may get a fresh insight into the employee's preferences and interests and build on them.

MISTAKE 68: BEING INTIMIDATED BY THE HOSTILE INTERVIEWEE

In any interview you may find yourself confronted by an individual with an angry manner. If the attitude is not deeply rooted, if it is more threat than aggressive intent, you can proceed without acknowledging the other's behavior, and it is likely to dissipate. But there are two circumstances that require you to act:

1. *The interview requires participation by the other, which will not be forthcoming as long as the mood persists.*
2. *The interviewee seems bent on an increasing intensity of hostility, possibly approaching physical violence.*

Case in Point

Fred R. is an angry man. He believes both fate and his boss are mistreating him. Even if he's right on both counts, his manager must put aside the business of the interview and deal with the behavior.

The hostility takes center stage because it blocks communication. And it does so in a pervasive way. For example, a simple, otherwise acceptable statement in the grip of temper becomes a provocation. The manager says, "Do you think you'll have trouble finishing that assignment on time?" The employee bristles: "Do you expect me to have trouble?"

Analysis

How do you deal with hostility? A common response is to meet anger with anger. This may be sound biology but poor management. While it may satisfy you to meet hostility with hostility, and perhaps subdue the other, there are more effective approaches. Knowing them can prepare you for the rare but upsetting situation when an interviewee turns rabid.

Effective Action

You may not have the time or training to probe for the character roots of the belligerence. However, a set of guidelines can help you face the immediate situation of the hostile interviewee:

1. Note differences in degree and kind. Assess what you're up against. One person's rage may be another's huff, some individuals are not as angry as they seem. Two reasons:

- Facial expression may register upset that may only look like anger. The manager may misread an expression or body posture: tension may be seen as aggressiveness.
- Some people suffer from free-floating hostility and register an angry mood unrelated to the present situation.

Since in neither of these cases are you the target, proceed with the interview. Only if you fail to progress should you call the turn on the other's mood.

2. Treat the symptoms. There may be a specific cause for the outburst. Your knowledge of the person and of incidents in his or her work life in the past days may help you pinpoint the irritant. There may have been a quarrel with an unsatisfactory outcome or a request for a privilege or a special assignment that was refused.

If you can't determine the cause, pose a tentative question: "You seem angry. Can you tell me why?" You have about a fifty-fifty chance of getting a satisfactory answer. If you're lucky, make some disposition of the matter: "We can go into the details on that later. Let's finish our present business first." One executive counsels a waiting game: "Sit there in silence. I find it usually gets the conversation on a remedial track." If appropriate, try to cool matters: "It will help if we calm down." ("We" is better than "you.")

3. Identify hidden hostility. Society usually exacts a penalty for hostile behavior. "Nobody likes an angry person," is the way one executive puts it. And so, in many cases, an individual with a hostile streak disguises it, even from himself or herself, by veiled behavior:

- Humor. The wisecracker fond of getting in a witty dig, "Just like Harry to screw things up" may seem innocuous, but it's gratuitous and it's mocking. Why kick a man when he's down or absent? Answer: to vent one's hostile feelings, either against the individual, or the world, or both.

• Rectitude. "A supervisor on my staff," one of our executive group recalled, "used to boast, 'I tell it like it is.' And he did. But behind the screen of righteousness he would verbally strike at people: 'You were stupid,' he tells a colleague. 'You never had a chance for that promotion. Helen had it sewed up.' "

In some cases you need not react to hostility. But in interviews, you're right in the line of fire. Being aware of the suppressed anger of others helps you see behind the words and realize the reasons for an unexpected attitude or unfavorable statements about others and decide on appropriate action.

4. Avoid feeding the mood. Some people are aroused by specific triggers. They may have pet likes and pet hates. Unless there is a reason to mention what for them may be sensitive subjects—another department, an unfavored colleague, a subject, such as promotions that he or she feels have been unjustly denied—exclude them from your discussion.

In dealing with people with a hostile streak, criticism becomes touchy. "You didn't do as well as I expected," may call for apologies or a request to hear more. However, the belligerent individual will find those fighting words. One remedy is to tone down the comment, since mild criticism for the fast-trigger person will seem twice as harsh and the person may become twice as explosive.

Remember these four steps to control. If for whatever reason, the person across the desk is more eager to fight than talk:

• Be aware of the attitude. Angry people are swept away by their mood. It's unlikely that an attempt to lighten the conversation or coax them out of their angry shell will work. Generally, your initial move is to
• Acknowledge the feeling. "You seem to be upset. . . ."
• Help the other ventilate. Encourage the other to express his or her feelings: "Can you tell me why you feel this way?"
• Create a helpful perspective. Help the interviewee to step back from the situation, see it long-range by suggesting mitigating factors: "Misunderstandings can foul things up," "I'm sure my assistant didn't mean it the way it sounds."
• Let the other decide about the impasse. Perhaps the hostile one

does not give in. Try handing over the reins: "I've tried to help you see the situation more constructively. If we can't get back to our subject, there is no point in continuing. What do you suggest we do?" If you get no response, fall back on the wisdom of the Roman philosopher Seneca, who counseled, "The greatest remedy for anger is delay." Cancel and reschedule the interview.

MISTAKE 69: BEING PRESSURED BY A REQUEST FROM A FRIEND

Friendships between managers and subordinates are common and may pose a problem. The manager usually goes by a no-favoritism rule and the subordinate supposedly accepts it. Often the manager leans over backward to avoid even the appearance of unfairness. But the intimacy of the interview may be irresistible to the friend. (For more on the friendship problem see Mistake 44, about friendship on the job.)

Case in Point

"It's bad enough," Clare Whitby tells her husband, "that Fay tried to use our friendship to get herself a plum assignment, but she acted as though she'd surely get it. When I told her I had decided to give it to Dave Wilson, she had the nerve to say, 'As a longtime friend, I expected you to give me the edge . . .' "

Mr. Husband wasn't sympathetic: "You should have told Fay flat out when you were made department head there would be no favored treatment for anyone."

"That's a sound principle," Clare said. "Suppose you make your own dinner."

Analysis

When you interview a subordinate or job candidate who is a friend, he or she may be tempted to trade on the relationship. In the one-on-one setup you may seem to be a captive, a sitting duck. Your friend has your total attention, distractions and interruptions are unlikely, and conditions are optimum for what may be seen as a benign conspiracy.

Expectation of favored treatment creates a crisis not only in the immediate situation, but in the aftermath. The relationship may be hurt, even destroyed, which calls for some kind of attention.

Your response to friendship used as a lever should be based on a clear policy. In reviewing yours, remember that the problem is two-fold. If you make a decision that is shaped by personal feelings, you may have to justify it to yourself and to others in the department. If you turn down the request, you may have to justify it to the friend.

Effective Action

The points below help you see how well prepared you are to pick your way through the emotional minefield:

1. Be aware of a basic conflict. Your feeling for a friend and responsibility to your organization may put you in a bind. It's the old love-versus-duty situation in business garb.

But don't confuse friendship with friendliness. The former may create an obligation that the latter doesn't. (Again, see Mistake 44 for more on this distinction.)

2. Don't let your guard down. With most friends, there's no question. But in some cases, the encouragement of the interview setting is irresistible, and a friend's ploys may appear in subtle ways. "You know I'm the best man for that job," when you know no such thing; or, during a raise request, "Madge [spouse] has been having a tough time managing family expenses on my present salary." That's really laying it on, but you have to respond:

- Without being defensive.
- Matter-of-factly.

Explain the reasons for your decision. One consolation, if you lose the friend as a result, is that his or her motives for the relationship immediately become suspect.

3. Make your tradeoffs knowingly. To minimize the hazards of favoritism:

- Offset the potential resentment of your friendships by friendliness to others.
- Let your friends know that they, like yourself, may have to pay a price. You may have to bend over backwards to avoid the appearance of favoritism and a friend may lose out. It's a necessary sacrifice.

4. Finally, you may want to offset the disadvantage the interview situation represents for you in this instance. At the very least, buy time. You may say, forthrightly, "I need time to consider your request. Let me think about it and we'll discuss it further tomorrow. Is two o'clock all right with you?"

MISTAKE 70: LETTING YOURSELF BE INTIMIDATED BY AN "ENEMY"

Few managers get by without one or two people who are less colleagues than antagonists. The interview's physical closeness or the subject matter, which may involve criticism of the interviewee, may exacerbate a touchy relationship.

Case in Point

Grace Santana checks her calendar and winces. She has an appointment for a project review with Rose Blair. The report is a poor one, and the unavoidable criticism will probably be taken personally. Blair resented Santana being made department head, and the ill feeling persists despite the manager's efforts to smooth things over. "Time heals all wounds," she tells herself, but the process is taking a long time.

Analysis

At stake is the goal of your meeting, threatened by confrontation and ill feeling. One executive says, "There is a colleague I'm literally afraid to meet one-to-one. I try to hold our meetings out in the open, the company cafeteria, even the reception room."

In salary discussions, requests for privileges, or planning new assignments, the dynamite is there, detonator and all. If you must criticize your "foe," that could be the ignition. Some managers may feel it's wise to make the session bland and inoffensive. The principle may be sound, the application shaky. Your reticence may be seen as timidity, may aggravate rather than sooth.

Effective Action

Change your view of the meeting from an occasion for conflict to one of opportunity. The pair dynamics of the interview (see Mistake 79), which may intensify hostility, can also be mobilized to remedy matters. Consider these points:

1. *Anticipate.* What created the hostility in the first place? It's a good question to ask yourself before going into the session. The very same circumstances that may intensify the ill feeling—the intimacy of the setting—give you an opening for salving wounds. Prethink how the business of the session might lend itself to breaking the ice.

2. *Facilitate.* Think through a tentative plan for your overtures. Knowing the other as you do, develop answers:

- Timing. Should you start off with your peace agenda, save it for the end, or inject it at an appropriate time during the discussion?
- Cooperation. Can you tie it into the scheduled subject? One possible approach: "Jack, don't you agree that our problems could be eased if we worked in a spirit of cooperation rather than competition? Our personal difficulties don't seem to matter very much in retrospect. Do you suppose we could forget the past and work together in a more constructive way?"

Admittedly, the suggested line may fall flat. However, this does not mean your relationship is worsened. Your knowledge of the other person can guide the words and manner that has the best chance to succeed.

3. *Alleviate.* A limited objective for a rapprochement may be more realistic. Instead of a complete transformation from ill feeling to friendliness, perhaps you can suggest a truce: "I know we've had our differences, but since there is so much at stake, let's agree to pull together on this project. . . ."

One executive finds the interview setting so conducive to repairing bridges, she goes out of her way to schedule one-to-one sessions with her less friendly associates. "I've been having a rough time with the head of a service department," she says. "I suggested a meeting to discuss a minor problem. Then I hauled out my secret agenda shaped to mollify him, and it did. All we needed was the chance to discuss our differences."

4. *Place your cards on the table.* "I've tried mollifying and getting agreement on putting the past behind us," asserts an executive, "but in one case my hardshell rival wouldn't have any. I got tired of pussyfooting and in our next meeting I closed the door, pushed the files and working papers aside and said, 'Ted, we've been fighting one another ever since the front office turned down your raise request. I

said you'd be in a stronger position after the reorganization went through. Now, while you're waiting to be rich, can you give me one good reason why we shouldn't turn in our weapons and let peace break out?' "

"The man says, 'Are you telling me I'll get that raise?' "

" 'Of course not,' " I said. " 'If I could do that, you'd have gotten it long ago.' He burst out laughing and held out his hand."

MISTAKE 71: BEING VICTIMIZED BY YOUR OWN EMOTIONS

No mechanism has yet been invented that can bar emotions from the work scene. But your own feelings can be the most destructive factor in an interview. As an executive, you often must exercise self-control in order to function responsibly. But self-control doesn't necessarily mean you swallow your feelings.

Case in Point

Executive Sam Borden is about to start a planning session with Danny Hall. As soon as they start, the manager realizes the other is trying to bait him, nothing obvious, but sly bits of behavior:

"I don't quite understand that. Would you mind explaining it again?" And then, suggestions that don't make sense: "Instead of doing the assembly here, why don't we . . . ?" The idea is far too costly, and Borden knows Hall knows it. The manager feels his anger and frustration boiling up.

Analysis and Action

Here again the intimacy of the interview causes an interplay of dynamics (see Mistake 79) that exacerbates the feeling between the two.

The particular test posed for you in this situation is that both you and the other may be either victim or victimizer. In the example, Borden is having his leg pulled and his nerves abraded by his subordinate's wily tactics. In other situations, managers may let their feelings outweigh fairness and good sense, and indulge their unbridled emotions, from twitting to torment, from playing a cat-and-mouse game to intimidation that indulges a sadistic bent.

You have to unleash your perceptiveness at full power to identify and then deal with your feelings, either in response to the interviewee's provocation or your own risibilities.

Effective Action

The manager must face up to the destructive potential of his or her own feelings. Some guidelines:

1. When the interviewee is being provocative, choose among three moves, noting that only the third applies managerial clout:

- Ignore the behavior, use a procedural remedy. For example, Borden might push ahead with the interview with the expectation that the give-and-take of the conversation will force the recalcitrant Danny Hall to pull in his horns. It might be said that even if the interview achieves its objectives, the penalties can be high: The other has seemingly "won" the encounter, the manager has chickened out on dealing with behavior that verges on insubordination. Possibly. But now the manager knows he has a problem with the subordinate, and he can handle a recurrence from a more considered stance.
- Recognize the obstructionism and rule it out of order. For example, Borden might say, "Danny, our time is very short. Let's wrap up this session as fast as we can and not linger over details." It might be said that this expedient only puts the battle on hold, and that's true. But it does take care of the immediate situation. You can decide what to do about a subordinate's negative feelings at another time.
- Be ready for confrontation. The manager can stop the session and deal with the misbehavior: "Danny, I have the feeling that you're dragging your feet on this. Any reason?" Chances are, the other will deny the statement. Borden can say, "Glad I'm wrong. Let's get on with it." He has made it difficult for Hall to continue his noncooperation. Of course, if the subordinate hauls out a hidden agenda, voices some reason for dissatisfaction, deal with it as you would any knot in a working relationship.

2. When you have no choice, broaden the focus and change the situation, which in this case means changing the emotion. What if the interviewer's feelings are not anger but sympathy? One executive recounts his experience in a termination interview:

The department head and I were old friends. I knew he had to go, but the idea was painful and I considered asking the head of personnel to tell him the bad news. But I decided I owed it to Henry to face him myself. As prepared as I thought I was, his reaction was so pathetic, I had to stop. The hell of it was, I had no place to go. I couldn't reverse the firing decision. And I couldn't break off the interview in the middle. I just gritted my teeth and somehow it was over. . . .

In some interviews it is possible to adopt an alternative the executive above felt he couldn't. You can stop, make some excuse, and say you will set up a continuation meeting at a later date. On a second go-round, whether it's anger or mental anguish, you will have had the time to fortify yourself.

3. Let yourself go. In some cases, you can diminish the crisis by venting your feelings. For example, Helen Glenn is in a counseling interview with a subordinate who discloses a pathetic family situation that arouses the manager's outrage and empathy. Glenn says, "Gloria, I can understand how you feel. There are very few people who could take the punishment that you have and still function both here and at home. It's admirable, but I feel you owe it to yourself to consider your own rights." In cases like this, the venting of sympathy helps both parties.

Managers have expressed rage, fear, excessive concern, and positive feelings such as admiration or encouragement strongly and directly, and as in the Helen Glenn-Gloria example, have derived double benefits. The specific circumstances help determine what you can say and how to say it.

The key to control of your emotions is not automatic suppression, but to be aware of them and to use them constructively. At the very least, exploit the incubator effect of the interview setup to become more aware of your levels and types of emotionality, such awareness being a factor in dealing with them.

PART IV

Staying on Top of Crises

Thousands of managers were conducting interviews when John F. Kennedy was assassinated or when the attempt on Ronald Reagan's life was made by John Hinckley. How did they react to the news? Managers were also interviewing on Black Monday, October 19, 1987, when the bottom dropped out of the stock market and the Dow lost over 500 points. What to do? Stop the session and rush to the nearest radio or TV? Take a temporary break? Take the day off? There were advocates of each choice. Which would have been yours?

Some managers took the events in stride and

continued with the meeting. They may not have been less upset. More likely they were motivated by a "show must go on" syndrome.

It's in Your Lap

Interviews proceed smoothly in the average case and in textbooks. But veteran executives will tell you of debacles caused by four-alarm fires or an interviewee's heart attack. You must make immediate decisions. Wrong ones can turn innocuous situations into total confusion; right ones can put things back on track.

The interview setting is a two-inhabitant microcosm, isolated, private, seemingly secure. But in some instances, when, for example, there is a serious accident or a natural disaster, the other person's life may be literally in the manager's hands. There are also situations that are not physically dangerous, but they throw you off balance because they make you flustered or uncomfortable: having to maintain your equilibrium when you are confronted with an unwarranted interruption or an emotional appeal from the interviewee.

Dealing With Agenda Busters

Whether the interruption comes from within or without, action is required. There may be no question as to what to do. For example, if there is a medical emergency you get help at top speed, whether it's from a staff member trained in first aid or the nearest doctor.

Not all crises are major nor do they all require life-or-death judgment. But the need for decision and action must be faced in every situation and advance consideration to all your options can lead you to the best decision in handling each case.

In coping with interview upsets, you may have to decide not only your own actions but those of

*your interviewees. If they are outsiders—a job can-
didate, a customer, a supplier, a visitor on professional business—it's your duty to secure their
safety.*

*In each case the threat is from a mistake—
lack of foresight, an error in judgment, delayed
decision, failure to take proper action—that causes
the damage. Each unit that follows aims to sharpen
your judgments and actions in dealing with the
unexpected.*

MISTAKE 72: OVERREACTING TO BLOOD AND SHATTERED GLASS

Interruptions may arrive on little cat feet or break in like a rampaging elephant. Don't let even the elephant paralyze you.

Case in Point

One of our executive panel members describes this unusual intrusion on an interview:

"Our plant is out in the country. I was in an intense negotiation with a supplier over some critically needed materials. Suddenly a grouse came winging in out of the woods and exploded right through the window. It was noisy, messy, and terrifying. There amid the glass shards lay the bleeding bird, its neck broken.

"The supplier started to leave, saying, 'I'll phone you tomorrow.'

" 'Hold it,' " I replied. " 'Our business is too important.' I moved our discussion into an empty office down the hall. Afterward, I took the man into town for a quiet drink. If I had stopped to deal with the mess and set another meeting date, we'd have been in trouble. Afterward I admired my presence of mind. Postponement would have interfered with a critical operation."

Analysis

Note the elements illustrated by the case:

- A blow from without. The suicidal grouse is certainly a one-in-a-million event. Rare as it is, it reminds you that forces from outside may intrude and must be dealt with.
- Obligation to the other. The supplier, the other person in the negotiating interview, was a visitor. This poses a special responsibility for the manager. It is up to him or her, especially in cases of physical upheaval, to shepherd the other out of harm's way, or at least to calm his or her fears.
- Anticipation of the other's upset. If the interviewee is on unfamiliar ground, any disruption that creates a physical hazard, broken glass, a fire, a ruptured steam pipe, is not only a threat but a disorientation factor. The manager should anticipate the other's confusion and the need for guidance and reassurance.

Effective Action

When the intrusion poses a physical threat, don't make the mistake of inaction or wait for help that may not arrive. Further:

1. *Don't let yourself be fazed.* Whether it's noise, smoke, or earthquake, let your responsibility as a manager keep you focused on constructive action. Don't give yourself time to worry, get the shakes, or to be otherwise engaged.

2. *Move fast.* Take the initiative. Particularly when the interviewee depends on you, issue direct orders. It can be anything from, "Follow me," as you go to safety or instructions to him or her as to how to get help—a colleague, doctor, the police, a security guard.

3. *Don't necessarily start cleaning up.* The executive in the Case of the Suicidal Grouse did well to move himself and the salesman out of the disaster area. Others would appear, armed with cleaning tools, better able to cope with the aftermath.

In some cases, it is necessary to deal with the influx of people from other offices, your secretary, assistant, and so on. Take the steps that will protect them or prevent them from actions that will harm instead of help.

MISTAKE 73: BEING STARTLED BY AN EMOTIONAL ERUPTION

It can happen at any time, in almost any type of interview. You touch on a subject that has special poignance for the other person, and tears erupt. Or it could be an outburst of rage. Another type of emotional behavior, depression, may show itself.

Case in Point

Eric Benning, in charge of the roll room in a plastics plant, is meeting with Pete Saltus, one of the roll operators. The shift supervisor has reported a quarrel between Pete and Roy Murn and added a comment to the written record: "With those exposed rolls going at high speed and all those guys using knives in their work, it could have been bad."

Saltus comes in, a patch on his chin, that Benning guesses covers a bruise from the brawl. One minute into the conversation and the manager realizes Pete is tied up in knots. "Why are you talking to me?" the operator exclaims. "Murn threatened me. Give him the going over!"

The manager spends the next fifteen minutes helping the roll room operator cool off. He then starts digging for the facts, and the anger and the murk begin to dissolve.

Analysis

Occasionally you are confronted by an overwrought interviewee. Not only is your agenda preempted, but you must face the problem of dealing with the person's mood. All your skill in dealing with people, especially upset people, must come into play.

Effective Action

Several industrial psychologists were consulted for their ideas for providing emotional first aid to people beset by an emotional storm. Here is the essence of their recommendations:

Crying or Related Behavior

1. Show concern, make clear your desire to help.
2. Give the other person time to regain composure. Don't exert pressure. Use a quiet, sympathetic tone of voice.
3. Ask, "What's wrong?" Don't insist on an answer.
4. Ask, "How can I help?" If the response is a shake of the head or, "You can't," say, "Try me." If reluctance persists, let matters rest. Offer water or a soft drink.
5. If the employee explains the cause of the tears, listen, and offer sympathy and understanding. Don't make judgments or prescribe.
6. When calm returns, give the interviewee the choice of continuing or rescheduling the interview.

Anger or Related Behavior

1. Be firm; don't respond in anger. Make clear your intention to cool things down before continuing with your conversation.
2. Ask the reason for the upset. Discourage tirades. Seek "just the facts," as an early TV detective used to say.

3. Listen to the complaint. This will further quiet matters. If the complaint is justified, do what you can to resolve it.
4. There may be a reversal of feeling if the employee regrets the outburst. Be ready to deal with shame or sheepishness. Alleviate the feeling by assuring, "It's just one of those things."
5. If professional counseling seems advisable, don't say, "See a psychiatrist," or anything similar. This suggests a diagnosis of abnormal behavior that will probably be resented. If, to your knowledge, the outburst is one of an ongoing chain, you might describe the situation to the company doctor or mental health adviser, who could suggest a follow-up.

Despondency

If the interviewee seems down in the mouth, withdrawn, or unresponsive:

1. Don't make a judgment. Ask, "Anything wrong?" You may get a negative reply. But stay with it a while longer. In a friendly way say, "I'd like to help."
2. Don't stop tears. Weeping can be a desirable alleviant.
3. Suggest a shortened version of your agenda or a meeting at a later time.
4. If you suspect a tangible reason, such as illness in the family, and the depression is deep enough to interfere with the work, suggest, "You may want to talk things over with someone." If your company has a medical department or outside medical service, suggest a visit and leave it to the nurse or doctor to refer the employee to a source of help.

For cases of unusual emotional behavior that aren't temporary, you might want to check with your boss or a medical or professional counselor to describe the case and get suggestions.

MISTAKE 74: BEING CONFUSED BY A PERSONAL APPEAL

Interviews usually take place at a matter-of-fact, businesslike level. But sometimes interviewees cast aside protocol and decorum, and the fullness of their ego needs comes at you like a battering ram. You may not be taken by surprise. You understand from your own feelings that individuality and an off-the-job self lurks just below workaday conformity. But as interviewer, a complicating element has been injected into the session, not to be disregarded or set aside.

Case in Point

You are in a discussion with Nancy Lim about her future. She's a good worker with an excellent potential, and you think her professional track is clear. But the interview is suddenly stopped cold. She erupts with feelings of dissatisfaction verging on despair: "I'm getting nowhere, I'm lost!" She asserts that her professional activities are out of line with her life aspirations. "Help me," she asks.

Analysis

You are caught between your responsibility as a manager and your feelings about the other as a human being. At issue is Nancy Lim's choice between growth on the job and ambitions that might leave you minus one excellent subordinate. In another instance, "Help me decide" may be the plea, or "I must have more money to cover my new expenses," or "Please talk to the employment director about my brother." Personal requests may cover a broad range, even going beyond matters you can control.

Effective Action

There is no one-size-fits-all answer to this problem. However, you do have some constructive moves to guide your subordinates' agonizing over a personal situation:

1. *Consider your dilemma.* Like your subordinates, you face a choice between two possible decisions: In your interest and the company's should you discourage the personal goals? Or, in sympathy with the personal desires, should you give the best advice you can to help them satisfy their needs, even against the company's interests?

2. *Decide what you think about the others' dilemmas.* A person who is tone deaf and can't read a note may want to be an orchestra conductor. How realistic are the ambitions or demands? You certainly don't want to make the decision for them, or even let them make their own, without spelling out and evaluating the choices.

3. *Encourage them to talk.* They may be confused and groping. The more they ventilate, the more they will clarify feelings and ideas, a royal road to better decisions.

4. *Help them think through the alternatives.* For example, you can raise questions about their goals and provide a clear assessment of their prospects in the company.

5. *Suggest the test of time.* It's not likely that the choice is one that must be made immediately. Propose that they do two things to gain a better basis for decisions:

- Explore the prospects and practicality of the expressed goals or desires.
- Sketch out some lines of activity that could clarify chances for achievement in their present jobs.

More is involved in this situation than just gathering information. A passage of time, even of a few months, especially if the employees gain new insights into true feelings about alternative directions, can provide a perspective that will help shape satisfactory decisions.

Your even-handed judgment will eventually prove to be your strongest move. Moves that neither subvert your loyalty to your organization nor ignore your subordinates' well-being or aspirations, even with some compromise, may be best.

Don't underestimate the possible benefits you stand to gain, in addition to the satisfaction of helping a person think through a personal crisis. Willingness and ability to deal with this type of problem reinforces the manager's leadership of the group.

MISTAKE 75: BEING FLUSTERED BY INTERRUPTIONS

Why are interruptions still a threat to the orderly procedure of interviews? Business manners and protocol are sufficiently established to prevent the thoughtless entry of a colleague, boss, or visitor into an interview session. Executive's assistants are usually adept enough to sidetrack phone callers. Even those who get to the manager on an open phone should be sufficiently savvy to back off in the few moments it takes to understand the situation. Part of the explanation points to the manager. He or she may know the solutions, but fail to apply them.

Case in Point

Manager Alice Schultz's door flies open and fellow manager, Howard Jensen, enters, although he sees she's interviewing a subordinate.

"Sorry, didn't know you were in conference . . ." Despite good intentions, the damage is done, the interruption has come at a critical point in the discussion. And it's made worse by Jensen saying, "While I'm here . . . this will only take a few seconds," and proceeds to go into an interdepartment matter of little urgency. When the colleague finally leaves, Schultz tries to pick up the thread, but the rapport at least for the while, has been broken.

Analysis

An interruption may even lack the off-setting virtue of importance. Executives, who, usually against their will, have experience in being disturbed offer explanations like these:

- "I really believe," says one, "that it's a perverse way of showing superior status. People who interrupt, at least among my colleagues, are never below me and only occasionally from the echelons above. It's those at about my level who want to show muscle that make a point of sailing in at whim."
- Says another, "Interrupters are usually people so wrapped up in themselves, they may not even be aware of their rudeness. I guess they won't change unless the interruptees let them have it. Spitballs would be the appropriate weapon."
- "It's ego," suggests a third. "They feel they come first. They don't even think they are doing something objectionable."

In addition to the motives of the interrupters, it's clear that laxness by the victim is another cause and calls for a check on privacy controls.

Effective Action

Whatever the cause, managers whose privacy is being invaded have some fence-mending to do. And the best approach may be that of those who mend fences. Leave the strong points alone, and zero in on the breaks. For example:

1. *Notify the guilty.* As in many situations, the Pareto Principle applies: a small percentage of those who can do the damage cause a large percentage of it. Without making it a big deal you can say to

those who have sinned: "You'd save us both time and embarrassment if you check to see if I'm free before dropping in."

2. *Rehearse the "security guard."* To a secretary, "Terry, you put Smith through to me this morning when I was in conference. Let's make sure that only those I OK in advance may interrupt when I'm interviewing. Exceptions are emergencies, and the boss, when he's hot about something. The same holds for visitors or anyone else who turns up in the office."

3. *Forestall possible invaders.* "I know you want to keep in close touch because of the tests you're running," you tell a subordinate, "but unless it's an emergency, try to confine the contacts to afternoons between two and four."

4. *Straighten out the boss.* "Ted, I'm holding my quarterly performance reviews between ten and twelve this week and next, so I'll be unavailable unless something special comes up."

5. *Deal with those who get through.* No safety screen is so fine a mesh that nothing penetrates. There may be occasional lapses. Be prepared to move briskly. Two cautions: (1) The interruption may be important or an emergency, so that you will want to act on it; and (2) It might be a superior whose priorities may be different from yours, and you won't want to put him or her off. Suggestions:

- Don't lose your cool, but do be firm.
- Explain simply: "I'm in conference. I'll get back to you later." Avoid specifying a time, such as ten minutes or half an hour. This suggests to interviewees that the session is slotted to the minute and the meter is ticking, which would destroy a desirable feeling of relaxation and the idea that your time is their time, both elements that encourage rapport.

MISTAKE 76: DISMISSING AN "UNSUITABLE" JOB CANDIDATE TOO ABRUPTLY

Underqualified or overqualified applicants may turn up when you hire. A few minutes into the interview comes the realization that the candidate is not for the job and vice versa. You're in a crisis position. What do you do?

Do you rise to your feet, briefly express regret, and escort the individual to the elevator? It's the simplest course, but not necessarily the best. There are other possibilities. It helps for you to know them and perhaps turn a crisis into a profit.

Case in Point

Jim Hoyt is hiring a computer programmer and apparently there's been a misunderstanding at the employment agency. The résumé of the tentatively smiling candidate shows an impressive educational background, including stints at the Sorbonne and Oxford, but degrees are in history and language. What an annoying mix-up! Hoyt is about to explain the contretemps and help the young woman bow out gracefully when she says, "The man at the agency said your company had a cadet training program. Are you in charge of it?"

He explains that he isn't, and yes, he has heard that the company was taking on trainees. "I'll find out who you should see," he says, picking up the phone.

"Wait," she says, "tell me what your department does."

Hoyt explains that his section is a key part of the company's computer system.

"Computers!" the young woman exclaims. "I'm in love with computers. Isn't there some job I could do here?"

Hoyt blinks and thinks. Why not explore the possibility of making this high-potential person a one-member trainee program? It could be an inspired idea or very dumb.

"Would you mind waiting," he says, and phones. His boss is free and Hoyt takes the résumé out with him to discuss the prospects. The boss's reaction: "Why not? You've got a little slack in your personnel budget, and it's my feeling that a person with her qualifications and high motivation could go right through the ceiling."

Analysis

The Jim Hoyt story is the stuff fairytales are made of. But it's a well-kept secret that the world of business is not entirely inhospitable to the unusual risk, and the 100-to-1 shot can come up a winner. The basic fact that suggests the unsuitable candidate situation need not end with a fast exit is that the human being always has much more potential than is ever used—some industrial psychologists say it's as low as 40 percent—and the business corporation has as many possibilities as a skyscraper-sized grab bag.

Effective Action

Consider taking advantage of the one-on-one situation to learn something from a job seeker who is not made to order for a job you are trying to fill. You might explore additional avenues of conversation:

1. *Learn something from the other.* There may be something in his or her job experience, educational background, or job training that could provide helpful information or insights. And of course, it needn't be a one-sided exchange. In learning more about the applicant, you might be able to make suggestions or supply leads that would assist in the job hunt.

Your focus need not be limited. Two other areas of possible interest:

- A grass-roots view of business in your industry. The fact that the candidate turns up in your office suggests possible experience in your field.
- The state of the job market. Is there a big demand for secretaries or whatever type of work within the other's experience?

2. *Explore the candidate's interests and capabilities.* Your company might be able to use him or her in another job, if not now, then in the future. This would hold for those with unusual qualifications. Keep a record of the meeting, and file the résumé. You might want to suggest a callback after a time, particularly if there is the chance of a job opening because of changes in your company's operations.

MISTAKE 77: BEING UNPREPARED FOR THE UNEXPECTED

This unit is a wrap-up of Part IV and focuses on some general aspects of crises. It also aims to refute the odd notion that you can't prepare for the unexpected.

Mistake 72, with its case of the suicidal grouse and other cases illustrating mishaps, suggest that upsets may come from a wide variety of sources. However, don't be intimidated. Awareness of the possibilities should replace wariness and jumpiness. Confidence in the interview can come with the "I've-been-there" feeling. Preparedness is better than unreadiness, knowledge is better than ignorance.

Case in Point

Executive Geraldine Ford stops in to see how the new department head weathered a first-time experience, conducting a progress review. One look and she expects the worst:

"How did it go?"

Larry Knox, complexion green, voice shaky, croaks, "Not too bad." Ford smiles and sits down. "Tell me about it."

Thawed a bit by the smile, Knox says, "Well, it didn't go exactly as planned. I had the checklist of questions you helped me develop, but Hal started telling me what an unfair deal he got from the previous manager . . ."

"Hidden agenda," Ford thinks to herself.

". . . then Gladys asked to get requisitions signed."

"He didn't tell Gladys, 'No interruptions,' " Ford surmises.

"Then I got a call from Accounting."

"Phone calls should have been held," the executive tells herself automatically.

"And then," Knox says, "the coffee pot boiled over, Hal Terry ran to take it off the heater, tripped, and cut his forehead. I took him to the doctor's office across the hall, then sent him home. Any suggestions?"

"You're learning," Ford says, and they both are convulsed by laughter. Then she says, "I mean it. You handled the one really unexpected development well. The other stuff is just a matter of experience."

Analysis

Notice that for the beginning manager, there were a number of unexpected events, all of which could have been prevented, and will be once he catches on. However, there are surprises whose shape or content you can't control. How, then, can they be prepared for? Answer, by expecting them. Not in particular, but in general. Don't expect tranquility, and you won't be startled by storm.

Effective Action

The problem of adjusting to the unexpected can be minimized by regarding it as a process. Here are guides to that consideration:

1. *Accept the proposition that the unexpected can happen.* In a recent movie, a character is told that X has been murdered. "That's impossible," he responds. The bearer of the tidings says, "But it's happened." "Then," says the other, "it's possible." Knowing about the crises that may disrupt your one-on-one meetings gives you a mindset

that takes some of the shock out of untoward events and makes you just that much more able to cope with them.

2. *Create in your mind what psychologists call a "field" with a range of possible ruptures of normal procedures.* Include the examples of the Part IV units, and add to them the incidents in your own experience, first hand or vicarious. This process immunizes you against being caught completely off guard. In a sense the exposure has immunized you.

3. *Assure yourself of your ability to cope.* The time and thought you have invested in analyzing the previous units is preparation for crises that exceeds that of the average manager. This exposure not only provides the know-how to act constructively, but also should give you the self-confidence that you can and will.

4. *Be ready to think on your feet.* The interview situation generally limits your time and resources for making decisions. Seldom can you delay deciding and acting for long.

Fast judgments are made, almost by definition, intuitively rather than by reasoning. But you can use reason as a check on your instinctive responses. For example, your good friend and interviewee throws you a curve: "You've got to give me the promotion. I'm asking as a longtime friend who has, to be crass about it, done you many favors. You owe me one, and this is it."

Your instinct may tell you, No. It's a raw and immoral request. But your reaction need not be instantaneous. You can ask yourself, "How good an assistant manager will he make? Who are the competitors? Can he work well with my boss?" You may find that the best candidate is the person you're looking at.

If you don't have the time to think through a judgment, make a tentative one and pretest briefly. Forget about the secondary factors; check the basics. Ask yourself, "Are there any key facts or information I could get in the time available?"

"Any similar cases to use for comparison?"

"Could we have a trial period?"

"Who could I consult for a quick opinion?"

"What might the consequences be, both pro and con, of this decision?"

And then be guided by the answers.

PART V

To Futurize: Concepts and Thinkpieces

Every art and science has its leading edge, beyond which lies a tantalizing territory of speculation and provocative ideas. That frontier is not always clearly marked. What makes one manager dream may be routine to another.

In any event, your vision of the field of interviewing can be brightened, your practice made more exciting by contemplating some ideas and procedures that are not fully explored and may even be untested. And even if tested, perhaps not by you.

The pages that follow offer a number of units that open windows on novel techniques that may enrich your interviewing skill. Starting with pair dynamics, *which, as far as this author knows, is an original term and deals with a concept that may change your idea of what goes on when you are in a one-on-one session, to a discussion of extrasensory perception as a means of learning what and how the other person is thinking and feeling, can become stimulating professional reading.*

The final unit, "How Good an Interviewer Are You?" is a self-rating quiz that may give you an up-to-the-minute measure of where you stand and what to do about it.

MISTAKE 78: BEING UNAWARE OF THE "NEW" INTERVIEWING

The traditional procedures are essential in interviewing, representing the know-how of countless practitioners over the years. However, the state of the art/science of interviewing has evolved new, innovative techniques. Including these in your repertory of skills will make a substantial difference in your face-to-face meetings, with greater success in achieving your objectives.

Case in Point

Manager Ed Bertrand uses a commonsense interviewing approach that he has just applied in hiring Grace Loden as his new secretary. His tried-and-true procedures, everything from carefully scrutinizing her résumé, having her demonstrate her shorthand and typing, and asking work-history questions to determine her reliability come up with strong positives. His satisfaction is short-lived. She quits before the month is out.

She explains, "I like working with you, but frankly, the pace of this office is too slow for me." (He is startled. Whoever heard of someone complaining of a slow work pace?) He doesn't realize it's Loden's way of saying the other people on the job are older, and she feels out of place in the group.

Ed Bertrand might have detected Loden's attitudes if he had watched out for Mistake 84, on one-sidedness.

She adds, "There was more overtime than I expected." (He remembered telling her about the overtime, and she had said it was all right.) Being unaware of Mistake 55, with its coverage of body language, he hadn't realized that she had agreed with reluctance. She had hoped there would be a minimum of late hours, but there had been considerable. The body language section also could have helped Bertrand understand why her bright, vivacious manner, conspicuous in the interview, seldom showed up on the job, where her moods were more often down than up. She had put on the show of ebullience to make a favorable impression.

Analysis

New additions to contemporary interviewing technique enrich the purely procedural aspects. They make the exchange less superficial, help get below the surface. Surface appearances can be made more meaningful by the deeper realities of things not said but important, of feelings hidden but crucial.

Interviewing at its most effective is a combination of sound procedures and use of perceptions and intuitions that pierce mere surface appearance and make for fuller communication. It is in the latter area that the interviewing practitioner will find the fresh approaches that add a new dimension to his or her skills.

Effective Action

The "new interviewing" can broaden your view of the one-on-one situation, making your perceptions and judgments sharper and more utilitarian. Certainly for important interviews it's advisable to take advantage of the newest concepts and techniques. A group of these follow in the pages ahead.

MISTAKE 79: BEING UNAWARE OF PAIR DYNAMICS

You're probably not alone in not being up on pair dynamics. *Dr. Kurt Lewin, whose ideas in the 1930s advanced the theory and practice of management, developed the group dynamics concept and its applications. The term* pair dynamics *has been coined as an offshoot of his concept.*

Lewin was struck by the unique behavior of people in groups and studied the special energies and forces (dynamics) brought on by the interactions of people in face-to-face assemblages. Some authorities assert that group dynamics theory applies to what they term a group of two, as well as larger ones. But in the context of interviewing it becomes clear that while there are interactions in a "group of two," these dynamics are different from those of larger groups. The old bit of folk wisdom that "Three is a crowd," suggests that the old folks were pretty keen observers and realized that the things that go on between two people change considerably when even one more person is included.

Case in Point

Notice the actions of two executives of the XYZ company planning a joint lunch. "Let's meet at P.J.'s," Ted says to Jake.

"Should we include Jerry?"

"No," Ted responds. "I want to talk shop, and we'll do better just the two of us."

Analysis

The two colleagues have often lunched as part of a trio but Ted feels the discussion will fare better in the dynamics—call it atmosphere, rapport, or mental entente—created when there are two present. What are the unique elements of pair dynamics? Consider these and evaluate them from your own experience:

1. The leadership factor. In one-on-one, the interview situation, leadership is different in kind and quality than for the group meeting. True, the interviewer-interviewee pair by their very designations, have superior-subordinate roles. And the interviewer, like the group leader, has a range of leadership styles, and may permit the interviewee to select the direction and pace of the conversation. But absent is the group leader's need to command the attention and cooperation of many individuals and the need to influence and balance the interests of group segments, to be concerned with the "politics" of the group.

2. Intimacy. When one individual relates to another, there is a sense of mental contact, usually mutual. In a larger group there is a parallel but the feeling is one of "groupness," of participation of a team effort. This is why the interview has a potential of interaction at a deep and open level, usually described by the term "rapport."

3. Field. An executive says of his experience of pair dynamics, "There is a sense of mental space that has a particular quality, especially during a good interview, when the two are on the same wavelength. It is more limited in scope than the group meeting, but it is warmer, friendlier, and more likely to strike sparks of ideas, perceptions and so on. There is something, a creative factor, that is aroused by the interaction of two brains working in harmony, or even in opposition."

Effective Action

You can apply the pair dynamics concept more knowingly (it's likely you've been using it for years) by considering points like these:

1. *Interview as incubator.* Consider pair dynamics as the validation

of the saying that "two heads are better than one." The executive in Point 3 above describes the one-on-one as a kind of incubation process, in which pair dynamics creates a productive atmosphere that favors constructive thinking. In some cases managers can benefit by using the "two heads" idea rather than a traditional view of interviewing, as a meeting of antagonists, verbal fencers, one on the attack, the other fending off the thrusts.

2. *Interplay of the senses.* "Do you agree?" the interviewer says to the other. "Yes," is the reply, but the manager notes the other's frown and realizes she must continue the discussion to get real acceptance.

3. *Give and take.* In interviews that are essentially negotiations, such as those for a raise, job performance, creation and evaluation of ideas, the discussion is a kind of seesaw dialogue. Be aware of the shifts, changes, ascent and descent of a cause or objective, understanding that these coincide with a forward movement aimed at an eventual agreement or goal.

4. *Communication.* With two people involved, each can plumb the depths of experience, creativity, and motivational power of the other by direct conversation. You don't have to take votes or worry about anyone being left out of discussions and decisions. There are just two of you, a strength of a closed communication loop. On the negative side, there is still the potential for misunderstanding, hostility, and noncooperation. But be aware of the benefits available by the positives.

5. *No limits.* When you understand the mechanisms of pair dynamics, you also can become aware of its lofty potential. You need not be mind-bound by the traditional formalities. In the one-on-one, you can "reach for the stars" in revelations and insights. For example, in a performance review, if the pair can raise the discussion to high levels of trust and confidence, the interviewer can elicit perceptions and aspirations from the other and possibly for the first time he or she will come to that greatest of personal achievements, self-understanding.

MISTAKE 80: NOT KNOWING YOU DON'T HAVE TO PLAY GOD TO GET THE PSYCHIC REWARDS THEREOF

The desire to play God is fought off by a high percentage of executives. They yearn for the rewards of a seeming godhood but most hesitate to do the things that are called "playing God" because they have been warned against it. Who says it's wrong? A collective

"They" have voiced their censure long enough for the scolding to permeate our culture. But some aspire and throw their weight around as Zeus might have.

The interviewing executive is particularly vulnerable to the urge to seem omnipotent. Dominating an interviewee may not match up to ruling a universe, but it can suffice. The good news is that managers can win the rewards without substituting for a deity. Two groups will find the information pleasing:

- *Those who have exerted a great deal of energy fighting off the urge and feel unrequited.*
- *Those who, consciously or unconsciously, behave as godlike as possible. Along with the satisfaction may come the aversion of colleagues and subordinates.*

Case in Point

Bryan Heath thinks he's quite the executive. Finishing a counseling interview with Bill Miller, he feels good. What a job he'd done on Bill. The subordinate had come into the meeting down-hearted and glum. At the end of the session Heath had asked, "How do you feel about things now?" "Better," Bill Miller had responded.

That night Bill Miller tells his wife, "I'm dumb to take that stuff from the boss. I'm tired of his, 'You're all wrong on that.' 'Now here's what I would do in your place,' and 'The thing you should be doing is. . . .'" He's trying to make a Bryan Heath out of me. I don't know how much longer I can stand it."

Analysis

What explains the Bryan Heaths of the world? Why do some people derive such pleasure out of forcing, persuading, or coaxing another person to "be like me." That's not the wording of the message, but that's the intent. Let's probe the specific acts of the God players:

- They tell people what to do and what not to do.
- They sit high on a seat of judgment, approving or disapproving, trimming off or adding on to others' ideas, values, and actions.
- They run the interview—right over the other person.

A single motivational link explains the behavior. Playing God is the ultimate aspiration, in order to gain a sense of power, of fulfillment, of security. It is possible for the executive to achieve these objectives without doing an ego-and-psyche transplant on a subordinate. The executive can minimize tendencies to dominate the interviewee, sublimate behavior (that eventually is destructive to both principals) by actions that can yield more constructive and permanent results.

Effective Action

In considering the recommendations that follow, keep in mind that they are subject to your own adaptations. If you don't have the slightest inclination to dominate an interviewee, whether in a counseling session, performance review, or in career guidance, the subject may be off the mark of your personal interests but still be in line with your professional ones. Subordinate managers or colleagues may act out the desire for total power. You may be in a better position to evaluate and decide what to do about it, if anything.

Three steps can help the manager avoid playing God and still win the benefits:

1. *Probe yourself.* You probably haven't asked yourself lately, "Do I use the interview situation as a stage to play a deity?" Do so now. How can you tell? Think back to your most recent interviews and consider:

- What was your attitude toward the interviewee? Was he or she seen as a fellow human being, an equal in humanity, if not in the relationship of superior and subordinate in the work setting?
- How did you feel about yourself in the situation? Relaxed and friendly, or uptight and wary, ready to take action at any attempt of the other to differ with you, to find you at fault, to best you in an argument?
- In hiring sessions, how do you regard the applicants? Poor sons of guns begging for a favor, a handout, a job? Or people worthy of respect for undertaking what is sometimes an ordeal requiring resolve and fortitude?

The less superiority you feel and show, the better. The fact of superiority may pertain, but the feeling of superiority is a negative factor in terms of a constructive relationship.

2. *Sublimate.* This is the principle that helps the manager gain the

rewards without donning the divine mantle. Remember, the God-inclined executive is explained not by the desire to be a deity but to get the supposed rewards of being one. What benefits come to the God-playing executive? The obvious ones, a feeling of power, of being in charge, of dominating others. Crucial point to note is that all focus on a single result: liking yourself, seeing yourself as a person of worth, having a self-image that you can find very good.

3. *Use winning procedures.* Rely on techniques that actually bring you the psychic rewards that the God-players hope to get. For example:

What events in an interview make you feel good? Naturally, they will vary with the type of session. In an exit interview, it may be that you were able to help the interviewee see his or her career situation in its most promising light. Or, during a performance review, you may have helped the subordinate jointly work out a program for self-development that replaced doubt with enthusiasm.

It's no coincidence that the two instances above show the manager helping the interviewee. The best executives accept the fact that stimulating subordinates to perform well is a direct measure of their own excellence. And perhaps God-likeness?

MISTAKE 81: BEING UNABLE TO SEPARATE THE REAL FROM THE PAPER PERSON

"He looks good on paper," is the way one personnel executive puts his quick appraisal of a job applicant sketched out by a résumé and references. He is right to make the distinction. The real person may vary widely from the image that emerges from reading his or her application. It's a distinction that haunts many a manager.

Case in Point

Jay Coty, owner of a New York design and construction firm, says,

> I and some of my managers find it difficult to alter the image created by résumés and the interview contact. In a way, this is saying that fiction is more vivid than reality. The individual isn't always interested in giving you an accurate self-portrait. He or she is after a job and seeks to get it by giving the impression of strong and relevant abilities, perhaps bending the facts to suit job requirements. That impression, paper or not, doesn't yield readily to subsequent facts.

Coty recalls his youthful effort to get a job until school started in the fall. "I was interviewed by a fast-food outfit that considered me a first-rate prospect." The interviewer felt Coty had management potential, highly desirable in that company.

"Why do you want this job?" he was asked.

"I love hamburgers and the romance of fast food," he responded, thinking fast. He got the job and quit six weeks later, to the chagrin of the company. Remarks Coty, "As an employer, I now sympathize with the food outfit. When interviewers hear something they like, they hate to give it up."

Analysis

Evaluating the image formed by résumés and other documents isn't simple. In addition to the sometimes misleading information submitted by job seekers, the interviewer is hampered by his or her own susceptibility and inability to separate image from flesh-and-blood. For example:

- Susceptibility. Managers are victims of their own likes and antipathies. Height, for example: "I won't hire a salesman under six feet," avers one sales manager, not realizing that what he really wants is a salesperson with a six-foot personality. Or pro and con bias about accents. An English-accented speech makes some executives drool, whereas the cadences of a middle European accent chills them. Chances for accurate conclusions suffer.
- Inability. "How do you judge people?" asks a manager, who, despite years of business experience, still confesses to difficulty in making hiring decisions. He has no natural instinct that helps him, nor does he have an experiential set of rules he can depend on. "Can't seem to get a handle on people," he says.

Effective Action

Pointers like those that follow can strengthen your hand:

1. *Be aware that even the innocent may be guilty.* A dishonest résumé isn't always the villain in the conflict between image and the real person. Even if a job applicant is honest, the paper-formed image would still differ from the real one. It's a practical impossibility for

anyone to depict a total person in a few pages of writing. And the hirer's interpretation of applications is subjective. Proof: Ask three people to examine a set of documents and you will get three different impressions of the person depicted.

2. *Look in two general directions for evidence:*

• *The paper image.* After a preliminary screening of applications and résumés, reexamine the documents of the surviving contenders. Key points to spotlight:

—Do claims hold up? For example, does the applicant who says she spent a year in study abroad reflect it in the interview?

—Is emphasis on experience credible? One executive says, "I was interviewing a forty-year-old person for a staff job. On reviewing his résumé, I noticed he stressed that he was president of his college class. If, after fifteen years or so in business, that represents one of his outstanding achievements, he can't have been much of an achiever.

—Are there contradictions? A man applying for a top executive job, and claiming high-salary positions in the past, submitted a covering letter with his résumé on ordinary paper with his home address and phone number typed at the top. That put me off him, not because of a personal reflection of his taste, but his poor understanding of business standards. At the very least, he should have realized his stationery would not be a plus.

• *The real person.* The second area of appraisal is the person in the flesh. Jay Coty suggests, "Look for behavior in the interview that demonstrates either favorable or unfavorable qualities. For example, I was looking for someone to take over part of the office load in my company. I asked an interviewee how he got on with his previous employer. 'That rotten battle-ax' he said, 'yelled at me all the time. She had a terrible temper,' and apparently, a poor employee." Coty continues, "After the candidate had said his piece, I felt he was probably lazy, inept, and certainly not able to work constructively with a boss."

A clue from an applicant might suggest a desirable trait. Coty relates, "In interviewing for a secretary, I had to leave a candidate alone in my office for a few minutes. When I returned, she was on the phone: "Call for you," she said. "I thought it might be important." I hired her because she showed initiative and had a sense of how to conduct business. She proved I was right."

3. *Evaluate the findings.* Sensing the worth of a human being, in

the context of hiring, isn't easy. Avoid the simplistic. Even a negative finding need not be a knockout factor. For example:

A VP of a shipping firm relates, "We were looking for a receptionist, and one of the applicants showed up for the interview with her hair unkempt and her dress in need of a cleaning. My assistant, who escorted her into my office, whispered an approving comment. After some conversation and an inspection of her references I went into another office and called her previous employer. She gave a highly favorable rating. I decided to hire. On the way back, my assistant met me in the corridor. "Did she tell you she'd been knocked down by a bicyclist right in front of the building?" he asked. "No," I replied, "but you should have." The executive had decided, correctly, that the candidate's untidy appearance was a rare departure from the norm.

Negative factors may be offset by positive ones. In one case, a check showed that a candidate had misstated her educational qualifications. She had only spent three years at a college from which she had claimed a degree. The hiring executive explained,

> I remember I myself had similarly lied about getting a degree in applying for my first job. It was wrong, of course, but it made me realize that it is naïve to automatically rule out a candidate with a high potential because of inaccurate information on an application. I hired the applicant after I learned that she had dropped out of school for financial reasons, which again was my experience.

Talk to executives who are hiring for a position that is difficult to fill, and you find that they are willing to cut corners about qualifications as long as they feel the candidate can do the job.

4. *Modify your commitment.* If you find yourself still caught between an impressive paper image and the real person who doesn't quite live up to expectations, you may want to make something less than a total commitment. In effect you say, "You're hired, but. . . ." The buts give you a margin of safety, and in key hiring situations, provide some latitude. Your options:

- Professional testing. For certain kinds of jobs, such as a high-pressure executive position, psychological testing organizations can provide a profile that suggests the emotional resources of the individual and predicts his or her ability to cope with ongoing tension. For key lower-echelon jobs, aptitude testing can help you decide on the potential of a candidate to advance to higher levels.
- A probationary period. It's certainly not one-sided. You can

honestly tell the individual that three or six months on a job will give both of you the opportunity to see how things work out. Where possible, provide goals by which the arrangement can be judged: achievement of a specific goal, such as monthly sales (for a salesperson); or, for a department head, lowering of absentee rate, improvement of quality performance.

MISTAKE 82: DISREGARDING THE ADVANTAGES OF PSYCHING YOURSELF UP

Athletes do it and attribute their victories to the process. Losers swear they became winners when they learned how to rev up their mental and physical motors by psyching themselves. The same technique can be used in interviewing. All that's needed is to know how to do it.

Cases in Point

1. Regard with sympathy the plight of executive Ken Brewster. He's due to interview Leon Deming, a subordinate to whom he relates poorly. In their performance review—the up-coming agenda—the boredom point was reached long ago for both of them. It's up to Ken Brewster to break out of his lethargy, but he can't seem to do it. And so the atmosphere of their meeting gives the word "perfunctory" a new incisiveness.

2. Admire executive Mary Yates. She can hardly wait for the performance review with Jack Oppenheim. His quarterly record looks good. She's hoping to push him along even further. And she knows that if she goes about it properly, she can infect him with her revved-up feelings. She begins to psych herself up.

Analysis

Mary Yates is correct in her approach and plan. The psyched-up individual, strengthened by belief in self, can be dynamite in the interview situation. The technique works because it intensifies key areas of an interviewer's capability. Note:

- The interviewer's mood is a major influence on the climate of the meeting.
- The pair dynamics (see Mistake 79) of the session becomes more volatile. More initiatives, breakthroughs, and constructive agreements are likely to occur.

It's one of those tempting procedures: You know it will work if you only knew how to do it.

Effective Action

Self-psyching isn't either a scientific or voodoo mystery. It's a procedure with a specific technique and specific purposes. Here's a recipe for action:

1. *Apply a two-step procedure.* It's a direct application of the principle, accentuate the positive, accompanied by a corollary, eliminate the negative.

- Eliminate the negatives. Think of and/or write out the relevant feelings and ideas that put you down. Take the case of executive Ken Brewster. His list might read like this:
  —Sense of defeat. He feels he hasn't been able to get anywhere with his subordinate, so why continue to try. Nonsense! Now he tells himself he can take action, he can dare a new approach in dealing with Deming.
  —Lack of cooperation. "Even if I can liven up, I'll be stopped cold by Leon's disinterest," he feels. Ridiculous! That's exactly what leadership can cure, and he's a leader.
  —Why bother? For some managers, this can be the worst de-motivator of all. "Things can't be so bad," they tell themselves, "because I've been living with them for months." And they add a sly argument: "The idea that I must take action is just in my own mind. I don't see other managers busting their backs to perform motivational miracles." It's the thought that bad is good enough that the Brewsters of the world have to fight.
  —Fear of failure. "What if I try and fail?" That is seen as adding insult to injury. Turn that around: If you don't try, you will certainly fail. Trying ensures that you will do better.
- Beef up the positives. For example:
  —Anticipate the excitement of tackling a challenge. Inspiring

Deming to involvement and ambitious action would be a strong confirmation of your leadership skills.

—Think how pleased X would be. Who is X? The one in whom you confide your hopes, your fears, your failures and successes. It could be your boss, a spouse, a close friend, your children. The listener to your cries of victory can be an important motivator in your life.

—Savor the feeling of success. "It has one of the best bouquets ever," says one wine-tasting executive. For many, the glow of a potential victory is the strongest incentive in the book.

Also note these additional points:

2. *Know why you're doing it.* Self-psyching for its own sake, although an interesting experience, has no place to go. You rev up for a reason. In the context of the interview, worthwhile benefits become available.

3. *Know the kind of person your psyched-up self will be.* Under the influence, the person you see in the mirror may not even look the same. Self-confidence and enthusiasm, two key results, are likely to change your appearance in subtle ways and surely the way you behave. Keep this in mind in presenting yourself. The interviewee is likely to respond differently from previous ways.

4. *Pick your targets.* The session for which the procedure has obvious application is in the performance review, where your intensified mood can produce echoes in the interviewee that can help smooth over failure, be ambitious in setting new goals, and become enthusiastic about the element of challenge.

However, do not rule out other possible applications. One executive recalls,

> I had gone through weeks of interviewing job applicants for a hard-to-fill job. My mind was worn to a nub and I guess I was in a depressed state. I certainly was, every time I faced a new applicant. But one morning I said to myself, "Pull out if it, fella." I put myself through what you call self-psyching, and whether it was a coincidence or not, the very next interview turned up a winner.

Any of your one-on-one meetings in which your confidence and enthusiasm could have an enlivening affect on the meeting climate or on the other person would make a logical occasion to elevate your own spirits.

5. *Develop new objectives.* To take full advantage of your enlivened

mental state, you may want to set more ambitious goals for your meeting. For example, you are likely to be able to inspire the other to set more far-reaching goals. In some cases it will not be improved performance as much as the possibility of increased or precedent-breaking creativity.

6. *Control the psyched-up you.* Avoid overwhelming your interviewee. The motivational high you give yourself may make you feel like Superman or Superwoman. You have probably increased your potential along one or two dimensions, but you're still not Lord of the Universe. Two things limit what you can do:

- The reaction of the other. Some people will be right there, ready to take off with you. Others may shrink at the unexpected apparition you have become for them. For each person you can sweep along with you on your high, there may be one who will draw back. The old ways—apathy, marginal performance, limited motivation—may never have looked safer or more desirable.
- The possibility of letdown. The "cure" may be temporary. That's not a stopper, just a realistic thought to give you pause. Some people may set new goals for themselves beyond their capabilities. Excessive strain followed by failure may be the result. Keep in mind that psychologists recommend medium-high goals as best for solid advances. Help your subordinate set his or her new practical targets.

MISTAKE 83: NOT CARING

The interview situation, as has already been noted, is one in which the physical proximity of the principals and the common interests and goals foster an atmosphere of harmony, even intimacy. Yet, some managers create a barrier that prevents the interviewee from either sending or receiving warmth or human feeling.

"He didn't give a hoot about me," a job applicant tells another. "I'll bet robots get a better reception from the mechanics that install them."

Perhaps the candidate expects too much. The accused interviewer might protest, "I just do my job. Crackers don't always come with caviar."

A case can be made for the importance of caring, not in the way one family member cares for another or the way that social workers care for their clients. In the latter instance caring takes on an almost medical connotation. The interview context requires a different type of solicitude. In the interview relationship there are practical reasons, in addition to the emotional ones, that make caring important, even crucial.

Case in Point

Manager Elaine Breen looks across the desk at Mel Vernon. The latter's frown irritates Breen. Why does Mel insist in getting so wrought up in discussing the work? Work is work, Breen thinks, and doesn't get any better by adding a strong dash of emotion.

"I care about what I do," she hears Vernon saying. "It isn't just a paycheck."

"If he thinks he's scoring points, he's way off," Breen thinks. She prides herself on her coolness. She considers aloofness—she sees it as objectivity—as a key element of her management style. She is not necessarily wrong, but she is limiting herself by an attitude that rules out the warmth, companionship, and the excitement of human endeavor, and also the benefits inherent in an enriching rapport. Mel Vernon's feelings, highly motivating, are left to shrivel on the vine.

Analysis

Elaine Breen is an extreme case. A psychiatrist might say she is affect-lame, suggesting that her pattern of emotions is not quite normal. People in that category may not cry at funerals, still less at weddings. Such people may have difficulty in expressing love or anger. While Breen sees herself as composed, others see her as frozen.

Caring adds a facilitating element in the atmospheric mix of the interview. But it is a special kind of caring, often confused with the generalized term, as in "He cares about people." It's helpful to understand the difference.

Effective Action

What caring is in the interview context, what it isn't, and how to use it is embodied in the following points:

1. *Realize that the bond may be conscious or unconscious.* Somewhat the same degree of caring may be felt by two executives, one aware of how he or she feels toward the interviewee, the second not cognizant

of it. However, for the executive desirous of vitalizing this element in his or her approach, it is at conscious mental levels that the process must take place.

2. *Understand the components of caring in interviewing.* Caring in the interview context is special because the interview isolates two individuals and puts them in direct confrontation. The pair dynamics (see Mistake 79) are unique. To begin with, "caring," as the term is used in its general sense, usually involves a general approach to people, and is, of course, exemplary. The feeling that optimally develops in the one-on-one situation involves three elements:

- Identification. We seldom cut ourselves off from our past. We remember ourselves as children, teenagers, in our early twenties. We remember ourselves as beginners in the world of business, as novices striving to progress, sometimes caught up in difficulties. The subordinate or job candidate may be us, 10 or 20 years removed, one or two echelons below. We tend to care for these people, even those that have just walked in for a job, because they are us.
- Self-interest. In many instances, what is good for the interviewee is good for us. If we smooth out a problem that improves a performance or motivates a subordinate to higher achievement, it redounds to our credit. And we benefit by our sponsorship. If our protégé wins the day, we've won.
- The future. Managers have a professional interest in tomorrow. Our planning, goal setting, and aspirations are all future-oriented. In many interviews, judgments and decisions are made that will influence what happens in the months and years ahead. Of course we care about the people we hire, promote, motivate. We are shaping the future for ourselves as well as others.

3. *Make caring an effective force.* Theoretically, it's possible for managers to care, and care deeply, about subordinates and keep it so completely internalized that no one, including themselves, are aware of it. For those executives who have no reason to disguise their benign feelings

- Tell. It needn't be effusive, but it can be vocalized: "I'm interested in the well-being of all the people in the department, and you are certainly no exception . . ."
- Show. "I think the systems analysis course could do a lot for you. I'm going to ask Personnel to pay half the tuition." The showing need not be a privilege or a favor. The time you spend

with a faltering newcomer, the readiness with which you listen to a subordinate's ideas, are convincing demonstrations of your caring.

- Results. Success may come thick and fast or be almost nonexistent. Either way, some managers develop a reputation for backing up their employees. Others are known as "people builders," because the sponsorship and help they lavish on their subordinates makes their departments known as breeders of success, or skyrocketing projects and successful people who put them across—because the manager cared. More for the project than the people? In most cases you can't separate the two. Central to the effort were countless interviews. It's what went on during those that lit the spark then added the fuel to keep the achievement-fires burning.

MISTAKE 84: BEING BLINDED BY ONE-SIDEDNESS

"There are two sides to everything," goes the adage. In interviewing this is literally true. To benefit from the total situation you need understanding, even empathy with the person on the other side of the desk.

Case in Point

Addie Gerassi has herself rated as a superior interviewer. She approaches each meeting with the confidence of a poker player who has drawn a fourth ace.

And yet, something is lacking. For example, in a recent interview with Ted Quiller, a subordinate dissatisfied with his assignments, she ends the session feeling that she has disposed of the other's complaints. But a week later Ted is back in her office, raising objections that supposedly had been eliminated. "I don't think," he mutters, leaving her office a second time, "she really understands what I'm talking about."

Analysis

In the case above, the cause of the imperfect communication rests with Gerassi. You can do a perfect job of communicating with the other person, make adequate preparations, ask the right questions, touch all the bases. But if your perceptions all go one way, entirely from your side, you are losing out on a crucial factor—the other person's viewpoint and values.

Effective Action

"Put yourself in the other's shoes," said lawyer Basil Henry Liddell Hart, in his *Advice to Statesmen*, "so as to see things through his eyes." This is easier said than done, but well worth trying. The rewards are tempting: better results for both you and the other person. Here are some assists:

1. *Prepare for an out-of-body experience.* You're probably familiar with the occultists' claim of being able to leave their own bodies and move freely in space. What's suggested here is not the spiritualist's experience but one based on the powers of your own mind. Reach out. Use your perceptions and intuitions about other people, your ability to release your mind from its ordinary restrictions. Difficult? No, you probably do it often, for example, when you shop for a gift and think, "How would Pat feel about a red scarf?" Or, "How would that job candidate get along with the wisecracking crew like the second-shift inspectors?" You try to answer by seeing through the other's eyes.

2. *Fit yourself into the other's shoes.* Begin by asking yourself questions directed at the specific interview situation you face. Keep in mind the individual across the desk. Use your knowledge of human nature as well as your familiarity with the person himself or herself. At appropriate times during the conversation ask yourself questions like these:

"How is he or she feeling?" based on your reading of gestures, body posture, tone of voice, and reactions to what you've said.

"What is he or she thinking?" Note facial expression, openness of what is said, its relevance. This is the point at which you assess the other's sincerity and honesty.

Pay special attention to the unexpected word, sentence, or new line of thought. These are likely to be key cues to the other person's state of mind, and if you don't understand the cues you may be off track. Figuring out the "why" of the behavior can yield useful insights. When in doubt use a direct query: "Why do you say that?"

3. *Apply the insights you get.* Let's return to the Gerassi-Quiller case. Manager Addie Gerassi, during the session looks at Quiller and makes the following observations:

- He looks upset. His statements are made angrily. He asserts that his last three assignments were routine and required a lot of fly-specking, not his favorite kind of work. Two of his colleagues have gotten tasks he felt were right up his alley.
- He is probably right in his contention. Accordingly, Gerassi decides, "I should do two things. First, make his next assignment one he'll be happy about. Second, make it as soon as possible. To make sure of the fit, let him share in selecting the task."

Although Gerassi thought she had satisfied Ted's complaint in their first session, it had ended with her telling him that she "would try to see that he got more challenging jobs in the future." From where he sat, that was less than a satisfactory resolution. The two elements lacking: fast action, and the certainty that his very next assignment would provide the involvement he was after.

4. *Consider handing over the reins.* One executive says, "When I'm at a loss to understand the other's real views and feelings, I sometimes pass over control. In a recent performance review I said, 'Tom, you know as much or more about the weaknesses and strengths of your performance as I do. Tell me how you feel about your last quarter's record. Take as much time as you need.' What came out was more constructive than anything I could have suggested."

MISTAKE 85: FAILING TO CONSIDER COMPETING MEDIA

The need to communicate with others is ongoing and covers a vast range of subject matter. Fortunately, you have a choice of media at hand. In addition to the interview, the two closest competitors are the telephone and the memo. Knowing how to select from among these can sharpen your communications practices in general.

Case in Point

Wilma Rivers, senior VP, marketing, finds three items on her To-Do list:

- "Give shipping a rundown on customer complaints on deliveries." She dashes off a memo with the information.
- "Get information from the design department on how the special order for XYZ Woolens is coming." She picks up the phone, dials design.

- "Discuss production problems we're having with our Hong Kong supplier with boss." She calls his secretary and asks for a meeting tomorrow morning.

How does she make the choices of media?

Analysis

Wilma Rivers, like most managers, makes her choices of media according to two criteria:

1. *Suitability of the medium to the message.* For example, the memo gives shipping a convenient written record of each customer's dissatisfactions. And she retains a copy that verifies the message and date it was sent.
2. *Personal preference.* Some people are most comfortable conversing on the phone, others like one-on-one get-togethers.

Your personal responses to the interview situation become an important part of your effectiveness in them. Some managers are interview shy, others thrive on them. The latter develop a special preference for the one-on-one get-together. The expert communicator is the one who knows when to use which method in given situations. Pinning down your personal preference, knowing your feelings about interviews and when to use them can improve your mastery of this most personal medium.

Effective Action

To interview or not to interview, that question is best answered by comparing the pros and cons of three communications methods that are most interchangeable:

Communication Method	Advantages	Disadvantages
Phone	Fast. You can do it at your desk or from any convenient phone location. You can ask questions and get answers.	Line may be busy, other person involved elsewhere. Usually no record of transaction.

| Note or memo | You have a record. You can prethink your message. You can add visuals, sketches, models, previous correspondence. | Subject to mailroom delay and inbox bottlenecks. Rigid, must get by on sender's writing skill. |
| Face to face | Personal contact. Meeting arranged at mutual convenience. You can control content and mood of exchange. Two-way communication offers the "two-heads" advantage. | One person may dominate. Wastes time when out of control. May cut you off from other pressing matters. Repetitions, as in a series of job interviews, can be boring. |

Keep in mind that the list above represents average practice. Since communicating skills tend to be highly individualized, make your selections based on your weak and strong points with each and requirements of the specific communication at hand.

MISTAKE 86: NEGLECTING YOUR ESP POWERS

Most people have an extrasensory perception capability. The ability to receive information by means other than your five senses, by mental telepathy, to use the more precise term, may be available to you. Even people with strong ESP potential may be unaware that they have it or can use it. ESP, mental telepathy, or mind reading is worthwhile exploring in our context of interviewing technique, because it can add an unusual and effective tool to your repertory.

Part of the difficulty in discussing ESP is that, despite its popularity, the prevailing ideas about it are vague. The definition is simple enough. The Dictionary of Psychology *defines mental telepathy as "knowledge conveyed from one individual to another by means other than the senses." Then comes this additional explanation, "Telepathic communication is presumed to be direct communication from one mind to another without the intervention of any known physical form of energy transmission."**

As far as the second half of the Dictionary's statement, forget it. The human body, as presently constituted, has no apparatus for sending or receiving messages not based on the senses. And as for the first part, the import depends largely on what is meant by the word "senses." There is a method that can help you read another person's mind. You use sight and hearing, but not in the conventional way.

* J. P. Chaplin, *Dictionary of Psychology* (New York: Dell, 1982).

Case in Point

Here is an example of mind reading that shows practical mental telepathy in action:

Gary Hazen gets a call from Tim Farr. Tim says he would like to meet for about ten minutes. Hazen says OK and wonders what Tim wants. Tim Farr walks in and Hazen knows immediately what's on the other's mind. He wants to reopen an argument that they had in the staff meeting the day before.

Mental telepathy is a sensing-and-evaluating system, rather than an automatic brainwave receiver for which today's human brain has no hardware. Here's how Hazen reads Farr's mind:

Farr had said nothing over the phone that suggested the reason for his visit. But as soon as he entered Hazen's office, the latter sensed his tension—tight lips, stiff body. This he perceived instantly, not by his cognitive mind but by his intuitive one.

"But wait a minute," you may say, "what you're describing is reading body language."

Yes and no. Hazen didn't consciously note the line of Farr's lips and compare it to others gathered in the past. That is the rational mind in action. Hazen's perception was instantaneous and intuitive.

See what happens in the second phase, which now brings in the rational mind to team up with the intuitive one. Hazen thinks back into the immediate past, "scans" the contacts he has had with Farr, and remembers the disagreement in the staff meeting. "That's what he's tense about," he decides and settles back to listen to the other's resumption of the argument, which is exactly what takes place.

Analysis

This example shows the mechanism for practical mind reading (PMR). It is a sensing-and-evaluation system. The sensing is intuitive and nonrational but is tied directly into the rational segment of the mind. It is the joined effort that helps us read another person's thoughts and feelings.

Many people use the word "intuition," but its actual meaning and how it differs from the cognitive mind is sometimes not clearly understood. There is a simple way to explain the difference based on humor and our reaction to it.

An anecdote is told about Vince Lombardi, the tough, assertive football coach of Notre Dame in its glory days. After long overtime practice on the field, the coach returns home late and tired. He gets into bed quietly, but his wife wakes up. After a moment she says, "God, your feet are cold."

"In bed," responds the great man, "you can call me Vince."

Even if you have heard the joke before, you may have laughed. The spontaneous laugh of a person responding to a one-liner is the work of the intuitive mind. You don't know why you've laughed, you just know the joke is funny. Now to find out why you laugh is a job for the cognitive mind, and that may take some time, or in some cases, remain forever elusive. It's fortunate for comedians that intuition is almost instantaneous. They'd grow grey and poor, waiting for their quips to wow the audience trying to figure out the point of a joke in order to appreciate it.

To further illustrate PMR note a crucial incident in a job interview:

"Oh yes," a job applicant says airily, "I've had considerable writing experience. I was editor-in-chief of my college magazine and had a job as reporter on my hometown newspaper two summers." The relaxed manner seems excessive.

"What was the name of the paper?" asks the interviewer. The job doesn't primarily require writing skill, but it would be a useful adjunct.

"*The Hadley Bugle.*"

The interviewer reads the other's mind, and in it he senses the thoughts and feelings of a prevaricator. For one thing, the man is too relaxed. If he were telling a straight story, the tension he is trying so hard to cover up wouldn't exist. A few hours later an assistant comes in with the information that there is no *Hadley Bugle* and the applicant hadn't even been on the college magazine staff, to say nothing of being editor-in-chief.

Of course, the PMR concept may be readily attacked. One argument raised against it: "Isn't what you describe just a logical deduction?" There's a simple rejoinder: "It matters less what you call it than what it can do for you. If by uniting your intuitive and cognitive abilities in the ways described, you can come up with perceptions as to what the person opposite you is thinking and feeling in a way you otherwise might not, the approach is worth some further attention."

Effective Action

The two illustrations provide a simple and followable method that you can test for yourself. Some further guidelines:

1. *The basic technique.* PMR works in two phases. The first part tells you how a person feels, his or her state of mind. The second phase gets your rational mind to process your intuitive perception and come up with a message.

2. *The critical points.* There are two. In phase one, you must end with a definite conclusion about the other's emotional state. You must be able to differentiate not only among the range of choices, but in degrees. If the person is angry, how angry? Mildly, wildly, or just irritated?

And in the second phase, your rational mind may not always be able to produce the "message" signaled by your perception, because there may not be enough data. You may not know enough about the person to interpret the emotion, so you can't decipher its meaning.

Practice will help in more ways than one. Even if you don't end up being a master of PMR, trying the process, say in your next four or five interviews, will certainly sensitize you and make you aware of the other person's vibes, and help you read them.

MISTAKE 87: BEING FLUSTERED WHEN YOU'RE AN INTERVIEWEE

You're an experienced and capable interviewer, and you pride yourself on your insight and flexibility. You know all the traditional strategies and some of the new tricky ones. Then suddenly you're a passenger, and someone else is in the driver's seat. Everything is familiar except your role. You're surprised at how you feel, not really bad, just peculiar. The interviewer doesn't help matters when you hear, "Good morning. I'm sure we'll both benefit from this meeting." That's one of your own favorite lines.

Case in Point

You're in a meeting with your boss, and although it isn't billed as such, you recognize the subject: Performance review. You know what his opening ploy is, so you think you'll help him out:

"Brad, I'm eager to tell you just how we're doing on the conversion program." You start to take some papers out of a folder and he says, "I believe that's coming along well. What I'd like to start with is the

Excelsior matter. Now I understand that your relations with their purchasing department have been a bit gritty. . . ."

You become defensive. "Actually, they're improving."

"I didn't say they weren't, but I think we should analyze just what the prospects are for the future."

"Fine. I'll turn in a report on that by the end of next week."

The boss shakes his head. "I want to discuss it now."

You make one or two other attempts to guide the conversation into relevant areas, and the boss shakes you off. What's wrong with the old goat, anyway?

Analysis

Possibly the only thing wrong with your boss is that he wants to call the shots. Since he has ideas about what your job priorities are, and they are at least as good as yours, it's not surprising that he wants the choice to be his.

Most managers do much more interviewing than time spent at the other side of the desk. The roles are not totally dissimilar, but it's the similarities that keep you off balance. You wish you had some guidelines on how to be a good interviewee. The picture you get of yourself seems to be coming from the wrong end of the telescope.

Effective Action

To add the hat of interviewee to your exective hatrack:

1. *Ask yourself, "Am I overly self-conscious?"* If you can slide into the interviewee's chair without qualm or question and you rate yourself zero in self-consciousness, go on to the second point. If it is a problem, work to make it less so by:

- Assuring yourself that a one-on-one meeting with you as inter-viewee is acceptable and doesn't undercut your managerial status.
- Not kidding yourself by thinking your efforts to "help" are efforts to help. More likely, they are attempts to avoid control by the other or to preempt it for yourself.

2. *Understand the reasons for the problem.* A parallel instance: Psychiatrists say with resigned grins, "Psychiatrists make the worst

psychiatric patients." To the extent that it's true, the following two points explain:

- Professional awareness. The patient can't help but be aware of the techniques being used, which is also true of the manager as interviewee. This perception is a distraction that interferes with the manager and adds an obstacle to easy functioning.
- Role reversal. Psychiatrist or executive, sitting on the "other side of the desk" feels uncomfortable because the other side seems like the wrong side.

3. *Be honest about your feelings.* This is an area where individual feelings vary widely. Executives were questioned on their reactions to being at the receiving end:

- One heartfelt one-word answer: "Uncomfortable." When asked to amplify, the executive said, "I guess I fell out of the habit of being a subordinate, and I became impatient being picked at with words. I tell you one thing, it sure makes me more aware and I now treat interviewees with more empathy, even compassion."
- "I found myself trying to go along with the interviewer, but it was like a game, and an unfamiliar one."
- "I anticipated the other's moves—that executive from a higher echelon was not very good at interviewing—and I tried to give 'correct' responses rather than those that expressed my true feelings and ideas. I was surprised at my duplicity."

Do your feelings mirror any of the above? Can you state your attitude as clearly? What does your answer tell you about yourself as manager and interviewer?

4. *Choose a balance between what you know and what you do.* A careful maneuver can help you get the best of two possible roles. Here's what is required:

- Suppress your tendency to play your customary role, of controlling the interview. Not that you need reminding, it's acceptance that is needed. Give unto the interviewer what is due, the privilege of moving the conversation along at the pace and direction desired by him or her.
- Be the best interviewee you can be. If you want to take initiatives, do it in ways that reinforce what your interviewer is trying for rather than to supersede or undercut. If he or she says, "Let's evaluate the record of customer complaints," do your best to make it an effective evaluation. If you are asked, "How would

you rate the performance of your correspondents group," make your response as objective and insightful as possible. Provide data, examples, ideas for future application, in other words, the kind of responses you would praise in a subordinate, when you're at the helm.

MISTAKE 88: NOT KNOWING HOW YOU'RE DOING

One's self-image is an important factor in shaping your management behavior. If you see yourself as a brisk, astute, and capable practitioner you will fare much better than if doubts of your abilities suffuse the way you see yourself.

Having some sense of how good an interviewer you are can do two things for you: (1) It can root your interviewing behavior in the firm ground of self-knowledge or (2) If you are not satisfied with the result, you may want to proceed to take the steps that lead to improvement.

The quiz below can provide both benefits. Answer all questions and make your replies as objective and candid as possible.

HOW GOOD AN INTERVIEWER ARE YOU?

	True	False
1. Generalizations about people based on large-group categories, such as gender, nationality, hair color, and such can be seriously misleading.	☐	☐
2. I always stick with first impressions.	☐	☐
3. Preparation is the best antidote to panicking in a crisis.	☐	☐
4. It is possible to observe an interviewee's behavior and learn how he or she is feeling.	☐	☐
5. Stress interviewing is a tried and true technique.	☐	☐
6. A courtesy interview is called that because you should be especially courteous while conducting it.	☐	☐
7. Interviewing has a clear field in the sense that it doesn't overlap or conflict with other types of business communication.	☐	☐

	True	False
8. Ending the interview and shaking the other's hand is a final wrap.	☐	☐
9. The big thing about the hidden agenda is that it must remain hidden.	☐	☐
10. The knockout factor idea can prevent needless continuation of a hiring interview.	☐	☐
11. Short and sweet is the best formula for an exit interview.	☐	☐
12. Extrasensory perception is fine in science fiction but has no place in interviews.	☐	☐
13. What happens in a subordinate's home life is of no concern to the manager, and still less a subject for an interview.	☐	☐
14. Pair dynamics is one of those impractical hotshot phrases that has little meaning or use.	☐	☐
15. You can psych yourself up for an interview in the same way an athlete does before a contest.	☐	☐

Your Total Score _____

[*Preferred Answers: 1.T, 2.F, 3.T, 4.T, 5.F, 6.F, 7.F, 8.F, 9.F, 10.T, 11.F, 12.F, 13.F, 14.F, 15.T.*
Scoring: Give yourself 10 points for each correct answer, and if you like, write it on the total score line above.
What your score suggests:
130–150. Your knowledge of interviewing is excellent. If your results are also, you are outstanding among your peers.
90–120. You're good, with only a slight susceptibility to mistakes. Double-think some of the tough situations and crises in your sessions, and you should do well.
Below 90. Your knowledge of the field is shaky and probably lands you in hot water from time to time. Consider looking up the subjects about which you gave incorrect answers in the Index, and see if mastering them fills in the weak points of your interviewing practices.]

INDEX